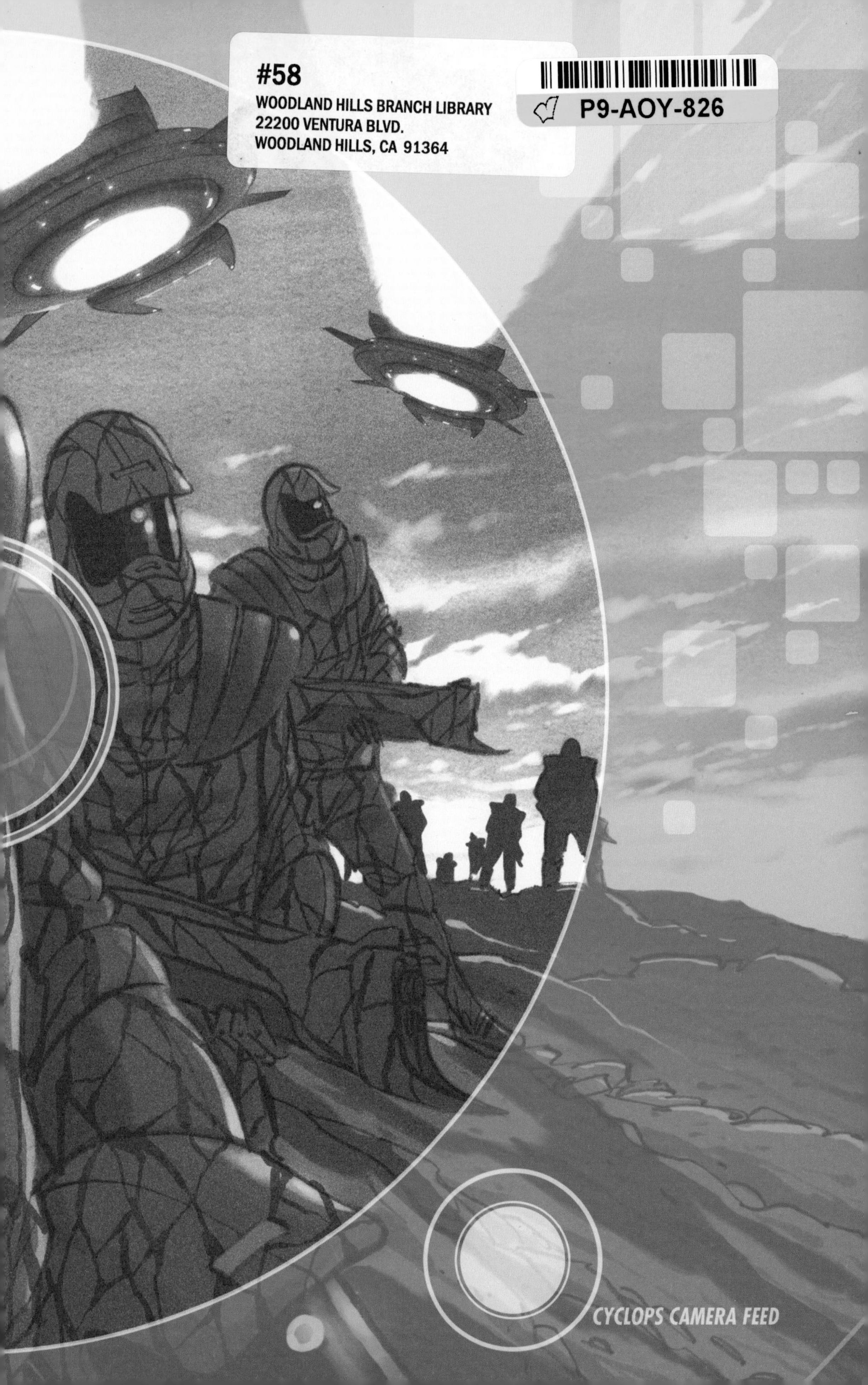
CYCLOPS CAMERA FEED

JACAMON & MATZ ゾッゾペズゼド

CYCLOPS™

01 VOLUME ONE

ARCHAIA ENTERTAINMENT LLC
WWW.ARCHAIA.COM

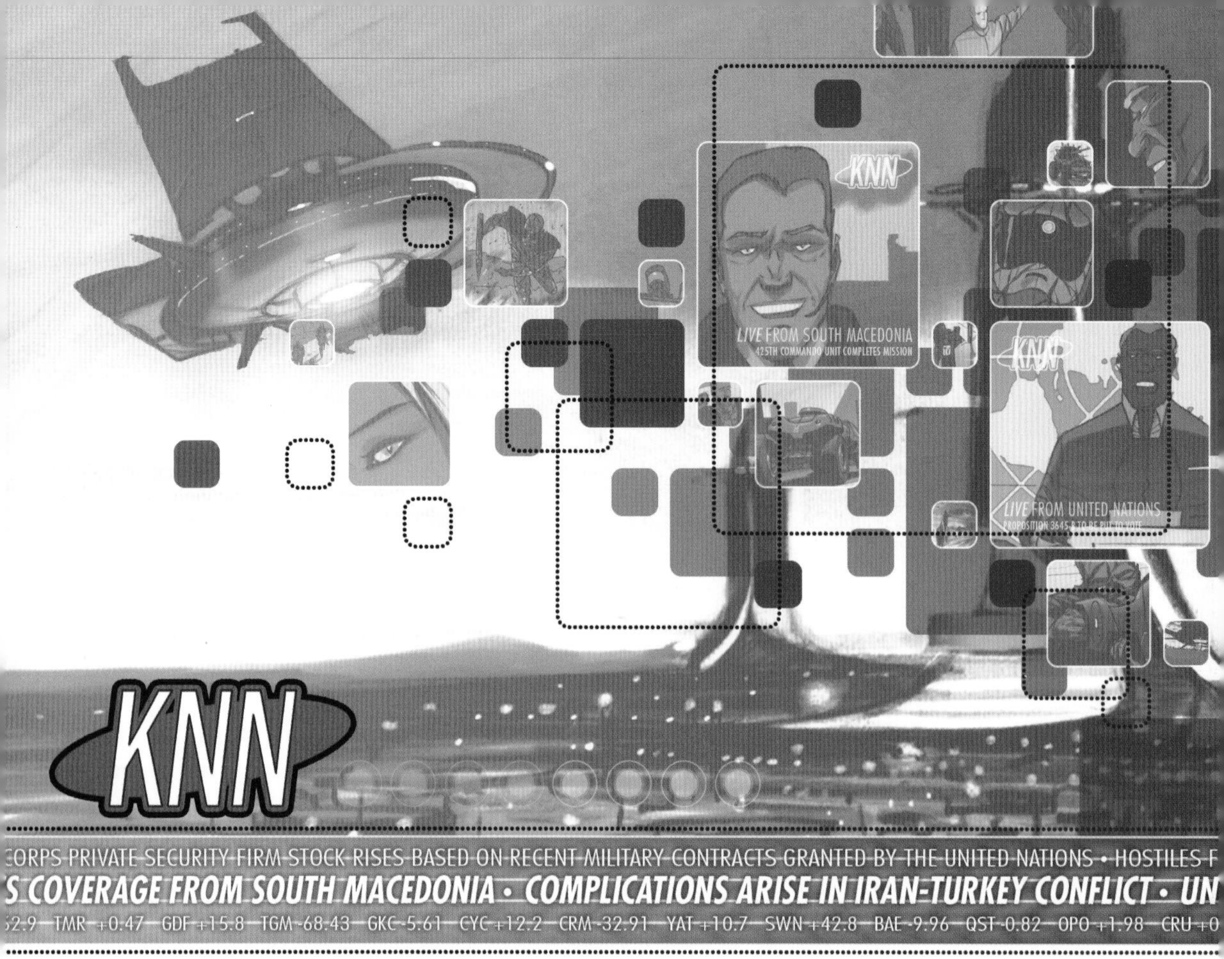
KNN
LIVE FROM SOUTH MACEDONIA
425TH COMMANDO UNIT COMPLETES MISSION
KNN
LIVE FROM UNITED NATIONS
KNN
ORPS PRIVATE SECURITY FIRM STOCK RISES BASED ON RECENT MILITARY CONTRACTS GRANTED BY THE UNITED NATIONS • HOSTILES F
S COVERAGE FROM SOUTH MACEDONIA • COMPLICATIONS ARISE IN IRAN-TURKEY CONFLICT • UN
2.9 TMR +0.47 GDF +15.8 TGM -68.43 GKC -5.61 CYC +12.2 CRM -32.91 YAT +10.7 SWN +42.8 BAE -9.96 QST -0.82 OPO +1.98 CRU +0

Published by **Archaia**

Archaia Entertainment LLC
1680 Vine Street, Suite 912
Los Angeles, California, 90028, USA
www.archaia.com

Originally published in France & Belgium
by CASTERMAN.

CYCLOPS VOLUME ONE. May 2011. FIRST PRINTING.

ISBN: 1-936393-11-5
ISBN 13: 978-1-936393-11-4

Printed in Korea.

ARCHAIA™

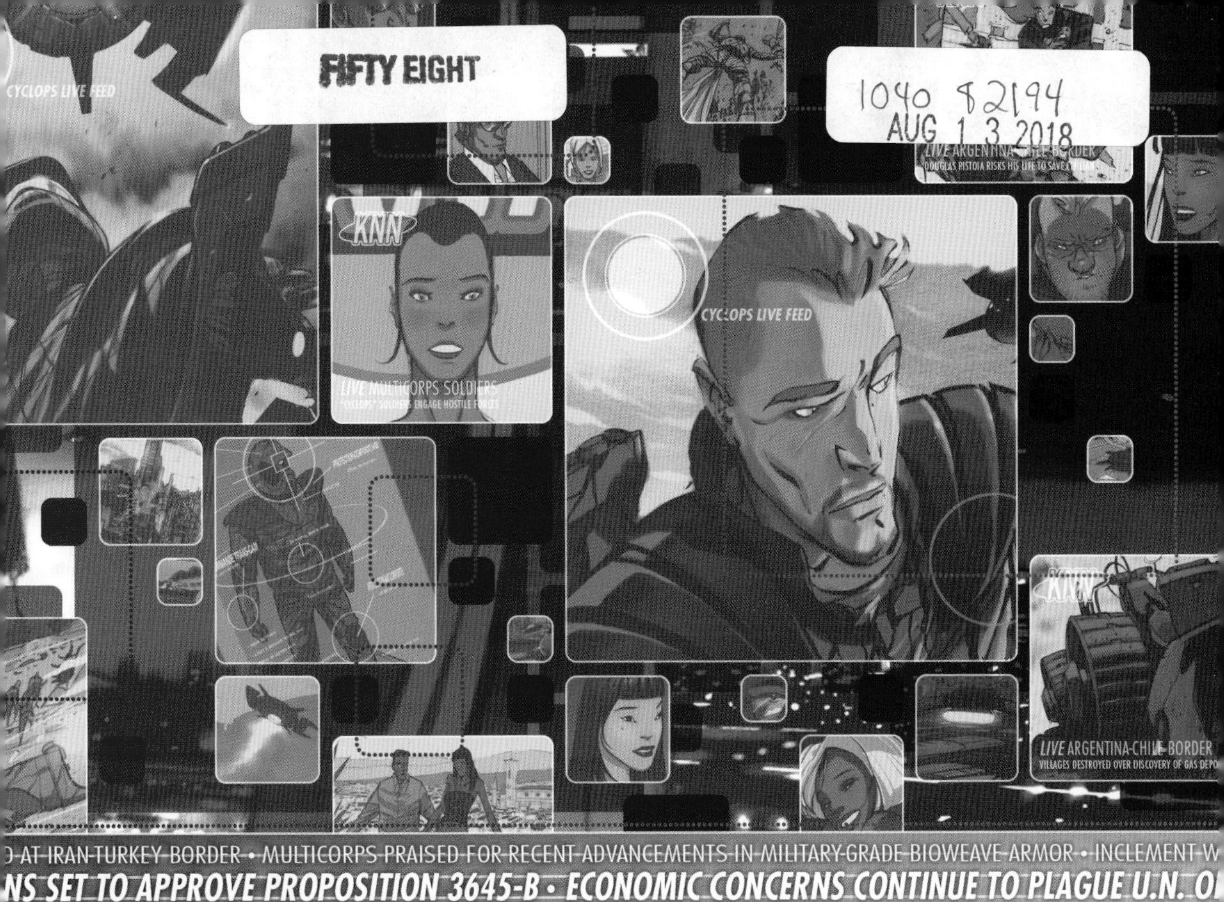
CYCLOPS LIVE FEED
KNN
LIVE MULTICORPS SOLDIERS
"CYCLOPS" SOLDIERS ENGAGE HOSTILE FORCES
CYCLOPS LIVE FEED
LIVE ARGENTINA-CHILE BORDER
DOUGLAS PISTOIA RISKS HIS LIFE TO SAVE CIVILIAN
KNN
LIVE ARGENTINA-CHILE BORDER
VILLAGES DESTROYED OVER DISCOVERY OF GAS DEPO
AT IRAN-TURKEY BORDER • MULTICORPS PRAISED FOR RECENT ADVANCEMENTS IN MILITARY-GRADE BIOWEAVE ARMOR • INCLEMENT W
NS SET TO APPROVE PROPOSITION 3645-B • ECONOMIC CONCERNS CONTINUE TO PLAGUE U.N. O
NAT 12.5 GWR +7.78 WET 0.19 ACB +107.3 KZT +10.4 LBP +83.4 DSP 10.87 GOW 0.97 IHT +8.83 RWO +43.1 FRD 0.36 SAS +10.72 MV

JACAMON & MATZ

CYCLOPS™

01 VOLUME ONE

Written by **MATZ**

Illustrated by **LUC JACAMON**

Translated by **Matz** and **Edward Gauvin**

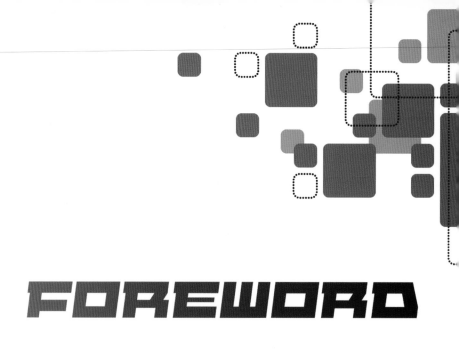

FOREWORD

I came up with the story for **Cyclops** somewhere around the turn of the millennium. I had already been toying with it for a while when Luc Jacamon told me he was getting tired of drawing **The Killer** day after day. He said he needed a break from the book. He said he'd like to draw something different, something in which he could design vehicles and weapons, outfits and interiors. So I dug up and suggested **Cyclops**. Luc instantly took a liking to it, so we started working on it right away.

The inspiration for **Cyclops** was mainly my general interest for history and geostrategy. The storytelling of Verhoeven's **Starship Troopers** (even though movie producers hate that reference, as the movie wasn't a big hit) and Ridley Scott's **Blade Runner** (producers love that reference) were also influential. I like the way these two movies smoothly throw us into a world apparently different than ours, but not that much if you take a closer look. They then use that world to deliver a message about ourselves and the world in which we live today.

Our world is an endless source of inspiration, even though it often goes beyond what we storytellers can come up with, and science fiction is a great tool to investigate it. The Iraq war showed it, and

then some. We French have very interesting characters, but you Americans also have fascinating ones, like Rumsfeld and Cheney. You couldn't really do guys like that in fiction. They're just too good. Bottom line is: fiction might not have anything on reality, but fiction can be an effective means to deal with reality and transcend it. I recently read a declaration by a former U.N. Secretary-General in which he explained that private military security would very probably be hired in the future to perform peace-keeping missions…so here we are! Who knows, maybe one day we will be considered visionaries! That would be funny... Or maybe not...

Cyclops was also a very interesting experience for two other reasons. First, because two books into it, Luc Jacamon had to leave. Main reason was that he couldn't keep up both **Cyclops** and **The Killer**. So he made a choice and chose **The Killer**. **Cyclops** went to sleep for a little while, until Gaël de Meyere came along. He's a young artist from Belgium. He showed us promising sketches and drawings, so we went for it. I believe the transition is rather seamless and efficient.

The second reason was that Warner Bros. and James Mangold showed interest in the project. I was lucky enough to meet Mangold and discovered an impressively smart man.

When we talked about the story, the whole series was not yet written. When I told him what I had in mind, he shared his ideas, which, I have to admit, were depressingly better than mine. They ended up triggering new ones.

My conversations with James Mangold made me think a little bit harder about the graphic novel as a medium itself. We have a freedom in comic books that movies don't have. We can show more, tell more, and differently. So I completely changed the ending of my story. I made it rougher, more accurate, and more hard-hitting – more what it should have been. And it's not one you'll find in a movie – if a movie ever gets made, which as I understand it, is a very fragile and mysterious process. But whatever happens, it was all worth the trip: meeting with James Mangold and Kathy Conrad, and now seeing these books hit American readers. That in itself is a trip!

But for now, as the books always will be the most important thing to me, I just hope the American audience will like the **Cyclops** series as much as **The Killer**!

— Matz

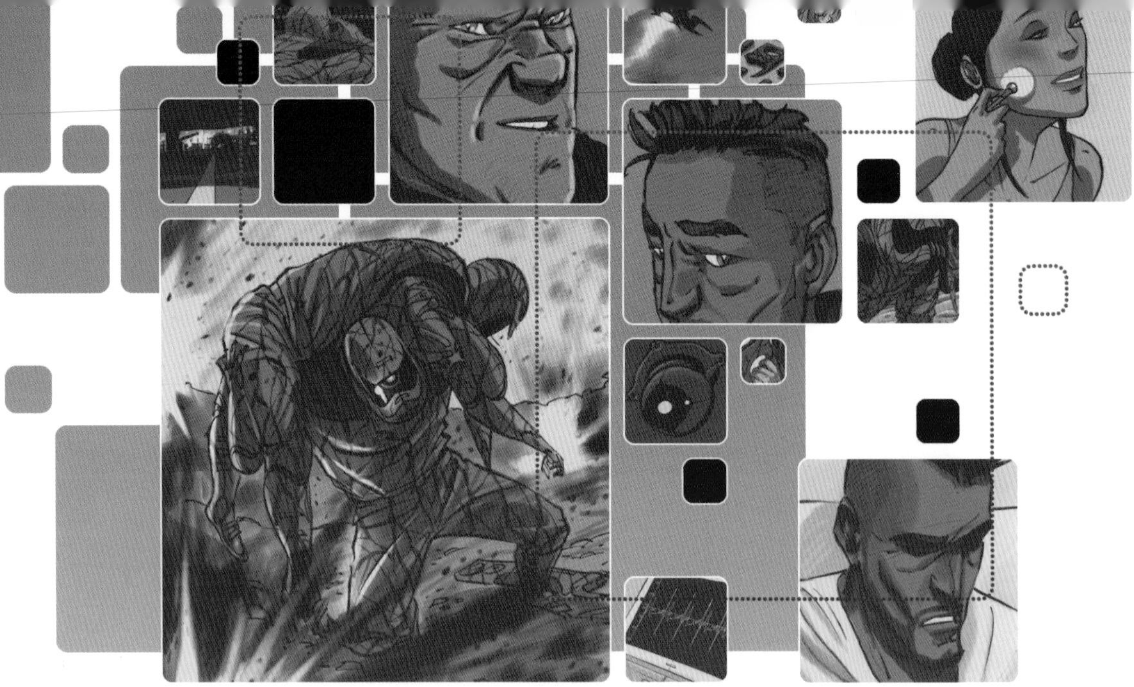

EPISODE ONE
01 THE RECRUIT

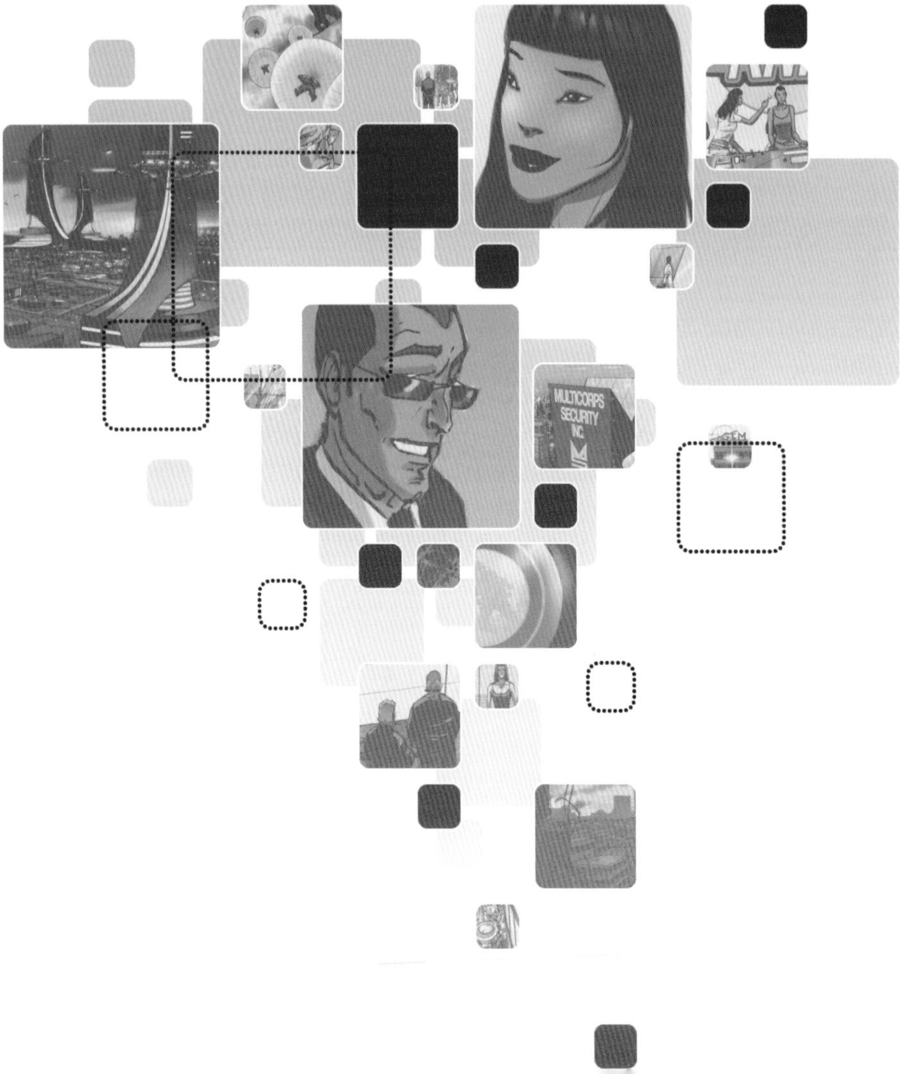
MULTICORPS SECURITY INC.

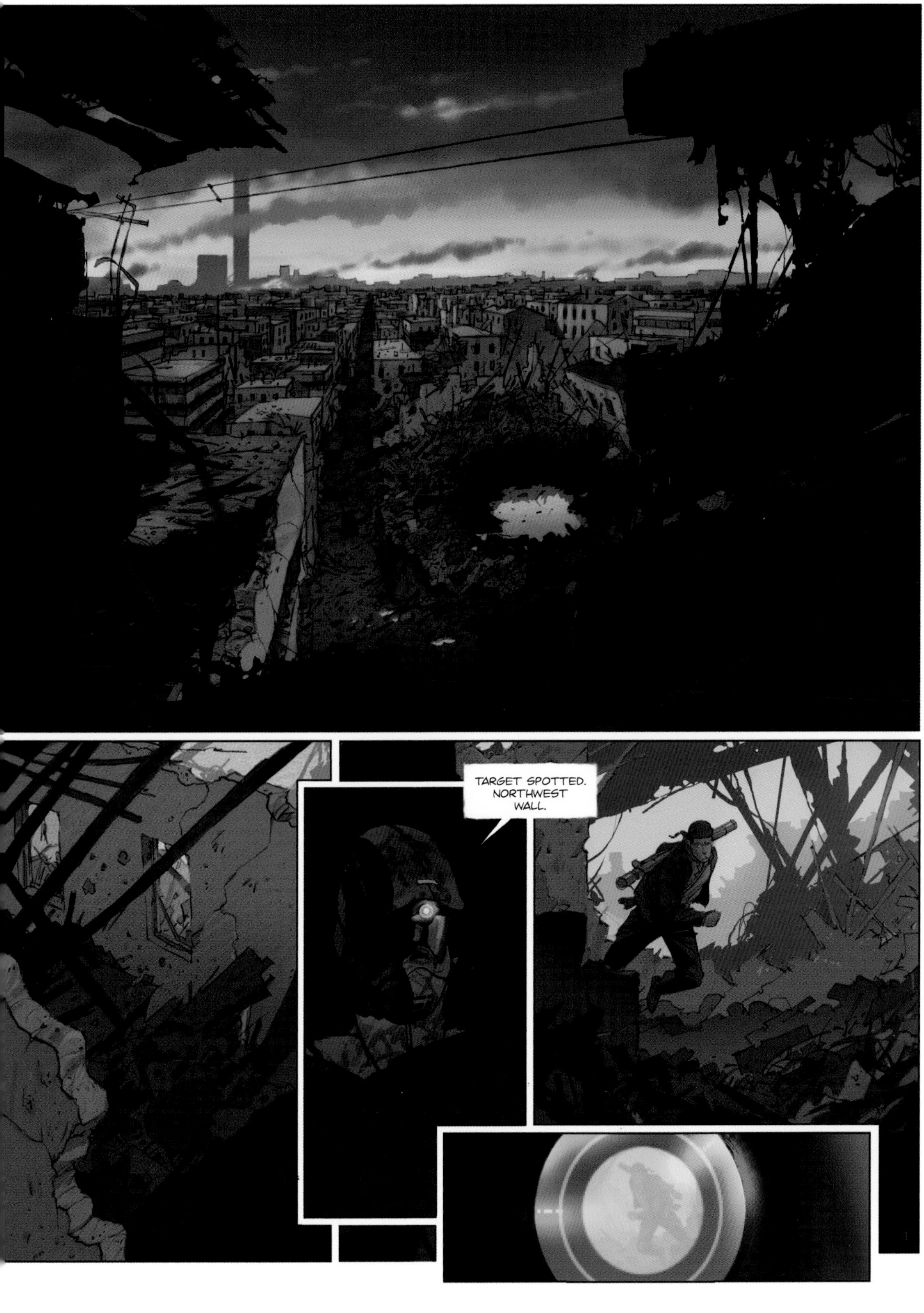
TARGET SPOTTED. NORTHWEST WALL.

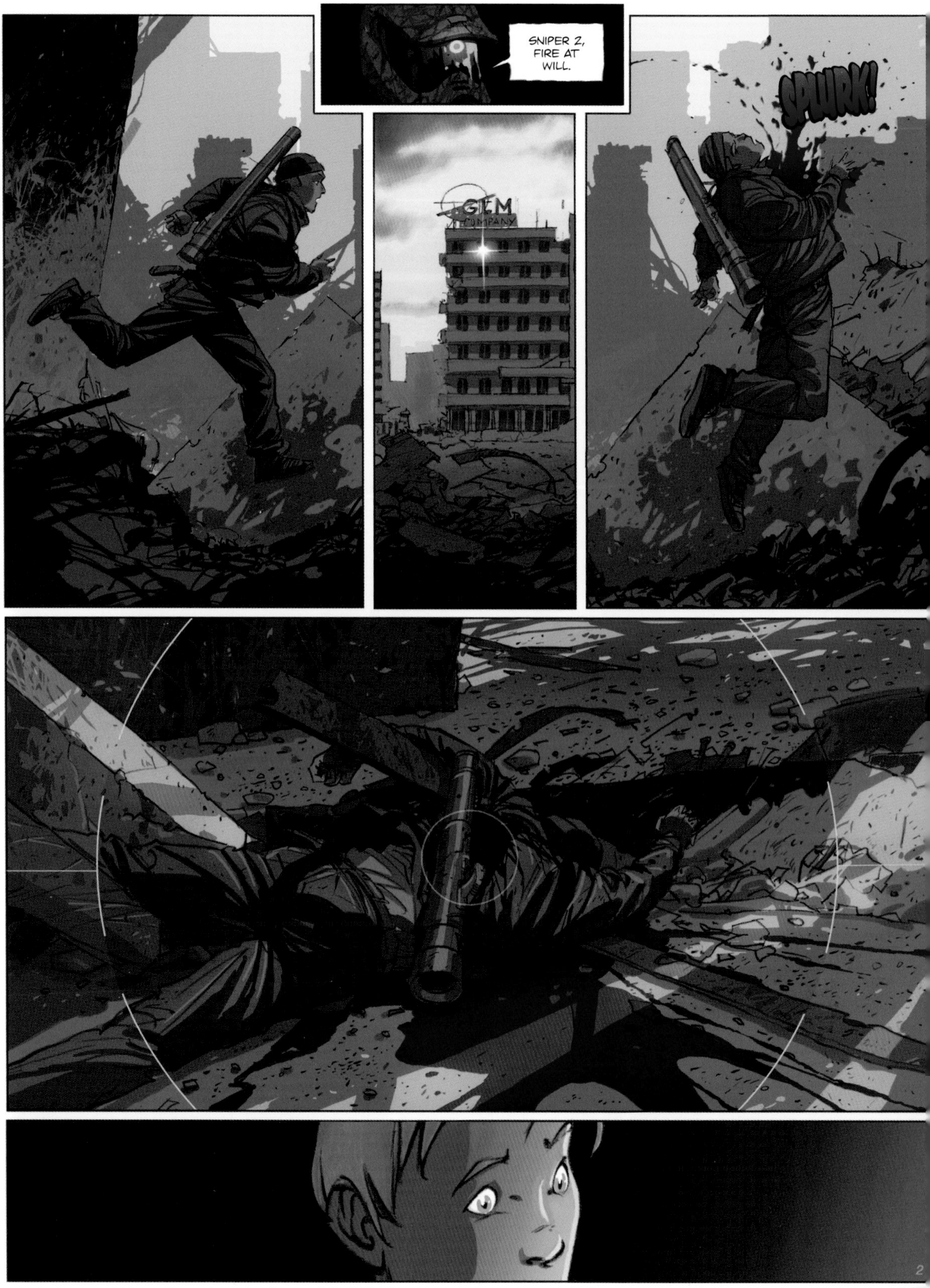
SNIPER 2, FIRE AT WILL.
SPLURK!

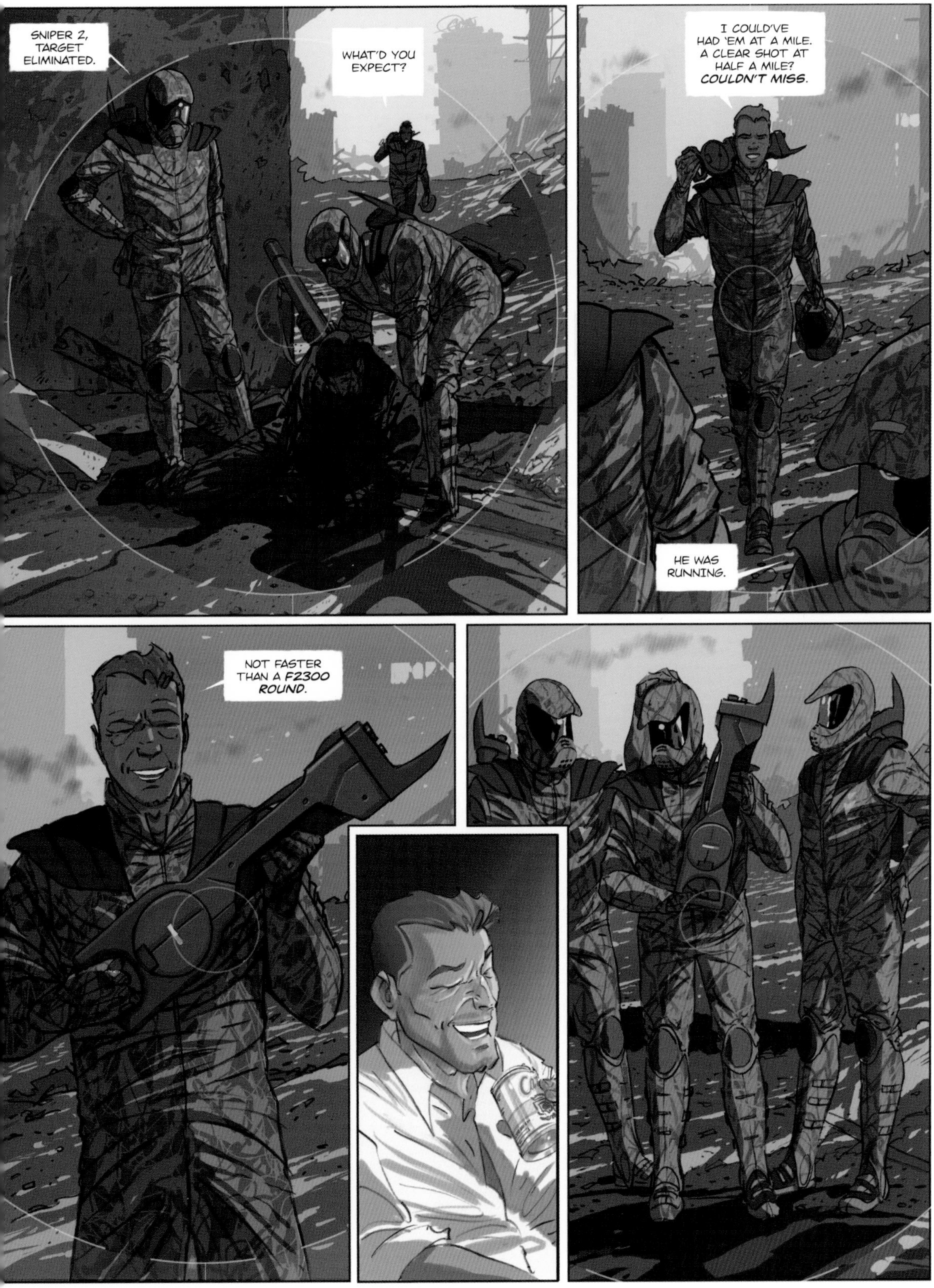
SNIPER 2, TARGET ELIMINATED.
WHAT'D YOU EXPECT?
I COULD'VE HAD 'EM AT A MILE. A CLEAR SHOT AT HALF A MILE? COULDN'T MISS.
HE WAS RUNNING.
NOT FASTER THAN A F2300 ROUND.

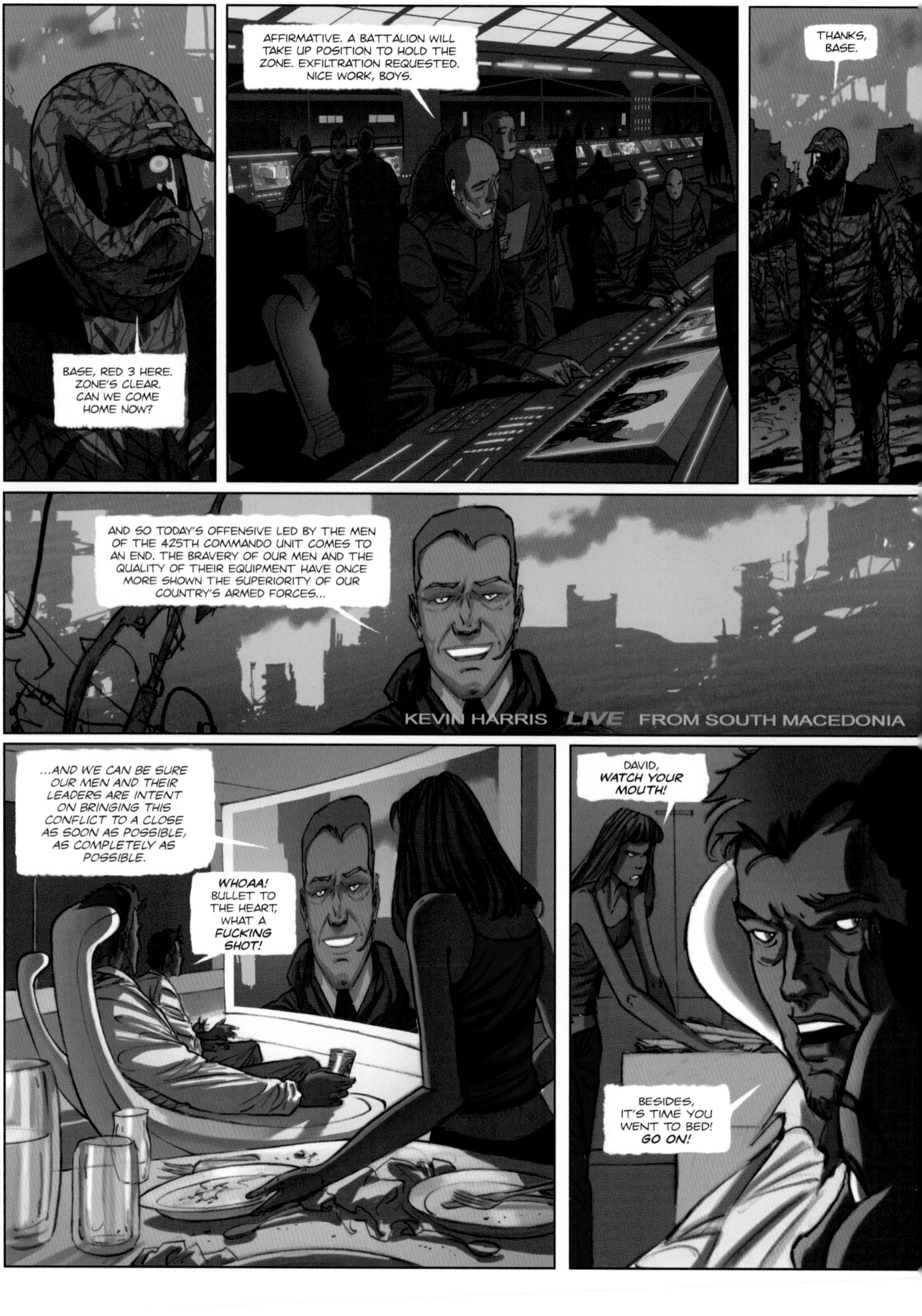
BASE, RED 3 HERE. ZONE'S CLEAR. CAN WE COME HOME NOW?
AFFIRMATIVE. A BATTALION WILL TAKE UP POSITION TO HOLD THE ZONE. EXFILTRATION REQUESTED. NICE WORK, BOYS.
THANKS, BASE.
AND SO TODAY'S OFFENSIVE LED BY THE MEN OF THE 425TH COMMANDO UNIT COMES TO AN END. THE BRAVERY OF OUR MEN AND THE QUALITY OF THEIR EQUIPMENT HAVE ONCE MORE SHOWN THE SUPERIORITY OF OUR COUNTRY'S ARMED FORCES...
KEVIN HARRIS LIVE FROM SOUTH MACEDONIA
...AND WE CAN BE SURE OUR MEN AND THEIR LEADERS ARE INTENT ON BRINGING THIS CONFLICT TO A CLOSE AS SOON AS POSSIBLE, AS COMPLETELY AS POSSIBLE.
WHOAA! BULLET TO THE HEART, WHAT A FUCKING SHOT!
DAVID, WATCH YOUR MOUTH!
BESIDES, IT'S TIME YOU WENT TO BED! GO ON!

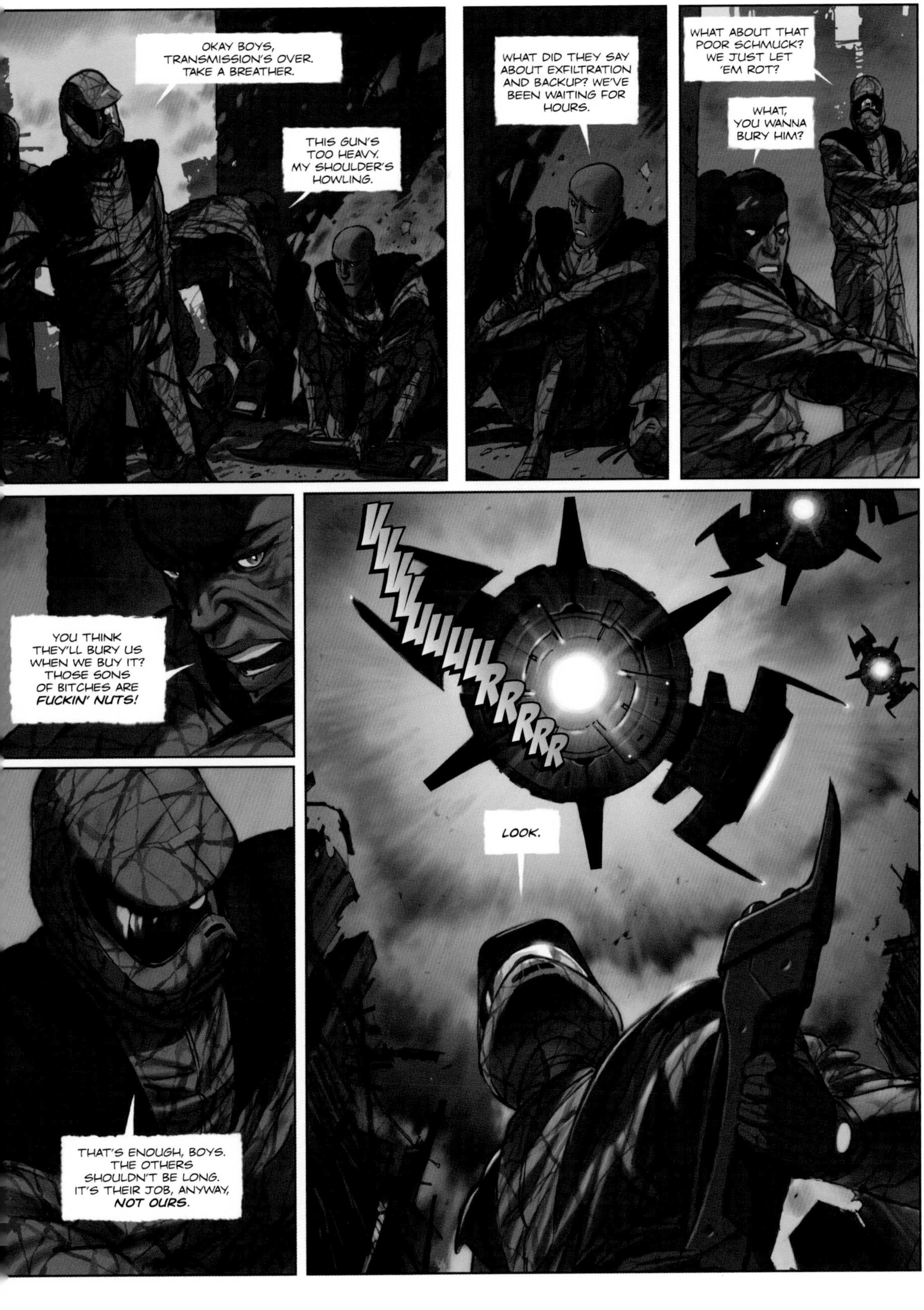
OKAY BOYS, TRANSMISSION'S OVER. TAKE A BREATHER.
THIS GUN'S TOO HEAVY. MY SHOULDER'S HOWLING.
WHAT DID THEY SAY ABOUT EXFILTRATION AND BACKUP? WE'VE BEEN WAITING FOR HOURS.
WHAT ABOUT THAT POOR SCHMUCK? WE JUST LET 'EM ROT?
WHAT, YOU WANNA BURY HIM?
YOU THINK THEY'LL BURY US WHEN WE BUY IT? THOSE SONS OF BITCHES ARE ***FUCKIN' NUTS!***
THAT'S ENOUGH, BOYS. THE OTHERS SHOULDN'T BE LONG. IT'S THEIR JOB, ANYWAY, **NOT OURS**.
VVVUUUUURRRRR
LOOK.

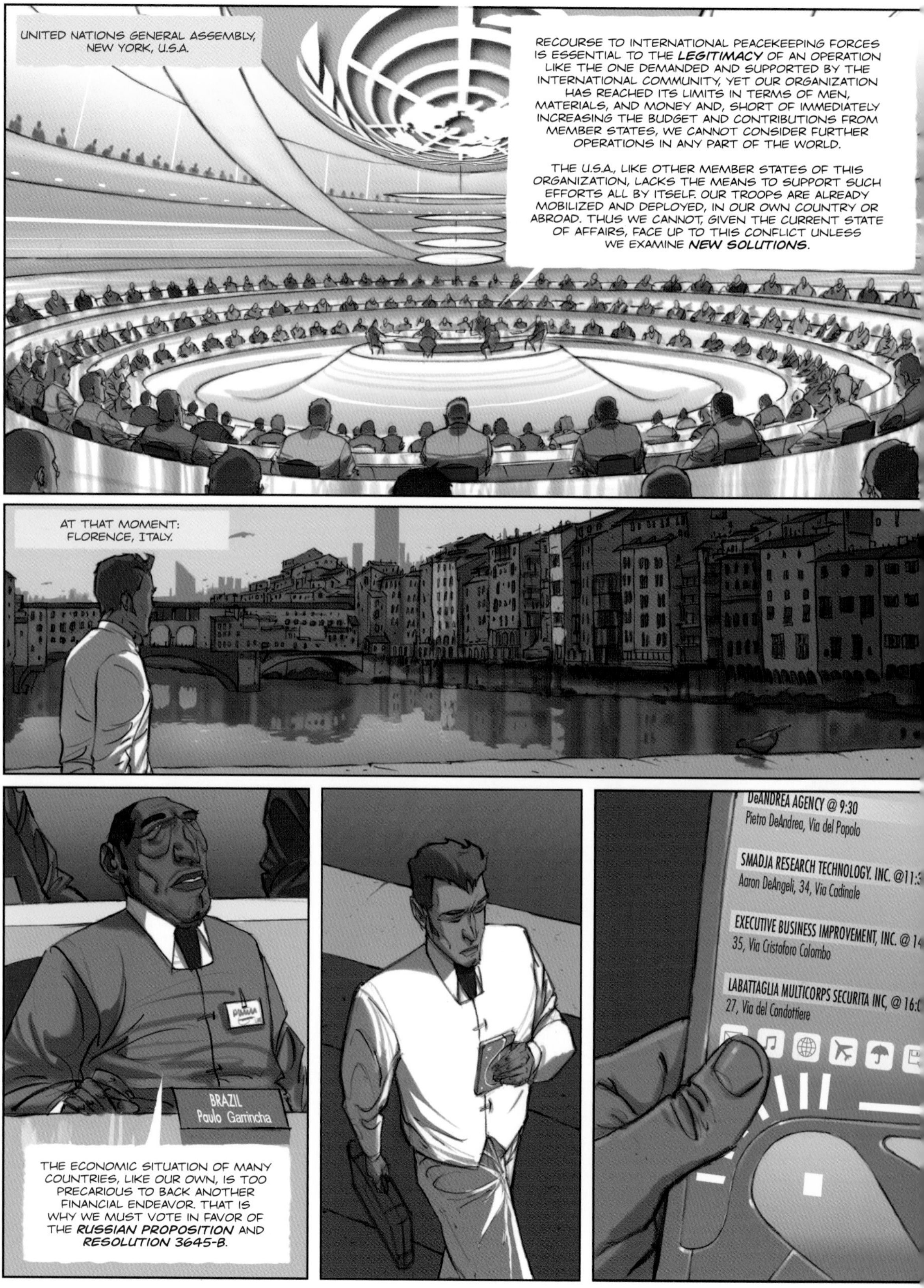
UNITED NATIONS GENERAL ASSEMBLY, NEW YORK, U.S.A.
RECOURSE TO INTERNATIONAL PEACEKEEPING FORCES IS ESSENTIAL TO THE **LEGITIMACY** OF AN OPERATION LIKE THE ONE DEMANDED AND SUPPORTED BY THE INTERNATIONAL COMMUNITY, YET OUR ORGANIZATION HAS REACHED ITS LIMITS IN TERMS OF MEN, MATERIALS, AND MONEY AND, SHORT OF IMMEDIATELY INCREASING THE BUDGET AND CONTRIBUTIONS FROM MEMBER STATES, WE CANNOT CONSIDER FURTHER OPERATIONS IN ANY PART OF THE WORLD.
THE U.S.A., LIKE OTHER MEMBER STATES OF THIS ORGANIZATION, LACKS THE MEANS TO SUPPORT SUCH EFFORTS ALL BY ITSELF. OUR TROOPS ARE ALREADY MOBILIZED AND DEPLOYED, IN OUR OWN COUNTRY OR ABROAD. THUS WE CANNOT, GIVEN THE CURRENT STATE OF AFFAIRS, FACE UP TO THIS CONFLICT UNLESS WE EXAMINE **NEW SOLUTIONS**.
AT THAT MOMENT: FLORENCE, ITALY.
BRAZIL
Paulo Garrincha
THE ECONOMIC SITUATION OF MANY COUNTRIES, LIKE OUR OWN, IS TOO PRECARIOUS TO BACK ANOTHER FINANCIAL ENDEAVOR. THAT IS WHY WE MUST VOTE IN FAVOR OF THE **RUSSIAN PROPOSITION** AND **RESOLUTION 3645-B**.
DeANDREA AGENCY @ 9:30
Pietro DeAndrea, Via del Popolo
SMADJA RESEARCH TECHNOLOGY. INC. @11:
Aaron DeAngeli, 34, Via Cadinale
EXECUTIVE BUSINESS IMPROVEMENT, INC. @ 1
35, Via Cristoforo Colombo
LABATTAGLIA MULTICORPS SECURITA INC, @ 16:
27, Via del Condottiere

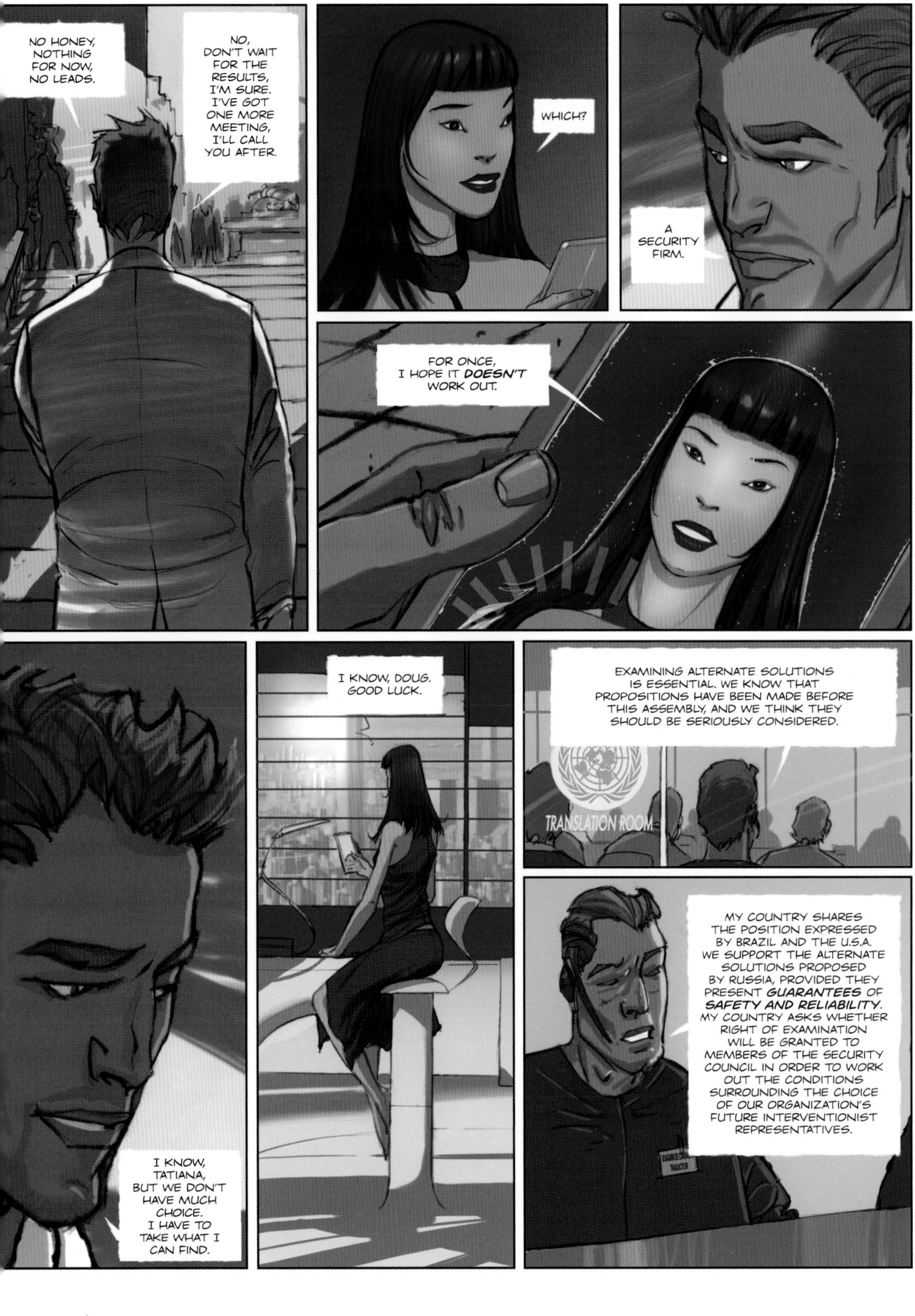
NO HONEY, NOTHING FOR NOW, NO LEADS.
NO, DON'T WAIT FOR THE RESULTS, I'M SURE. I'VE GOT ONE MORE MEETING, I'LL CALL YOU AFTER.
WHICH?
A SECURITY FIRM.
FOR ONCE, I HOPE IT DOESN'T WORK OUT.
I KNOW, TATIANA, BUT WE DON'T HAVE MUCH CHOICE. I HAVE TO TAKE WHAT I CAN FIND.
I KNOW, DOUG. GOOD LUCK.
EXAMINING ALTERNATE SOLUTIONS IS ESSENTIAL. WE KNOW THAT PROPOSITIONS HAVE BEEN MADE BEFORE THIS ASSEMBLY, AND WE THINK THEY SHOULD BE SERIOUSLY CONSIDERED.
TRANSLATION ROOM
MY COUNTRY SHARES THE POSITION EXPRESSED BY BRAZIL AND THE U.S.A. WE SUPPORT THE ALTERNATE SOLUTIONS PROPOSED BY RUSSIA, PROVIDED THEY PRESENT GUARANTEES OF SAFETY AND RELIABILITY. MY COUNTRY ASKS WHETHER RIGHT OF EXAMINATION WILL BE GRANTED TO MEMBERS OF THE SECURITY COUNCIL IN ORDER TO WORK OUT THE CONDITIONS SURROUNDING THE CHOICE OF OUR ORGANIZATION'S FUTURE INTERVENTIONIST REPRESENTATIVES.

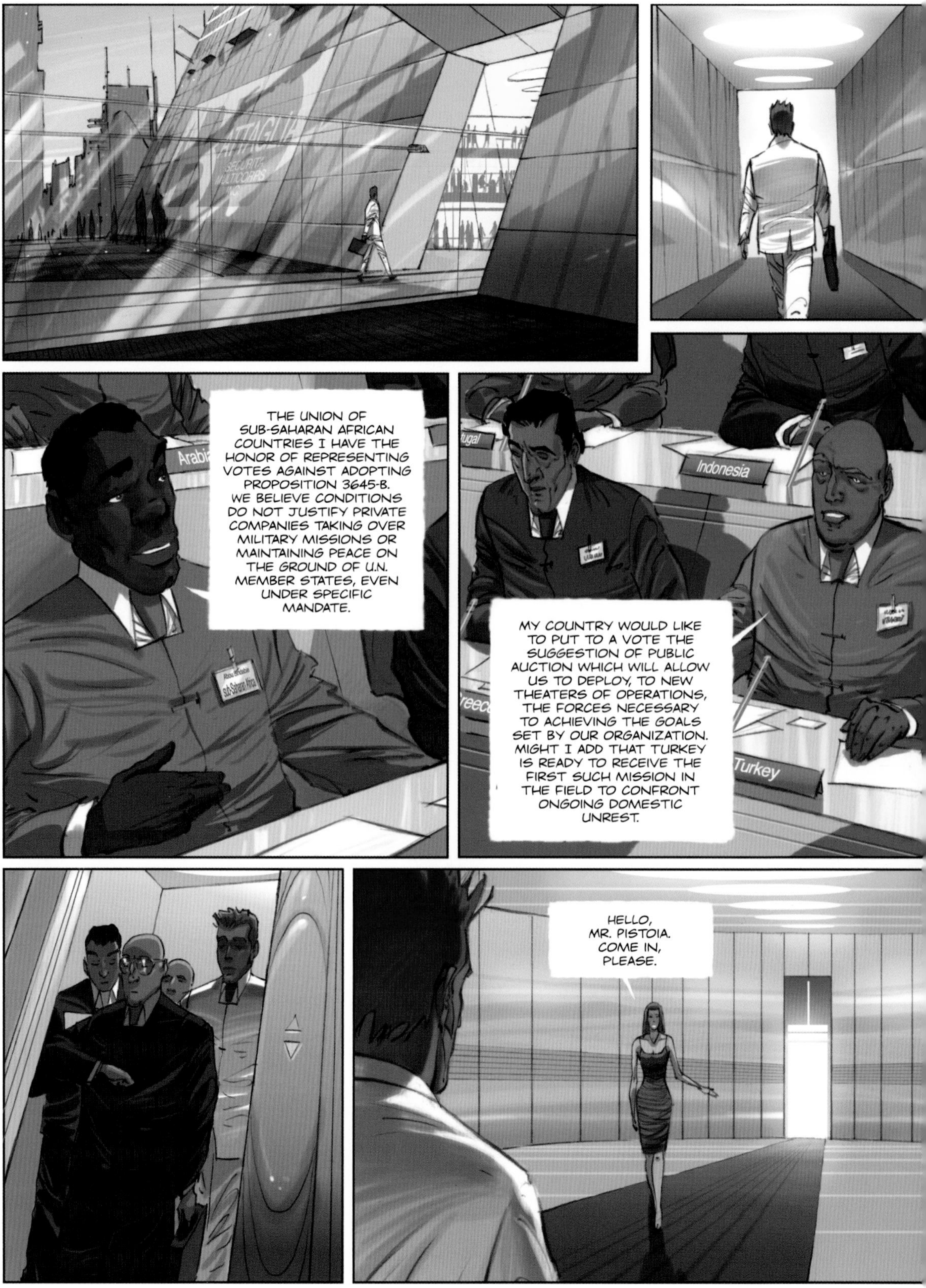
CATTAGLIA
SECURITY MULTICORPS
THE UNION OF SUB-SAHARAN AFRICAN COUNTRIES I HAVE THE HONOR OF REPRESENTING VOTES AGAINST ADOPTING PROPOSITION 3645-B. WE BELIEVE CONDITIONS DO NOT JUSTIFY PRIVATE COMPANIES TAKING OVER MILITARY MISSIONS OR MAINTAINING PEACE ON THE GROUND OF U.N. MEMBER STATES, EVEN UNDER SPECIFIC MANDATE.
Arabia
Indonesia
MY COUNTRY WOULD LIKE TO PUT TO A VOTE THE SUGGESTION OF PUBLIC AUCTION WHICH WILL ALLOW US TO DEPLOY, TO NEW THEATERS OF OPERATIONS, THE FORCES NECESSARY TO ACHIEVING THE GOALS SET BY OUR ORGANIZATION. MIGHT I ADD THAT TURKEY IS READY TO RECEIVE THE FIRST SUCH MISSION IN THE FIELD TO CONFRONT ONGOING DOMESTIC UNREST.
Turkey
HELLO, MR. PISTOIA. COME IN, PLEASE.

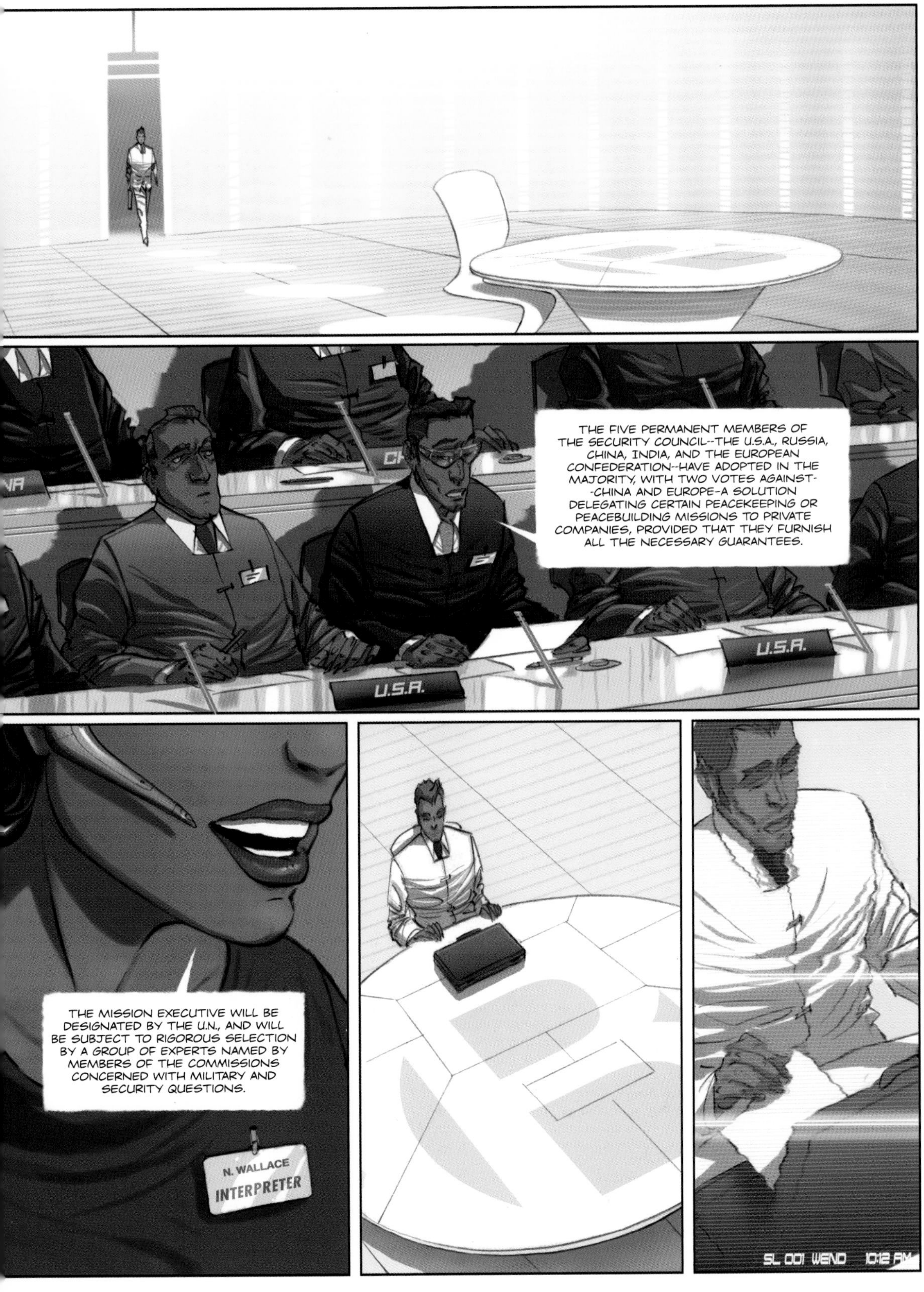
CH
NA
THE FIVE PERMANENT MEMBERS OF THE SECURITY COUNCIL--THE U.S.A., RUSSIA, CHINA, INDIA, AND THE EUROPEAN CONFEDERATION--HAVE ADOPTED IN THE MAJORITY, WITH TWO VOTES AGAINST--CHINA AND EUROPE-A SOLUTION DELEGATING CERTAIN PEACEKEEPING OR PEACEBUILDING MISSIONS TO PRIVATE COMPANIES, PROVIDED THAT THEY FURNISH ALL THE NECESSARY GUARANTEES.
U.S.A.
U.S.A.
THE MISSION EXECUTIVE WILL BE DESIGNATED BY THE U.N., AND WILL BE SUBJECT TO RIGOROUS SELECTION BY A GROUP OF EXPERTS NAMED BY MEMBERS OF THE COMMISSIONS CONCERNED WITH MILITARY AND SECURITY QUESTIONS.
N. WALLACE
INTERPRETER
SL 001 WEND 10:12 AM

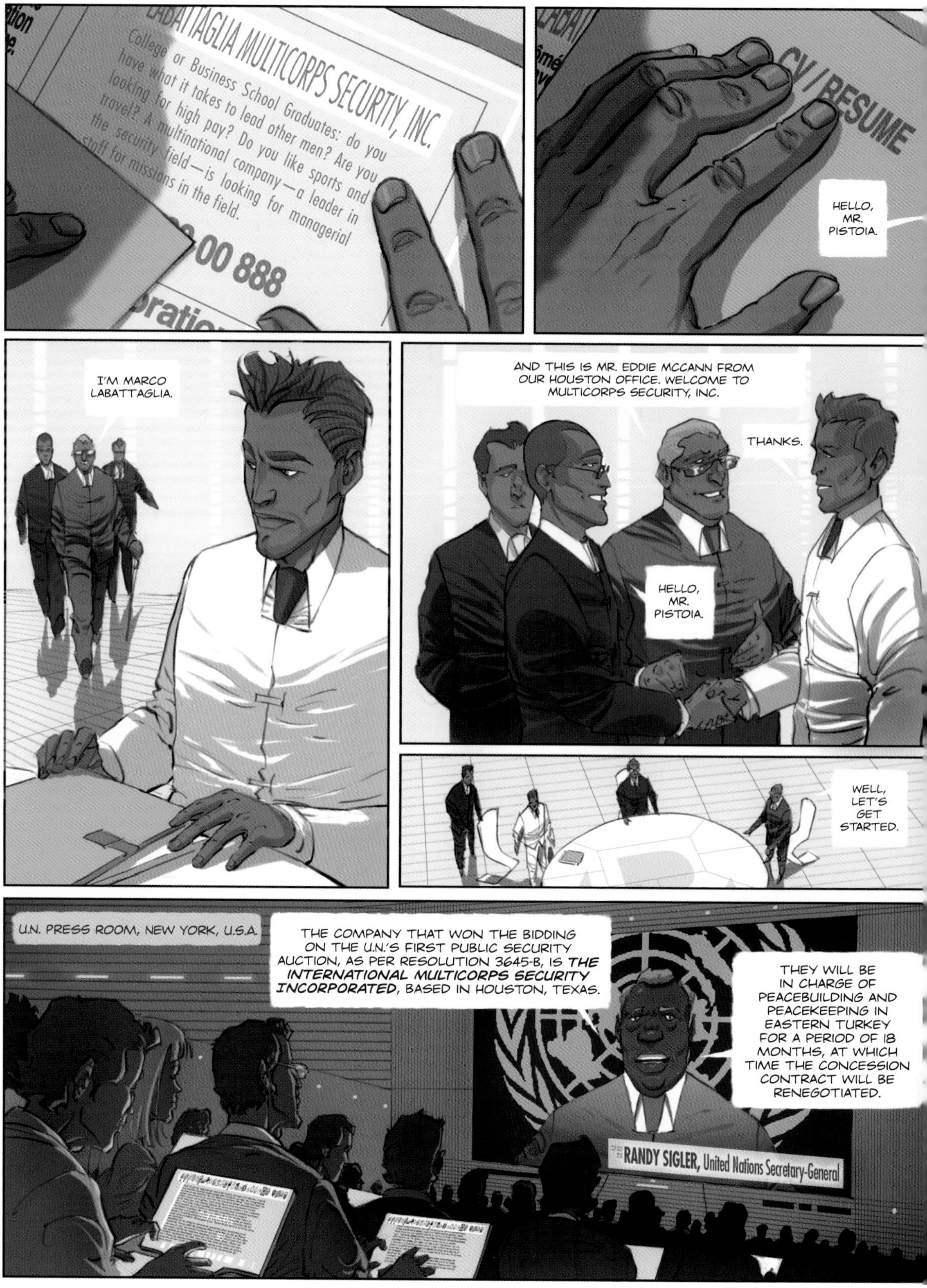
LABATTAGLIA MULTICORPS SECURTIY, INC.
College or Business School Graduates: do you have what it takes to lead other men? Are you looking for high pay? Do you like sports and travel? A multinational company—a leader in the security field—is looking for managerial staff for missions in the field.
00 888
CV / RESUME
HELLO, MR. PISTOIA.
I'M MARCO LABATTAGLIA.
AND THIS IS MR. EDDIE MCCANN FROM OUR HOUSTON OFFICE. WELCOME TO MULTICORPS SECURITY, INC.
THANKS.
HELLO, MR. PISTOIA.
WELL, LET'S GET STARTED.
U.N. PRESS ROOM, NEW YORK, U.S.A.
THE COMPANY THAT WON THE BIDDING ON THE U.N.'S FIRST PUBLIC SECURITY AUCTION, AS PER RESOLUTION 3645-B, IS *THE INTERNATIONAL MULTICORPS SECURITY INCORPORATED*, BASED IN HOUSTON, TEXAS.
THEY WILL BE IN CHARGE OF PEACEBUILDING AND PEACEKEEPING IN EASTERN TURKEY FOR A PERIOD OF 18 MONTHS, AT WHICH TIME THE CONCESSION CONTRACT WILL BE RENEGOTIATED.
RANDY SIGLER, United Nations Secretary-General

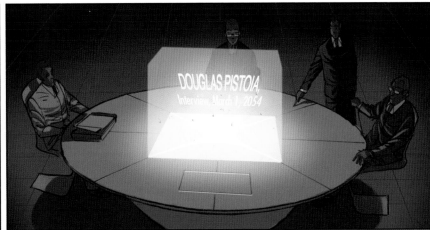

DOUGLAS PISTOIA,
Interview, March 1, 2054

DOUGLAS PISTOIA, YOU HAVE RECEIVED THE HIGHEST GRADE IN ECONOMICS AND HUMAN SCIENCES, AND IN MOST OTHER AREAS. YOU ARE THE FIRST IN YOUR YEAR. ALLOW ME TO CONGRATULATE YOU: IT'S BEEN A LONG TIME SINCE SUCH A HIGH GRADE WAS EARNED BY A STUDENT AT OUR SCHOOL.

THANK YOU, HEADMASTER. I'LL TRY TO BE WORTHY OF OUR SCHOOL.

DOUGLAS' PARENTS. HIS MOTHER, AMERICAN, JANET MAE HAWTHORNE, BORN IN LOS ANGELES. HIS FATHER, GAETANO PISTOIA, BORN IN MILAN. DOUGLAS WAS BORN FEBRUARY 2, 2030, IN NEW YORK. DUAL CITIZENSHIP: AMERICAN AND EUROPEAN.

HE PERFORMED BRILLIANTLY IN HIS STUDIES AT BOSTON UNIVERSITY, BUT GREW UP IN ITALY.

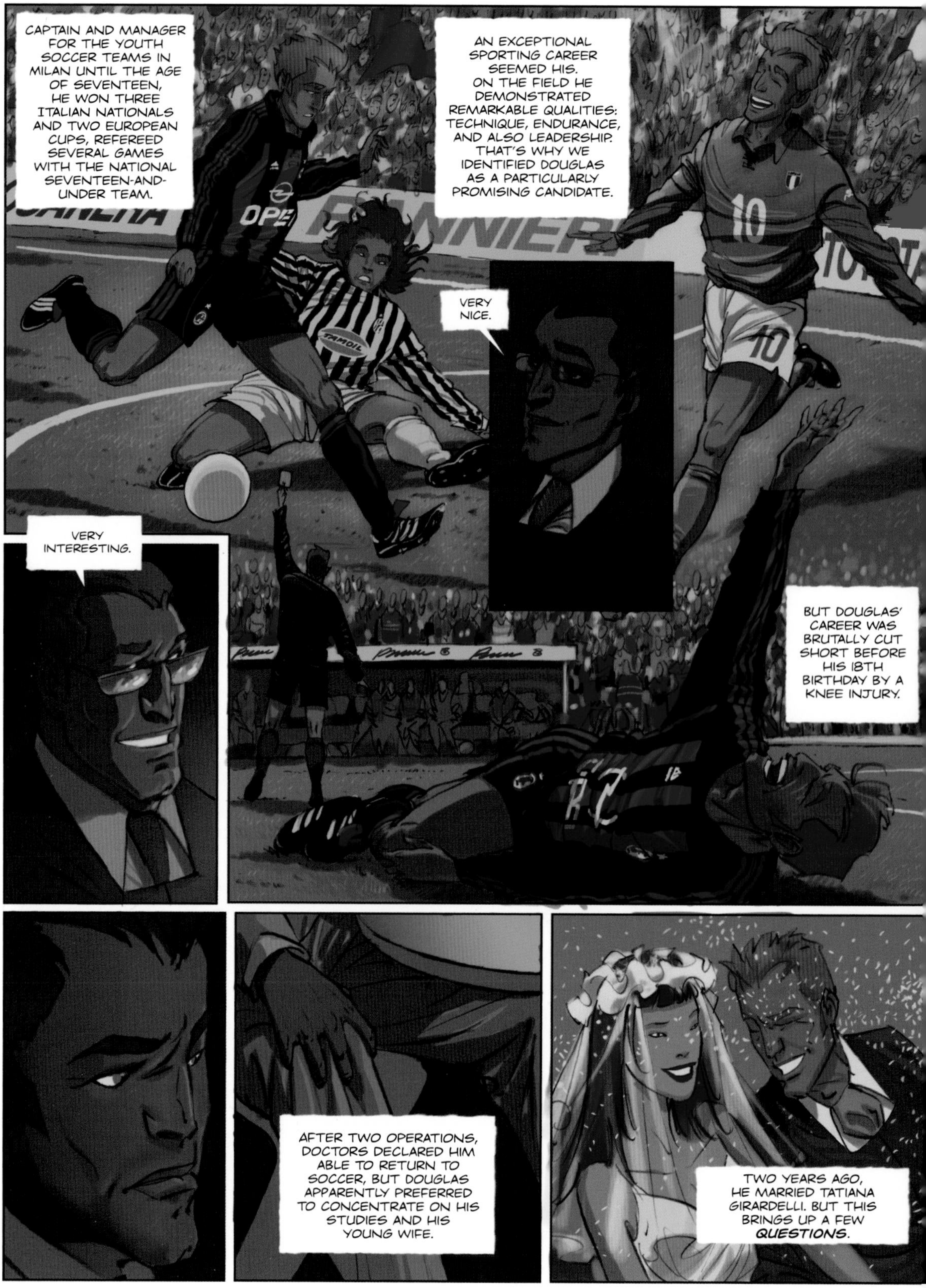
CAPTAIN AND MANAGER FOR THE YOUTH SOCCER TEAMS IN MILAN UNTIL THE AGE OF SEVENTEEN, HE WON THREE ITALIAN NATIONALS AND TWO EUROPEAN CUPS, REFEREED SEVERAL GAMES WITH THE NATIONAL SEVENTEEN-AND-UNDER TEAM.
AN EXCEPTIONAL SPORTING CAREER SEEMED HIS. ON THE FIELD HE DEMONSTRATED REMARKABLE QUALITIES: TECHNIQUE, ENDURANCE, AND ALSO LEADERSHIP. THAT'S WHY WE IDENTIFIED DOUGLAS AS A PARTICULARLY PROMISING CANDIDATE.
VERY NICE.
VERY INTERESTING.
BUT DOUGLAS' CAREER WAS BRUTALLY CUT SHORT BEFORE HIS 18TH BIRTHDAY BY A KNEE INJURY.
AFTER TWO OPERATIONS, DOCTORS DECLARED HIM ABLE TO RETURN TO SOCCER, BUT DOUGLAS APPARENTLY PREFERRED TO CONCENTRATE ON HIS STUDIES AND HIS YOUNG WIFE.
TWO YEARS AGO, HE MARRIED TATIANA GIRARDELLI. BUT THIS BRINGS UP A FEW QUESTIONS.

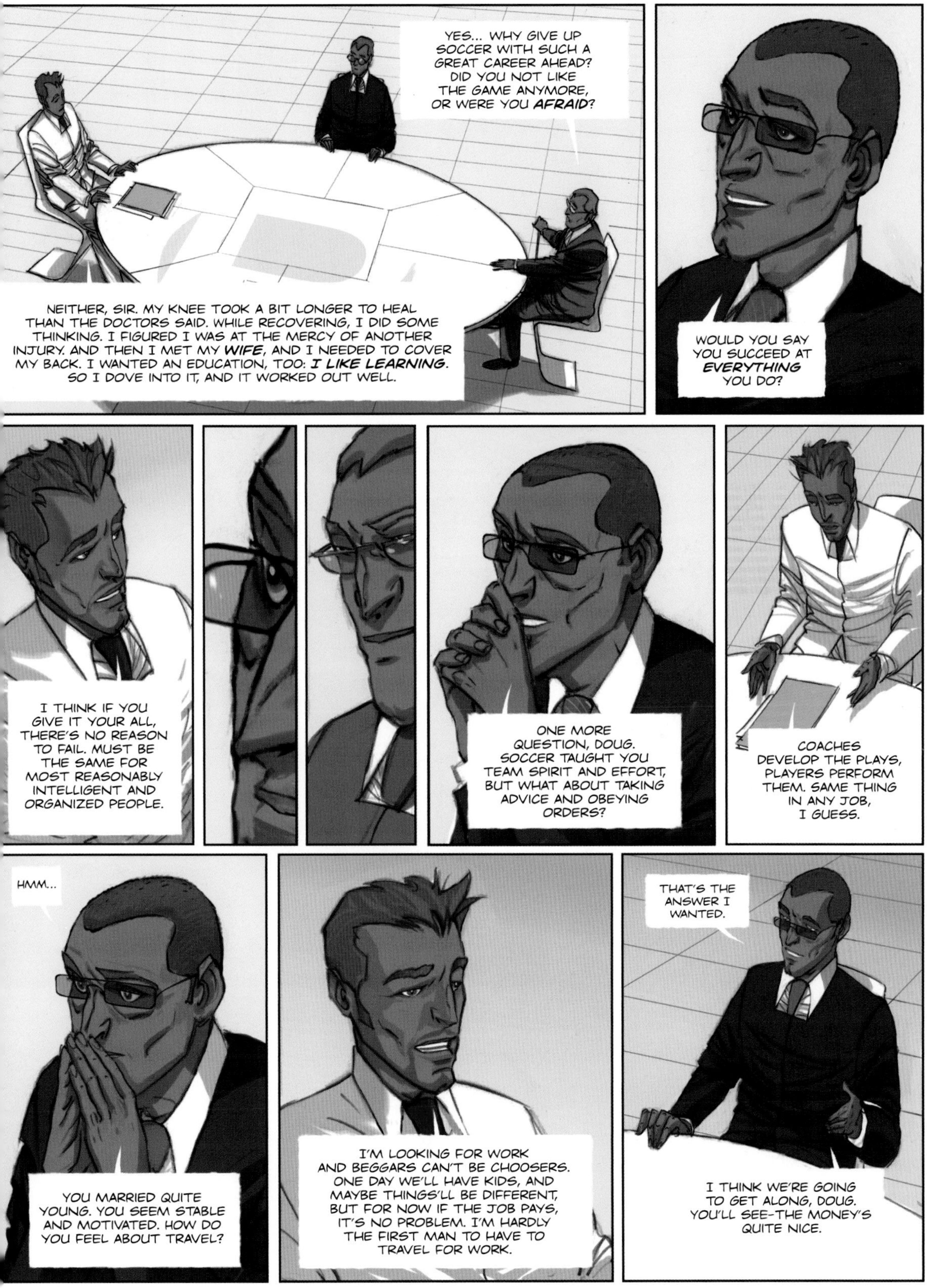
YES... WHY GIVE UP SOCCER WITH SUCH A GREAT CAREER AHEAD? DID YOU NOT LIKE THE GAME ANYMORE, OR WERE YOU *AFRAID*?
NEITHER, SIR. MY KNEE TOOK A BIT LONGER TO HEAL THAN THE DOCTORS SAID. WHILE RECOVERING, I DID SOME THINKING. I FIGURED I WAS AT THE MERCY OF ANOTHER INJURY. AND THEN I MET MY *WIFE*, AND I NEEDED TO COVER MY BACK. I WANTED AN EDUCATION, TOO: *I LIKE LEARNING*. SO I DOVE INTO IT, AND IT WORKED OUT WELL.
WOULD YOU SAY YOU SUCCEED AT *EVERYTHING* YOU DO?
I THINK IF YOU GIVE IT YOUR ALL, THERE'S NO REASON TO FAIL. MUST BE THE SAME FOR MOST REASONABLY INTELLIGENT AND ORGANIZED PEOPLE.
ONE MORE QUESTION, DOUG. SOCCER TAUGHT YOU TEAM SPIRIT AND EFFORT, BUT WHAT ABOUT TAKING ADVICE AND OBEYING ORDERS?
COACHES DEVELOP THE PLAYS, PLAYERS PERFORM THEM. SAME THING IN ANY JOB, I GUESS.
HMM...
YOU MARRIED QUITE YOUNG. YOU SEEM STABLE AND MOTIVATED. HOW DO YOU FEEL ABOUT TRAVEL?
I'M LOOKING FOR WORK AND BEGGARS CAN'T BE CHOOSERS. ONE DAY WE'LL HAVE KIDS, AND MAYBE THINGS'LL BE DIFFERENT, BUT FOR NOW IF THE JOB PAYS, IT'S NO PROBLEM. I'M HARDLY THE FIRST MAN TO HAVE TO TRAVEL FOR WORK.
THAT'S THE ANSWER I WANTED.
I THINK WE'RE GOING TO GET ALONG, DOUG. YOU'LL SEE-THE MONEY'S QUITE NICE.

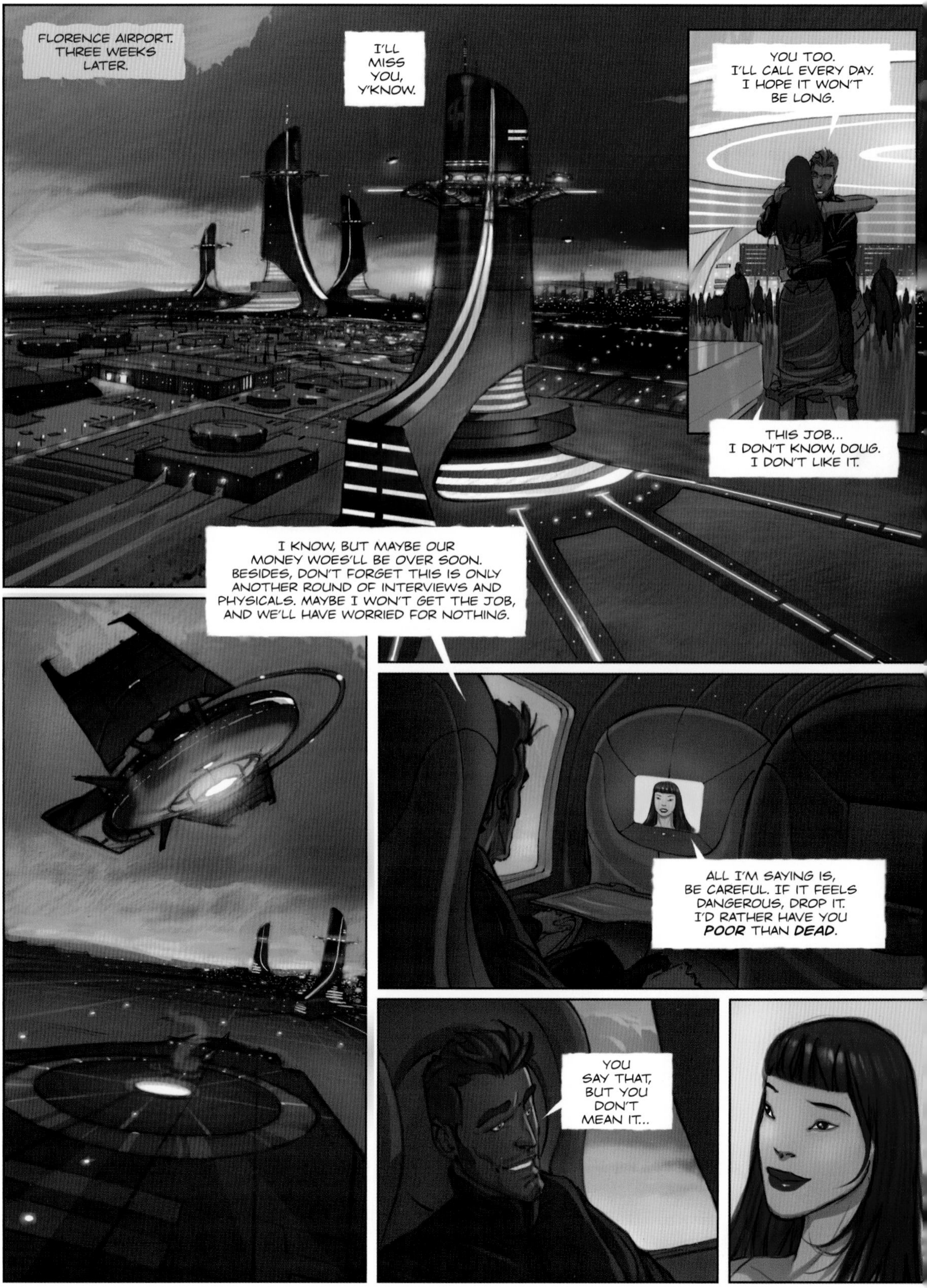
FLORENCE AIRPORT. THREE WEEKS LATER.
I'LL MISS YOU, Y'KNOW.
YOU TOO. I'LL CALL EVERY DAY. I HOPE IT WON'T BE LONG.
THIS JOB... I DON'T KNOW, DOUG. I DON'T LIKE IT.
I KNOW, BUT MAYBE OUR MONEY WOES'LL BE OVER SOON. BESIDES, DON'T FORGET THIS IS ONLY ANOTHER ROUND OF INTERVIEWS AND PHYSICALS. MAYBE I WON'T GET THE JOB, AND WE'LL HAVE WORRIED FOR NOTHING.
ALL I'M SAYING IS, BE CAREFUL. IF IT FEELS DANGEROUS, DROP IT. I'D RATHER HAVE YOU POOR THAN DEAD.
YOU SAY THAT, BUT YOU DON'T MEAN IT...

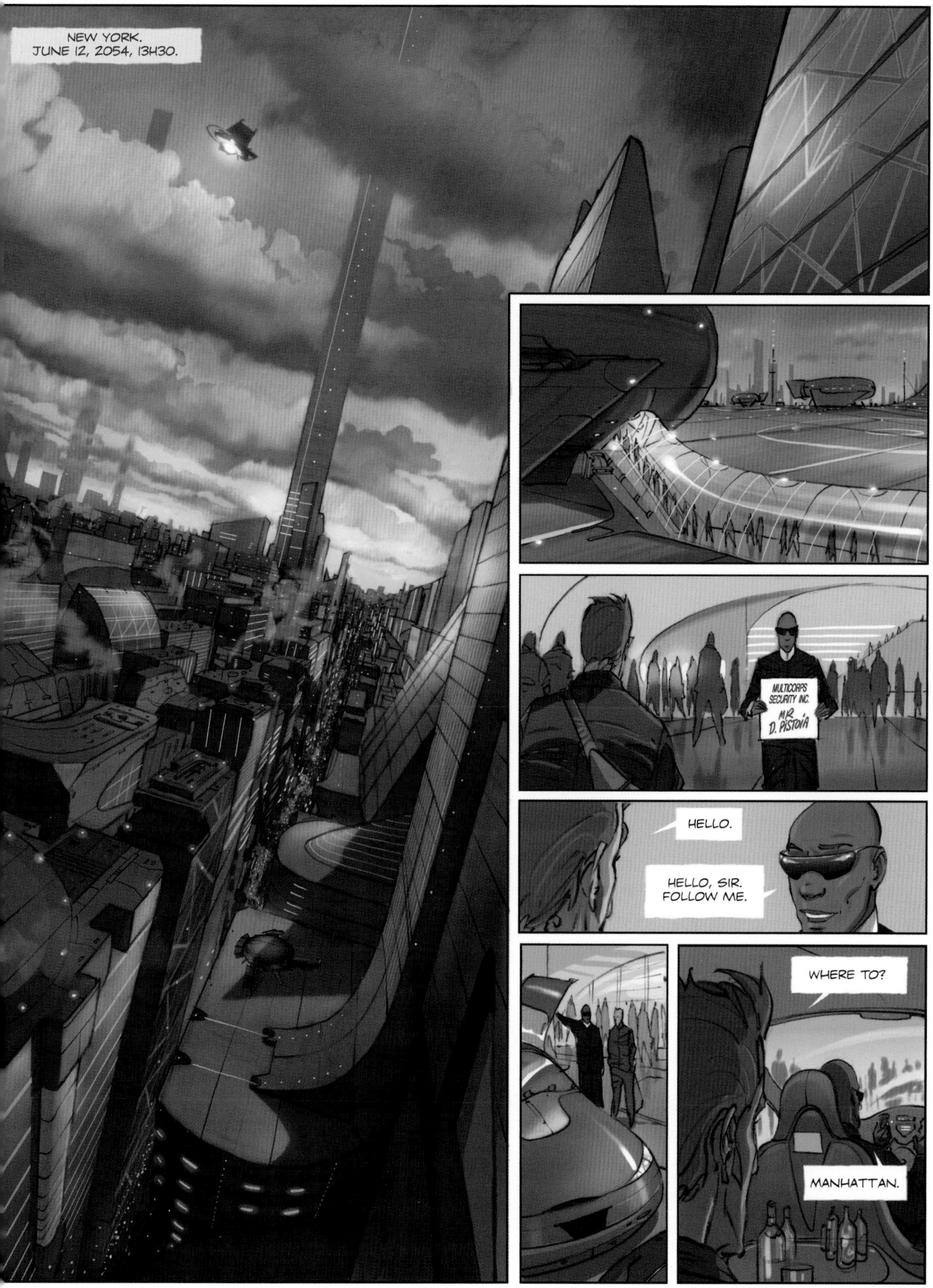
NEW YORK.
JUNE 12, 2054, 13H30.
MULTICORPS SECURITY INC. MR D. PISTOIA
HELLO.
HELLO, SIR. FOLLOW ME.
WHERE TO?
MANHATTAN.

MULTICORPS SECURITY, INC. TRAINING CAMP. PHOENIX, ARIZONA.

IF YOU'RE HERE, YOU'VE PASSED THE SECOND ROUND OF INTERVIEWS. THAT MEANS YOU'RE CLOSE TO THE GOAL. ALL YOU HAVE TO DO IS PASS THE FITNESS TEST.

FILL OUT THE HEALTH QUESTIONNAIRE, THEN WE'LL GO ON TO THE EXERCISES. THE SELECTION PROCESS IS TOUGH, BUT WORTH IT.

YOU WON'T REGRET IT. SO TRY TO KEEP UP.

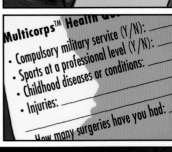

Multicorps™ Health que...
• Compulsory military service (Y/N): ___
• Sports at a professional level (Y/N): ___
• Childhood diseases or conditions: ___
• Injuries: ___
How many surgeries have you had:

HERE AT MULTICORPS, THE PRINCIPLE IS **SIMPLE**. BEFORE ASSIGNING YOU TO ONE OF OUR OFFICES TO BE THE GOOD LITTLE EXECUTIVES YOUR STUDIES HAVE PREPARED YOU FOR, WE SEND YOU INTO THE FIELD. THAT WAY, WE SEE WHAT YOU'RE WORTH, AND YOU CAN TAKE STOCK OF THE REALITY YOU'LL BE IN.

REMEMBER, MULTICORPS IS A *U.N. REPRESENTATIVE*.

THE RULES ARE CLEAR: YOU DON'T HAVE THE RIGHT TO SHOOT FIRST, BUT IF SHOT AT, YOU CAN SHOOT BACK. YOU'RE **SOLDIERS OF PEACE**, BUT YOU'RE NOT SITTING DUCKS. USE YOUR INTELLIGENCE AND YOUR JUDGMENT TO CONFRONT SITUATIONS.

IF YOU DECIDE TO SHOOT, I SUGGEST A BULL'S EYE. FOR TWO REASONS: DON'T MAKE MISTAKES THAT MIGHT COMPROMISE THE WHOLE OPERATION, AND DON'T LET ON THAT YOU'RE NOT ON TOP OF THE SITUATION.

NICE SHOT, PISTOIA.

AN UNDERSTANDING OF YOUR ROLE IS AT THE HEART OF YOUR TRAINING. MULTICORPS WILL INAUGURATE THE **PRIVATIZATION** OF THE INTERNATIONAL SECURITY MARKET.

I DON'T THINK I NEED TO TELL YOU HOW IMPORTANT THIS MISSION IS, AND THE **FINANCIAL REPERCUSSIONS** OF AN ENTERPRISE LIKE THIS. THAT'S ALSO WHY WE'RE ONLY SENDING HANDPICKED INDIVIDUALS.

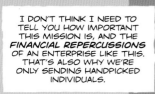

DOESN'T THAT MAKE US MERCENARIES?

IF YOU ASK ME, MERCS DON'T EXIST... OR THEY'RE **EVERYWHERE**. ANY MAN WHO GOES TO A JOB EVERY MORNING THAT HE WOULDN'T DO IF HE WEREN'T PAID IS A MERC--EXCEPT HE'S NOT AS WELL PAID. DON'T EVEN MENTION GUYS WHO KISS THE BOSS' ASS ALL DAY BECAUSE THEY'RE SCARED SHITLESS OF BEING FIRED.

I DON'T THINK THAT'S THE RIGHT QUESTION TO ASK. BESIDES, YOU'RE ONE OF THE GOOD GUYS. YOU'RE PERFORMING AN INVALUABLE SERVICE FOR THE INTERNATIONAL COMMUNITY.

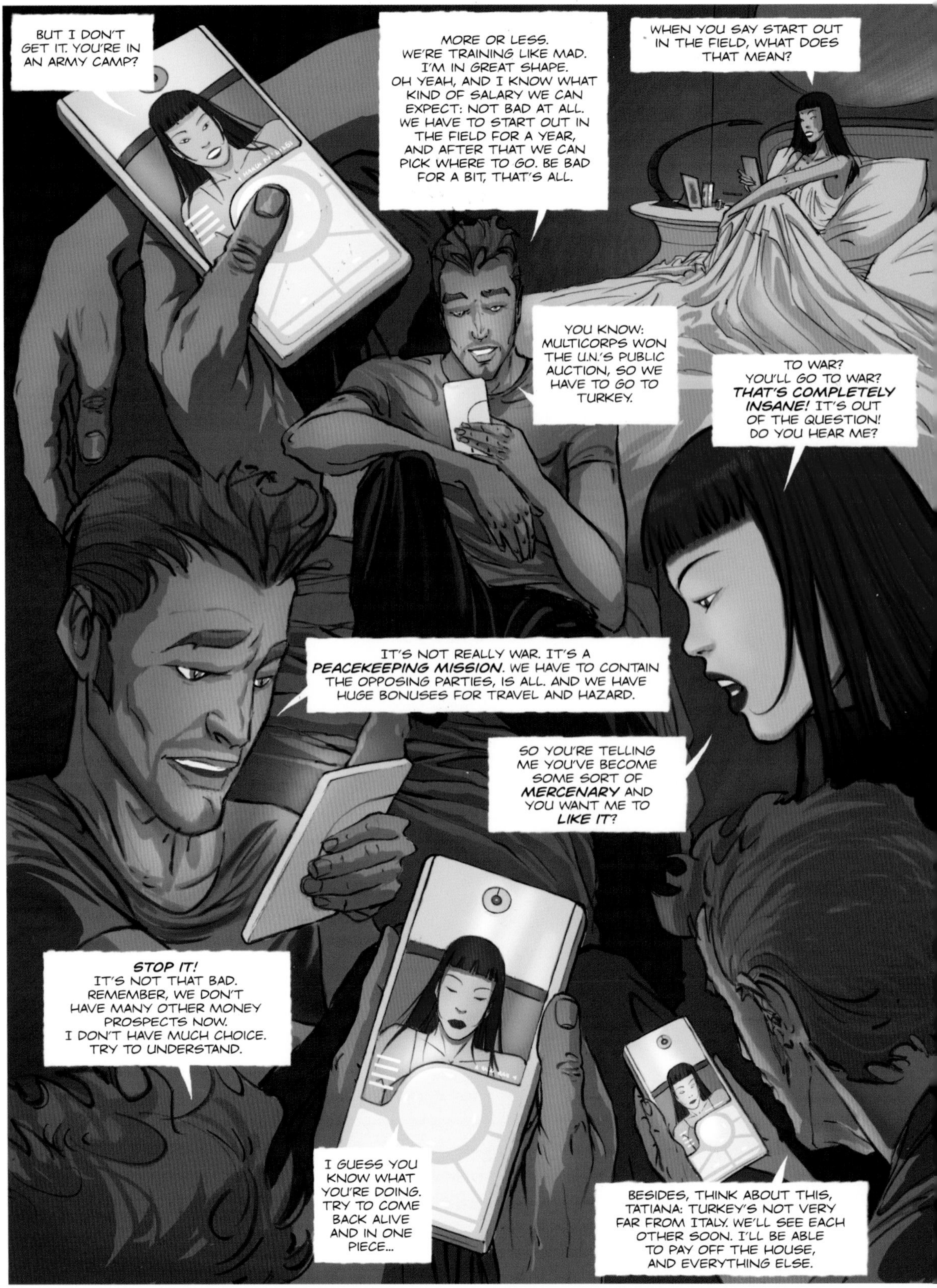
BUT I DON'T GET IT. YOU'RE IN AN ARMY CAMP?
MORE OR LESS. WE'RE TRAINING LIKE MAD. I'M IN GREAT SHAPE. OH YEAH, AND I KNOW WHAT KIND OF SALARY WE CAN EXPECT: NOT BAD AT ALL. WE HAVE TO START OUT IN THE FIELD FOR A YEAR, AND AFTER THAT WE CAN PICK WHERE TO GO. BE BAD FOR A BIT, THAT'S ALL.
WHEN YOU SAY START OUT IN THE FIELD, WHAT DOES THAT MEAN?
YOU KNOW: MULTICORPS WON THE U.N.'S PUBLIC AUCTION, SO WE HAVE TO GO TO TURKEY.
TO WAR? YOU'LL GO TO WAR? THAT'S COMPLETELY INSANE! IT'S OUT OF THE QUESTION! DO YOU HEAR ME?
IT'S NOT REALLY WAR. IT'S A PEACEKEEPING MISSION. WE HAVE TO CONTAIN THE OPPOSING PARTIES, IS ALL. AND WE HAVE HUGE BONUSES FOR TRAVEL AND HAZARD.
SO YOU'RE TELLING ME YOU'VE BECOME SOME SORT OF MERCENARY AND YOU WANT ME TO LIKE IT?
STOP IT! IT'S NOT THAT BAD. REMEMBER, WE DON'T HAVE MANY OTHER MONEY PROSPECTS NOW. I DON'T HAVE MUCH CHOICE. TRY TO UNDERSTAND.
I GUESS YOU KNOW WHAT YOU'RE DOING. TRY TO COME BACK ALIVE AND IN ONE PIECE...
BESIDES, THINK ABOUT THIS, TATIANA: TURKEY'S NOT VERY FAR FROM ITALY. WE'LL SEE EACH OTHER SOON. I'LL BE ABLE TO PAY OFF THE HOUSE, AND EVERYTHING ELSE.

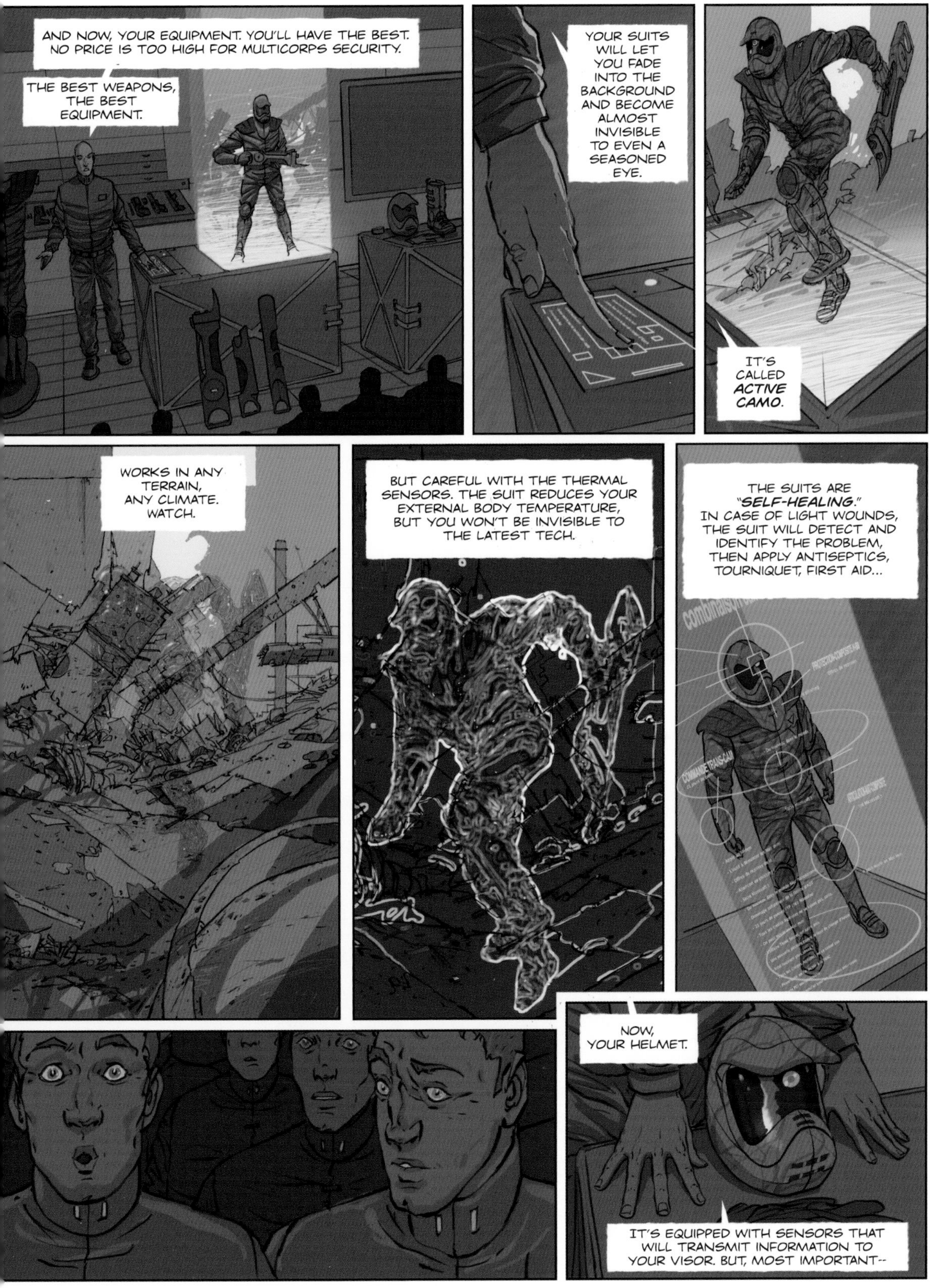
AND NOW, YOUR EQUIPMENT. YOU'LL HAVE THE BEST. NO PRICE IS TOO HIGH FOR MULTICORPS SECURITY.
THE BEST WEAPONS, THE BEST EQUIPMENT.
YOUR SUITS WILL LET YOU FADE INTO THE BACKGROUND AND BECOME ALMOST INVISIBLE TO EVEN A SEASONED EYE.
IT'S CALLED ***ACTIVE CAMO***.
WORKS IN ANY TERRAIN, ANY CLIMATE. WATCH.
BUT CAREFUL WITH THE THERMAL SENSORS. THE SUIT REDUCES YOUR EXTERNAL BODY TEMPERATURE, BUT YOU WON'T BE INVISIBLE TO THE LATEST TECH.
THE SUITS ARE "***SELF-HEALING***." IN CASE OF LIGHT WOUNDS, THE SUIT WILL DETECT AND IDENTIFY THE PROBLEM, THEN APPLY ANTISEPTICS, TOURNIQUET, FIRST AID...
NOW, YOUR HELMET.
IT'S EQUIPPED WITH SENSORS THAT WILL TRANSMIT INFORMATION TO YOUR VISOR. BUT, MOST IMPORTANT--

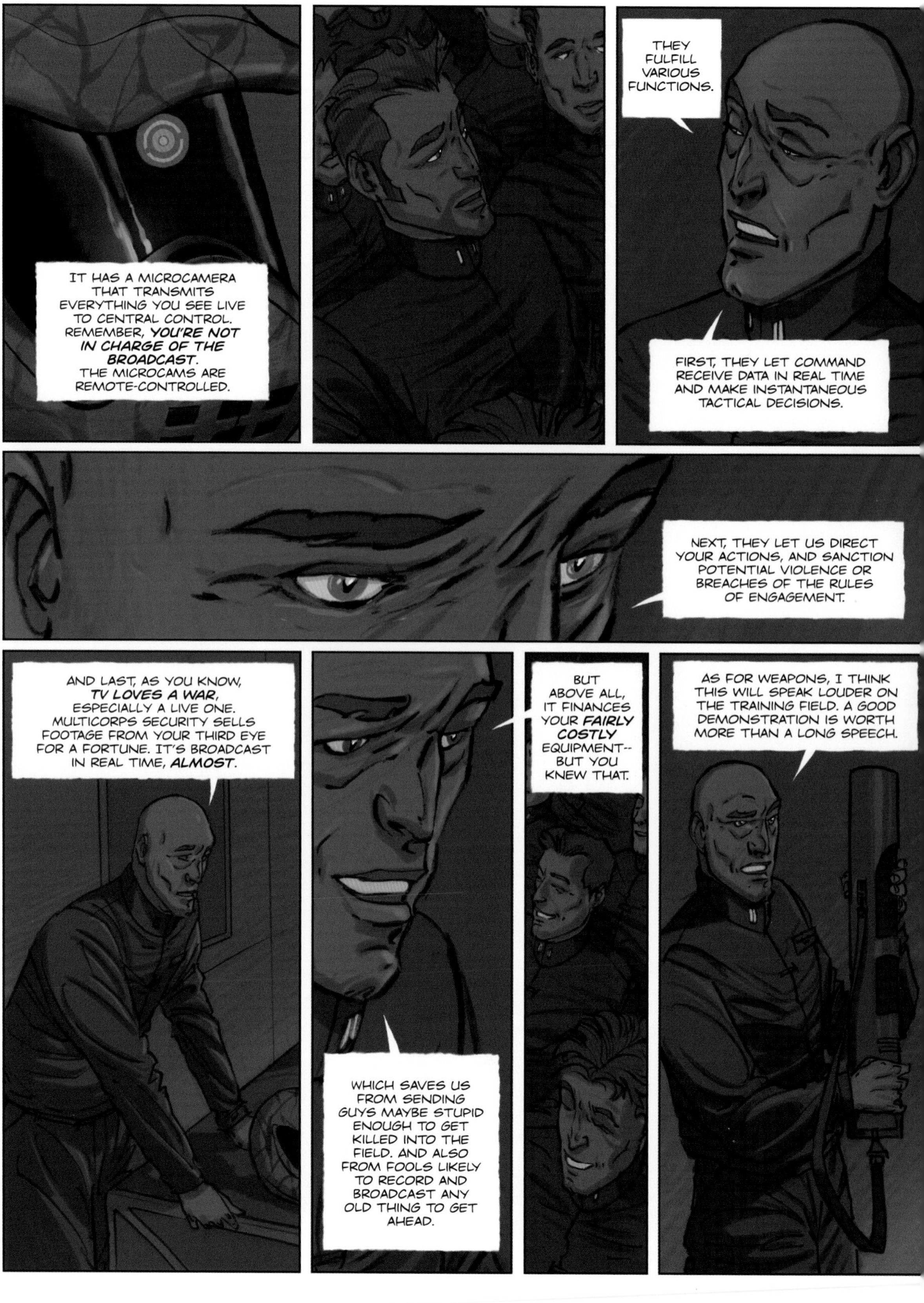
IT HAS A MICROCAMERA THAT TRANSMITS EVERYTHING YOU SEE LIVE TO CENTRAL CONTROL. REMEMBER, ***YOU'RE NOT IN CHARGE OF THE BROADCAST***. THE MICROCAMS ARE REMOTE-CONTROLLED.
THEY FULFILL VARIOUS FUNCTIONS.
FIRST, THEY LET COMMAND RECEIVE DATA IN REAL TIME AND MAKE INSTANTANEOUS TACTICAL DECISIONS.
NEXT, THEY LET US DIRECT YOUR ACTIONS, AND SANCTION POTENTIAL VIOLENCE OR BREACHES OF THE RULES OF ENGAGEMENT.
AND LAST, AS YOU KNOW, ***TV LOVES A WAR***, ESPECIALLY A LIVE ONE. MULTICORPS SECURITY SELLS FOOTAGE FROM YOUR THIRD EYE FOR A FORTUNE. IT'S BROADCAST IN REAL TIME, ***ALMOST***.
WHICH SAVES US FROM SENDING GUYS MAYBE STUPID ENOUGH TO GET KILLED INTO THE FIELD. AND ALSO FROM FOOLS LIKELY TO RECORD AND BROADCAST ANY OLD THING TO GET AHEAD.
BUT ABOVE ALL, IT FINANCES YOUR ***FAIRLY COSTLY*** EQUIPMENT--BUT YOU KNEW THAT.
AS FOR WEAPONS, I THINK THIS WILL SPEAK LOUDER ON THE TRAINING FIELD. A GOOD DEMONSTRATION IS WORTH MORE THAN A LONG SPEECH.

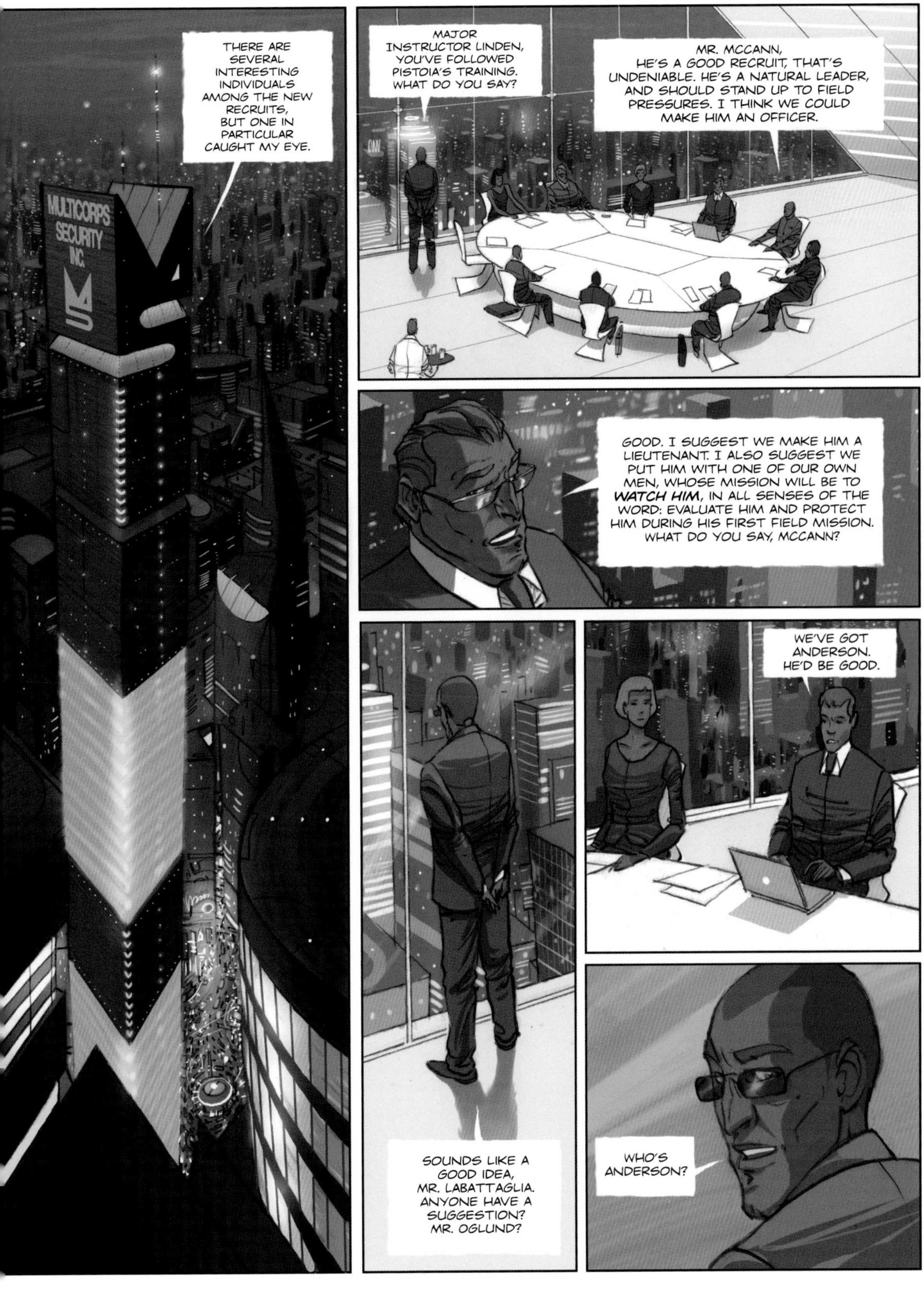
THERE ARE SEVERAL INTERESTING INDIVIDUALS AMONG THE NEW RECRUITS, BUT ONE IN PARTICULAR CAUGHT MY EYE.
MULTICORPS SECURITY INC.
MAJOR INSTRUCTOR LINDEN, YOU'VE FOLLOWED PISTOIA'S TRAINING. WHAT DO YOU SAY?
MR. MCCANN, HE'S A GOOD RECRUIT, THAT'S UNDENIABLE. HE'S A NATURAL LEADER, AND SHOULD STAND UP TO FIELD PRESSURES. I THINK WE COULD MAKE HIM AN OFFICER.
GOOD. I SUGGEST WE MAKE HIM A LIEUTENANT. I ALSO SUGGEST WE PUT HIM WITH ONE OF OUR OWN MEN, WHOSE MISSION WILL BE TO ***WATCH HIM***, IN ALL SENSES OF THE WORD: EVALUATE HIM AND PROTECT HIM DURING HIS FIRST FIELD MISSION. WHAT DO YOU SAY, MCCANN?
SOUNDS LIKE A GOOD IDEA, MR. LABATTAGLIA. ANYONE HAVE A SUGGESTION? MR. OGLUND?
WE'VE GOT ANDERSON. HE'D BE GOOD.
WHO'S ANDERSON?

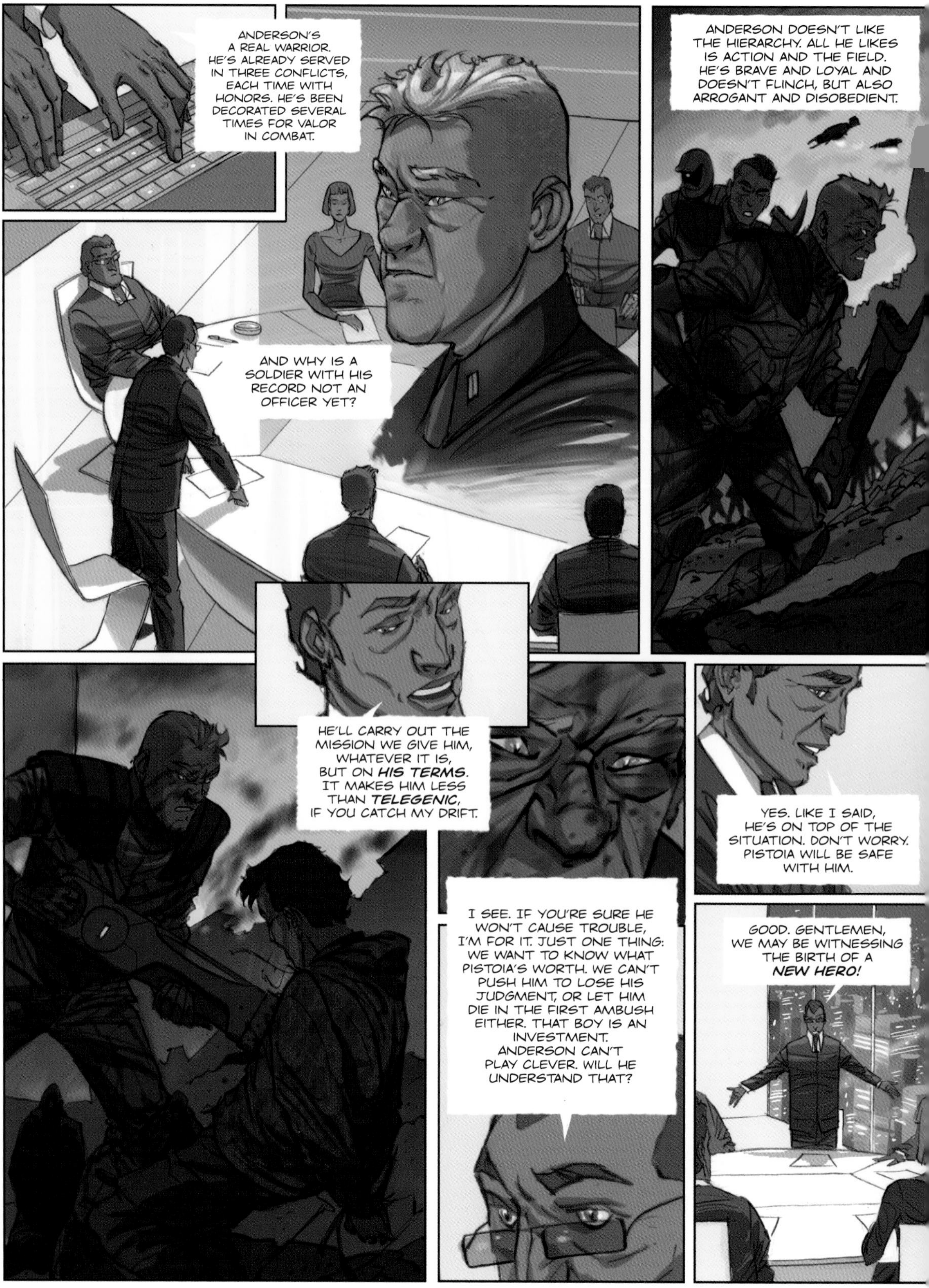
ANDERSON'S A REAL WARRIOR. HE'S ALREADY SERVED IN THREE CONFLICTS, EACH TIME WITH HONORS. HE'S BEEN DECORATED SEVERAL TIMES FOR VALOR IN COMBAT.
AND WHY IS A SOLDIER WITH HIS RECORD NOT AN OFFICER YET?
ANDERSON DOESN'T LIKE THE HIERARCHY. ALL HE LIKES IS ACTION AND THE FIELD. HE'S BRAVE AND LOYAL AND DOESN'T FLINCH, BUT ALSO ARROGANT AND DISOBEDIENT.
HE'LL CARRY OUT THE MISSION WE GIVE HIM, WHATEVER IT IS, BUT ON **HIS TERMS**. IT MAKES HIM LESS THAN ***TELEGENIC***, IF YOU CATCH MY DRIFT.
YES. LIKE I SAID, HE'S ON TOP OF THE SITUATION. DON'T WORRY. PISTOIA WILL BE SAFE WITH HIM.
I SEE. IF YOU'RE SURE HE WON'T CAUSE TROUBLE, I'M FOR IT. JUST ONE THING: WE WANT TO KNOW WHAT PISTOIA'S WORTH. WE CAN'T PUSH HIM TO LOSE HIS JUDGMENT, OR LET HIM DIE IN THE FIRST AMBUSH EITHER. THAT BOY IS AN INVESTMENT. ANDERSON CAN'T PLAY CLEVER. WILL HE UNDERSTAND THAT?
GOOD. GENTLEMEN, WE MAY BE WITNESSING THE BIRTH OF A ***NEW HERO!***

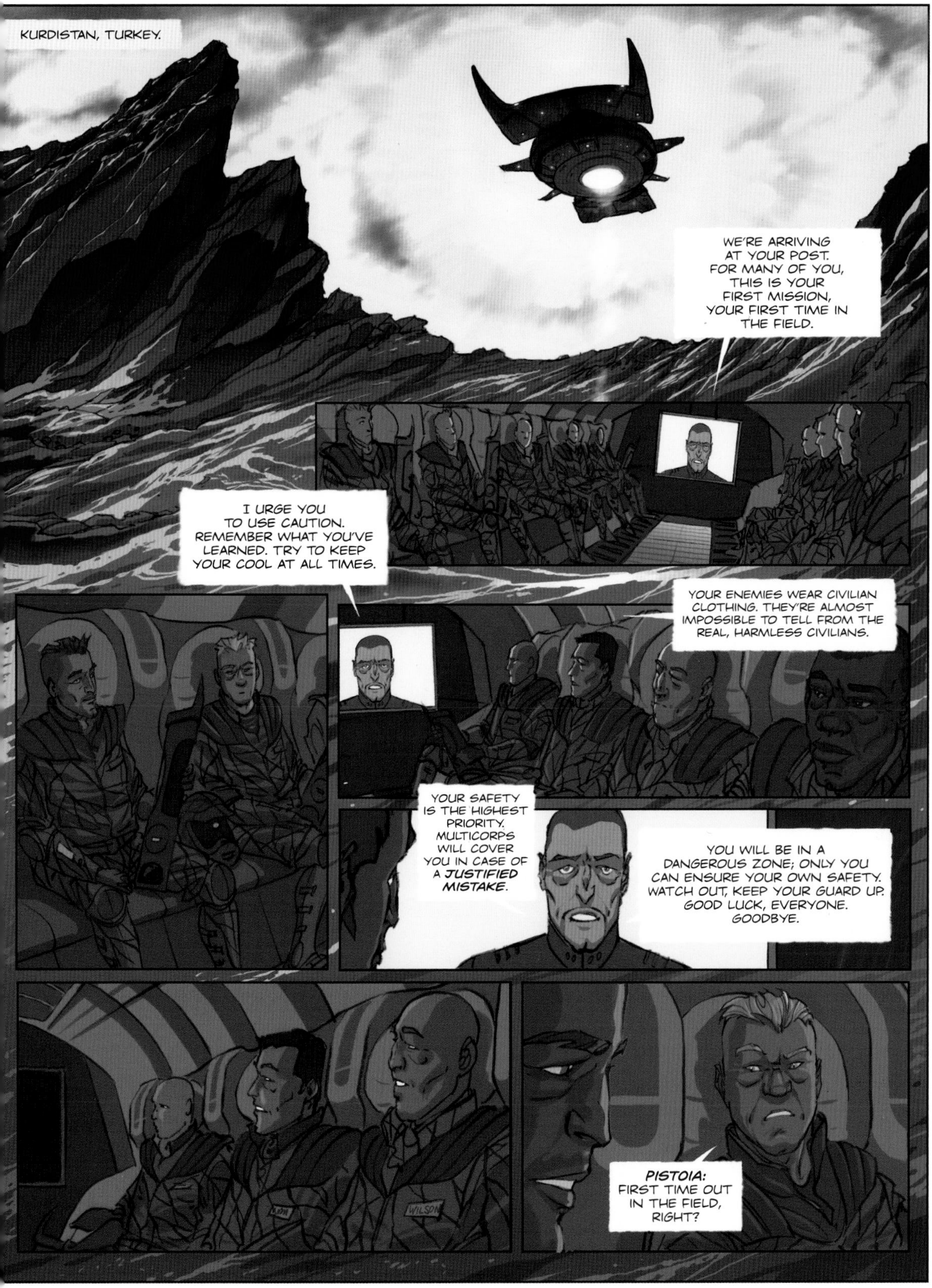
KURDISTAN, TURKEY.
WE'RE ARRIVING AT YOUR POST. FOR MANY OF YOU, THIS IS YOUR FIRST MISSION, YOUR FIRST TIME IN THE FIELD.
I URGE YOU TO USE CAUTION. REMEMBER WHAT YOU'VE LEARNED. TRY TO KEEP YOUR COOL AT ALL TIMES.
YOUR ENEMIES WEAR CIVILIAN CLOTHING. THEY'RE ALMOST IMPOSSIBLE TO TELL FROM THE REAL, HARMLESS CIVILIANS.
YOUR SAFETY IS THE HIGHEST PRIORITY. MULTICORPS WILL COVER YOU IN CASE OF A ***JUSTIFIED MISTAKE***.
YOU WILL BE IN A DANGEROUS ZONE; ONLY YOU CAN ENSURE YOUR OWN SAFETY. WATCH OUT, KEEP YOUR GUARD UP. GOOD LUCK, EVERYONE. GOODBYE.
WILSON
PISTOIA: FIRST TIME OUT IN THE FIELD, RIGHT?

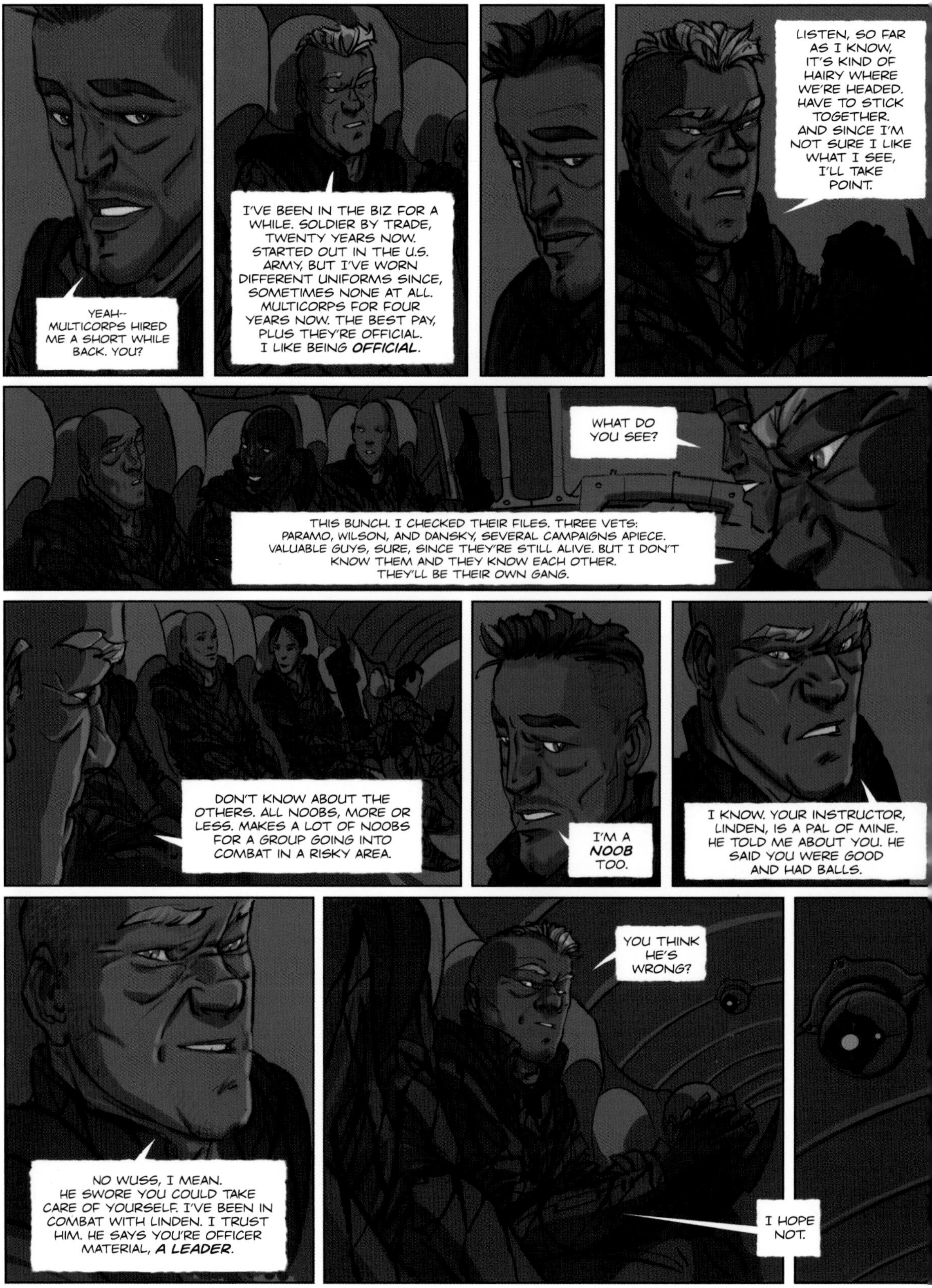
YEAH-- MULTICORPS HIRED ME A SHORT WHILE BACK. YOU?
I'VE BEEN IN THE BIZ FOR A WHILE. SOLDIER BY TRADE, TWENTY YEARS NOW. STARTED OUT IN THE U.S. ARMY, BUT I'VE WORN DIFFERENT UNIFORMS SINCE, SOMETIMES NONE AT ALL. MULTICORPS FOR FOUR YEARS NOW. THE BEST PAY, PLUS THEY'RE OFFICIAL. I LIKE BEING OFFICIAL.
LISTEN, SO FAR AS I KNOW, IT'S KIND OF HAIRY WHERE WE'RE HEADED. HAVE TO STICK TOGETHER. AND SINCE I'M NOT SURE I LIKE WHAT I SEE, I'LL TAKE POINT.
WHAT DO YOU SEE?
THIS BUNCH. I CHECKED THEIR FILES. THREE VETS: PARAMO, WILSON, AND DANSKY, SEVERAL CAMPAIGNS APIECE. VALUABLE GUYS, SURE, SINCE THEY'RE STILL ALIVE. BUT I DON'T KNOW THEM AND THEY KNOW EACH OTHER. THEY'LL BE THEIR OWN GANG.
DON'T KNOW ABOUT THE OTHERS. ALL NOOBS, MORE OR LESS. MAKES A LOT OF NOOBS FOR A GROUP GOING INTO COMBAT IN A RISKY AREA.
I'M A NOOB TOO.
I KNOW. YOUR INSTRUCTOR, LINDEN, IS A PAL OF MINE. HE TOLD ME ABOUT YOU. HE SAID YOU WERE GOOD AND HAD BALLS.
NO WUSS, I MEAN. HE SWORE YOU COULD TAKE CARE OF YOURSELF. I'VE BEEN IN COMBAT WITH LINDEN. I TRUST HIM. HE SAYS YOU'RE OFFICER MATERIAL, A LEADER.
YOU THINK HE'S WRONG?
I HOPE NOT.

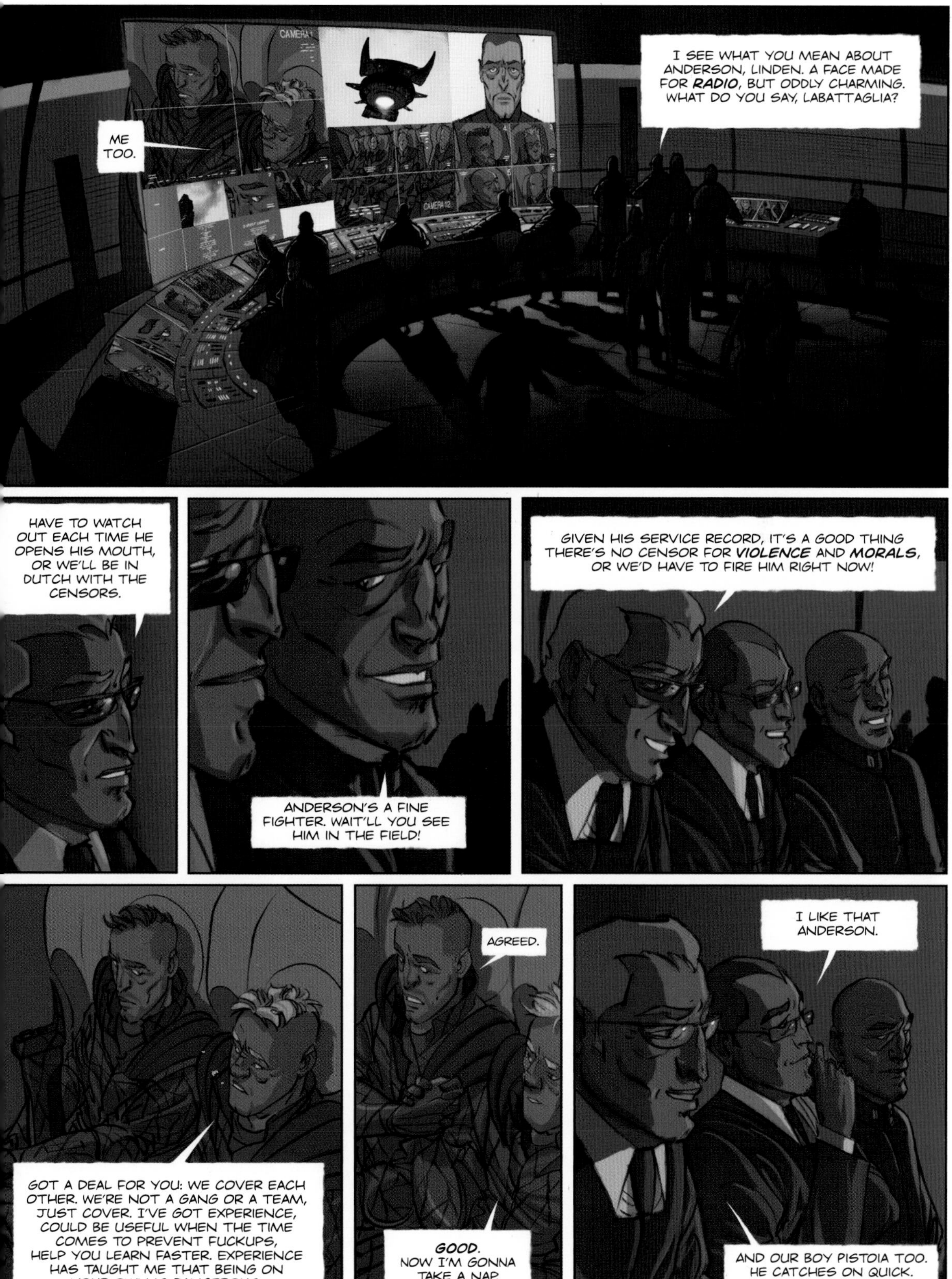
I SEE WHAT YOU MEAN ABOUT ANDERSON, LINDEN. A FACE MADE FOR **RADIO**, BUT ODDLY CHARMING. WHAT DO YOU SAY, LABATTAGLIA?
ME TOO.
CAMERA 1
CAMERA 12
HAVE TO WATCH OUT EACH TIME HE OPENS HIS MOUTH, OR WE'LL BE IN DUTCH WITH THE CENSORS.
ANDERSON'S A FINE FIGHTER. WAIT'LL YOU SEE HIM IN THE FIELD!
GIVEN HIS SERVICE RECORD, IT'S A GOOD THING THERE'S NO CENSOR FOR **VIOLENCE** AND **MORALS**, OR WE'D HAVE TO FIRE HIM RIGHT NOW!
GOT A DEAL FOR YOU: WE COVER EACH OTHER. WE'RE NOT A GANG OR A TEAM, JUST COVER. I'VE GOT EXPERIENCE, COULD BE USEFUL WHEN THE TIME COMES TO PREVENT FUCKUPS, HELP YOU LEARN FASTER. EXPERIENCE HAS TAUGHT ME THAT BEING ON YOUR OWN IS DANGEROUS.
AGREED.
GOOD. NOW I'M GONNA TAKE A NAP.
I LIKE THAT ANDERSON.
AND OUR BOY PISTOIA TOO. HE CATCHES ON QUICK. NICE PICK, LINDEN.

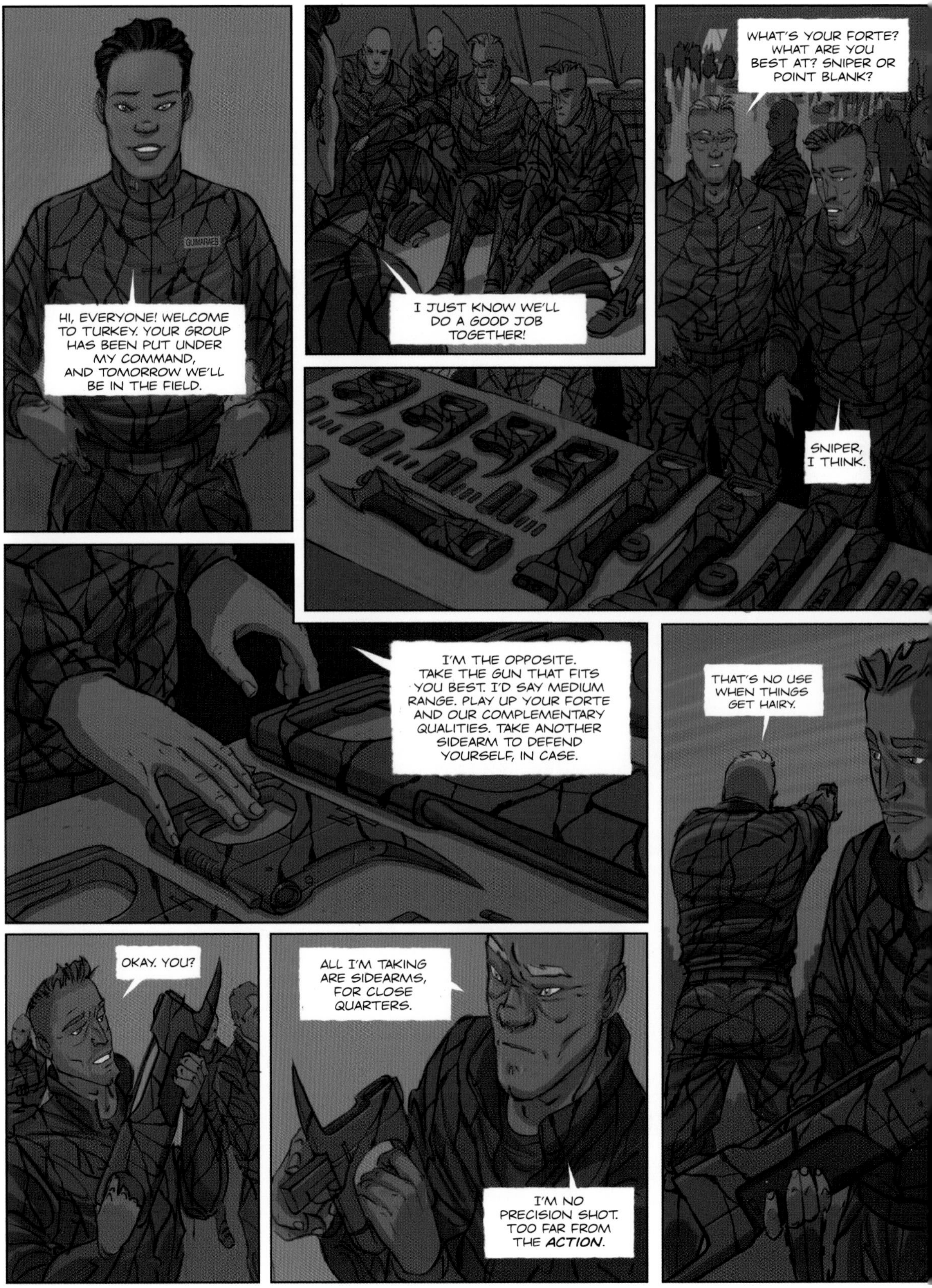
GUIMARAES
HI, EVERYONE! WELCOME TO TURKEY. YOUR GROUP HAS BEEN PUT UNDER MY COMMAND, AND TOMORROW WE'LL BE IN THE FIELD.
I JUST KNOW WE'LL DO A GOOD JOB TOGETHER!
WHAT'S YOUR FORTE? WHAT ARE YOU BEST AT? SNIPER OR POINT BLANK?
SNIPER, I THINK.
I'M THE OPPOSITE. TAKE THE GUN THAT FITS YOU BEST. I'D SAY MEDIUM RANGE. PLAY UP YOUR FORTE AND OUR COMPLEMENTARY QUALITIES. TAKE ANOTHER SIDEARM TO DEFEND YOURSELF, IN CASE.
THAT'S NO USE WHEN THINGS GET HAIRY.
OKAY. YOU?
ALL I'M TAKING ARE SIDEARMS, FOR CLOSE QUARTERS.
I'M NO PRECISION SHOT. TOO FAR FROM THE *ACTION*.

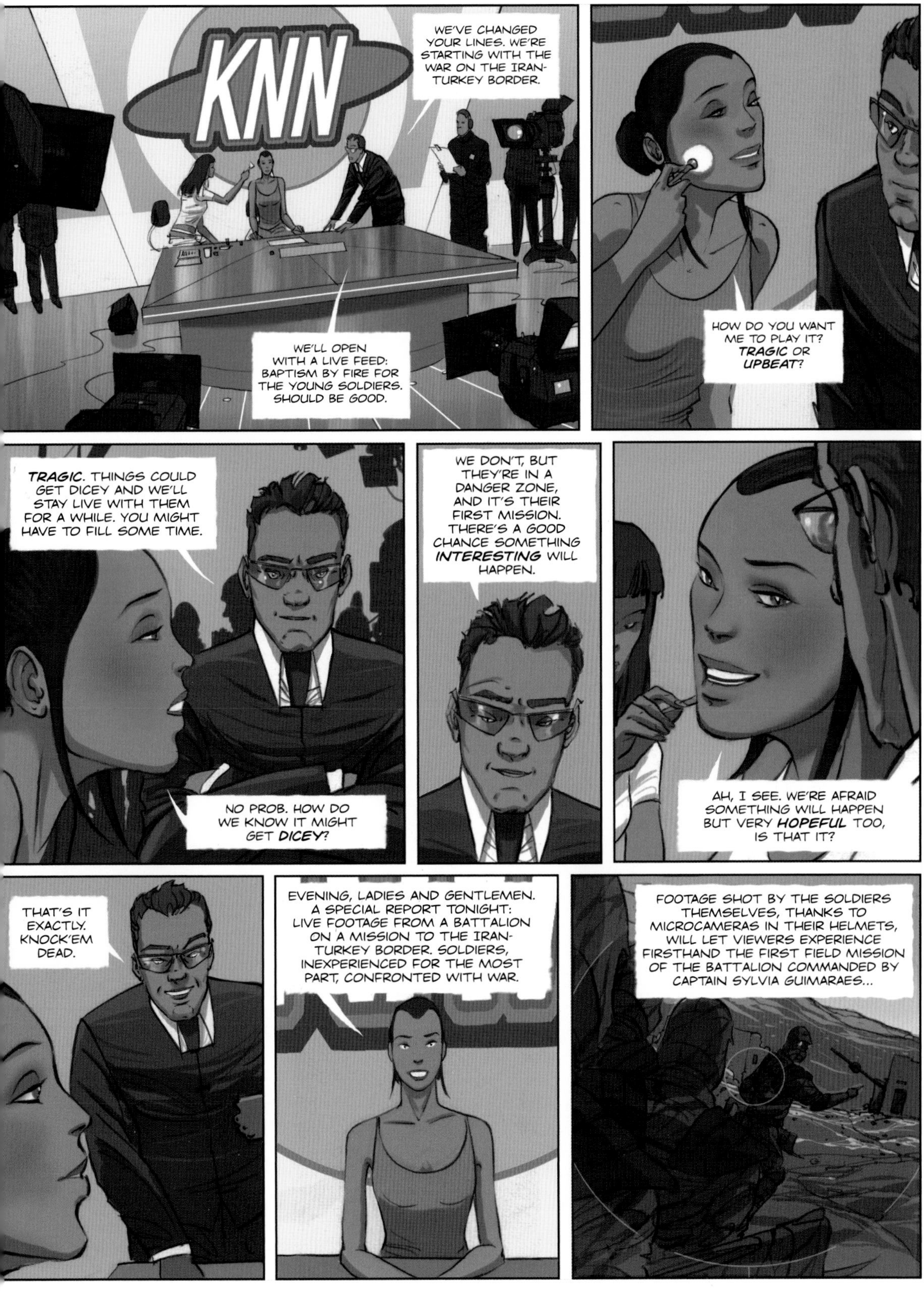
KNN
WE'VE CHANGED YOUR LINES. WE'RE STARTING WITH THE WAR ON THE IRAN-TURKEY BORDER.
WE'LL OPEN WITH A LIVE FEED: BAPTISM BY FIRE FOR THE YOUNG SOLDIERS. SHOULD BE GOOD.
HOW DO YOU WANT ME TO PLAY IT? TRAGIC OR UPBEAT?
TRAGIC. THINGS COULD GET DICEY AND WE'LL STAY LIVE WITH THEM FOR A WHILE. YOU MIGHT HAVE TO FILL SOME TIME.
NO PROB. HOW DO WE KNOW IT MIGHT GET DICEY?
WE DON'T, BUT THEY'RE IN A DANGER ZONE, AND IT'S THEIR FIRST MISSION. THERE'S A GOOD CHANCE SOMETHING INTERESTING WILL HAPPEN.
AH, I SEE. WE'RE AFRAID SOMETHING WILL HAPPEN BUT VERY HOPEFUL TOO, IS THAT IT?
THAT'S IT EXACTLY. KNOCK'EM DEAD.
EVENING, LADIES AND GENTLEMEN. A SPECIAL REPORT TONIGHT: LIVE FOOTAGE FROM A BATTALION ON A MISSION TO THE IRAN-TURKEY BORDER. SOLDIERS, INEXPERIENCED FOR THE MOST PART, CONFRONTED WITH WAR.
FOOTAGE SHOT BY THE SOLDIERS THEMSELVES, THANKS TO MICROCAMERAS IN THEIR HELMETS, WILL LET VIEWERS EXPERIENCE FIRSTHAND THE FIRST FIELD MISSION OF THE BATTALION COMMANDED BY CAPTAIN SYLVIA GUIMARAES...

...ONSCREEN RIGHT NOW. SHE CAN'T HEAR US, OF COURSE, BUT WE CAN HEAR EVERYTHING THE SOLDIERS SAY.

YOU KNOW WHAT TO DO?

YES, SIR!

THEN LET'S GO!

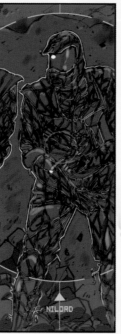

PISTOIA! ANDERSON! ADVANCE!

TIME TO GO TO WORK, LADIES. *COVER THEM!*

KRABOOM!

KRABOOM!

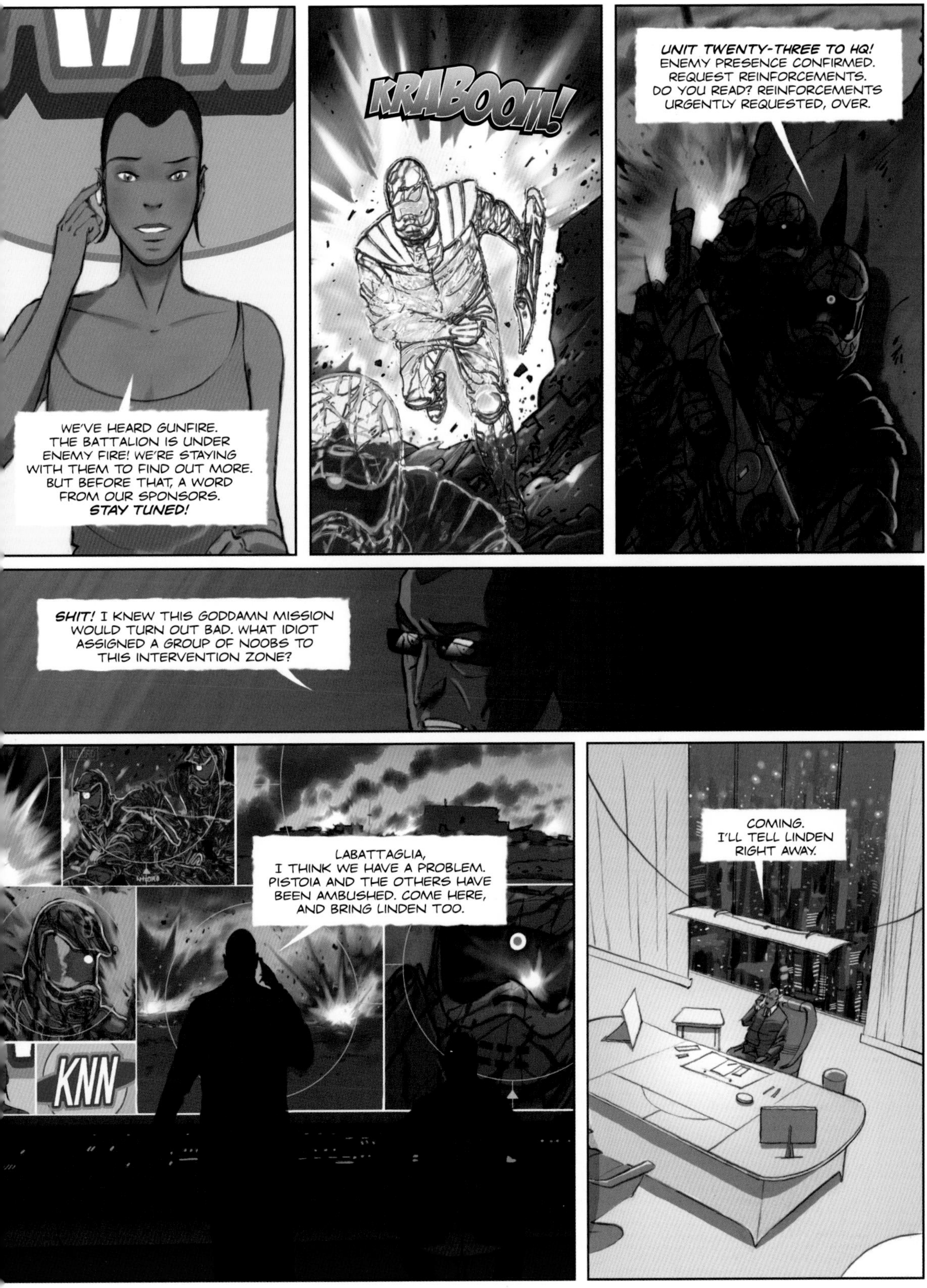
WE'VE HEARD GUNFIRE. THE BATTALION IS UNDER ENEMY FIRE! WE'RE STAYING WITH THEM TO FIND OUT MORE. BUT BEFORE THAT, A WORD FROM OUR SPONSORS. STAY TUNED!
KRABOOM!
UNIT TWENTY-THREE TO HQ! ENEMY PRESENCE CONFIRMED. REQUEST REINFORCEMENTS. DO YOU READ? REINFORCEMENTS URGENTLY REQUESTED, OVER.
SHIT! I KNEW THIS GODDAMN MISSION WOULD TURN OUT BAD. WHAT IDIOT ASSIGNED A GROUP OF NOOBS TO THIS INTERVENTION ZONE?
LABATTAGLIA, I THINK WE HAVE A PROBLEM. PISTOIA AND THE OTHERS HAVE BEEN AMBUSHED. COME HERE, AND BRING LINDEN TOO.
KNN
COMING. I'LL TELL LINDEN RIGHT AWAY.

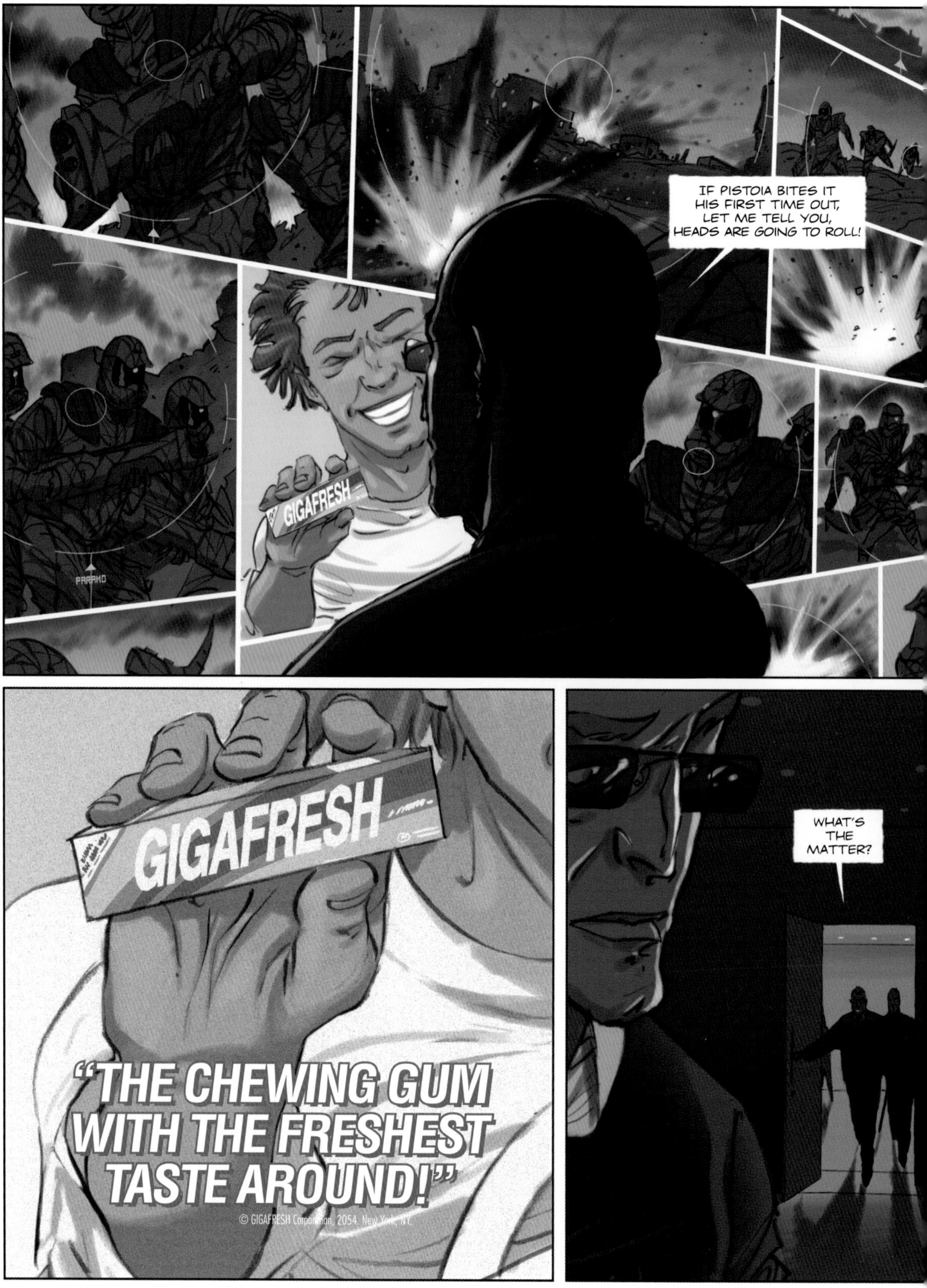
GIGAFRESH
PARAMO
IF PISTOIA BITES IT HIS FIRST TIME OUT, LET ME TELL YOU, HEADS ARE GOING TO ROLL!
GIGAFRESH
"THE CHEWING GUM WITH THE FRESHEST TASTE AROUND!"
© GIGAFRESH Corporation, 2054. New York, NY.
WHAT'S THE MATTER?

OUR PRETTY LITTLE PLAN IS GOING DOWN THE TUBES!

LET ME TALK TO ANDERSON.

HE'S LISTENING. GO ON.

ANDERSON, YOU THERE? IT'S LINDEN. HOW'S IT LOOK?

WE WALKED RIGHT INTO A TRAP. ME AND PISTOIA ARE PINNED BEHIND A WALL. THE OTHERS ARE UNDER COVER. IF WE SHOW OURSELVES, WE'RE TOAST.

LISTEN UP, ANDERSON. LABATTAGLIA HERE. DO YOUR BEST TO GET PISTOIA OUT, YOU HEAR?

I KNOW.

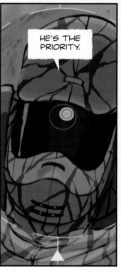

HE'S THE PRIORITY.

ALSO KNOW THAT YOUR OPERATION'S BEING BROADCAST LIVE THE WORLD OVER.

SO BE CAREFUL, ANDERSON. GOT IT?

LOUD AND CLEAR, MR. MCCANN. I'LL DO MY BEST.

LET'S GET BACK TO UNIT TWENTY-THREE, IN THE CLUTCHES OF AN INVISIBLE ENEMY.

CAPTAIN GUIMARAES SEEMS TO BE TRYING TO REJOIN HER TWO MEN ISOLATED AND UNDER FIRE FROM THE ENEMY.

NILORO

WHAT ARE YOU DOING, DOUG? WHAT WERE YOU THINKING?

BLAM!

BLAM!

WHAT DO YOU SEE, ANDERSON?

.55 CALIBER. I'D KNOW THE SOUND ANYWHERE. AND NOT MANY SNIPERS USE ONE, OR EVEN HAVE ONE AROUND HERE.

THREE SNIPERS AT 11 O'CLOCK, CAPTAIN.

WE'RE FUCKED, CAP. HAVE TO WAIT FOR REINFORCEMENTS OR AN AIRSTRIKE AND PRAY THEY DON'T HIT US.

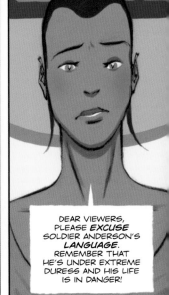

DEAR VIEWERS, PLEASE *EXCUSE* SOLDIER ANDERSON'S *LANGUAGE*. REMEMBER THAT HE'S UNDER EXTREME DURESS AND HIS LIFE IS IN DANGER!

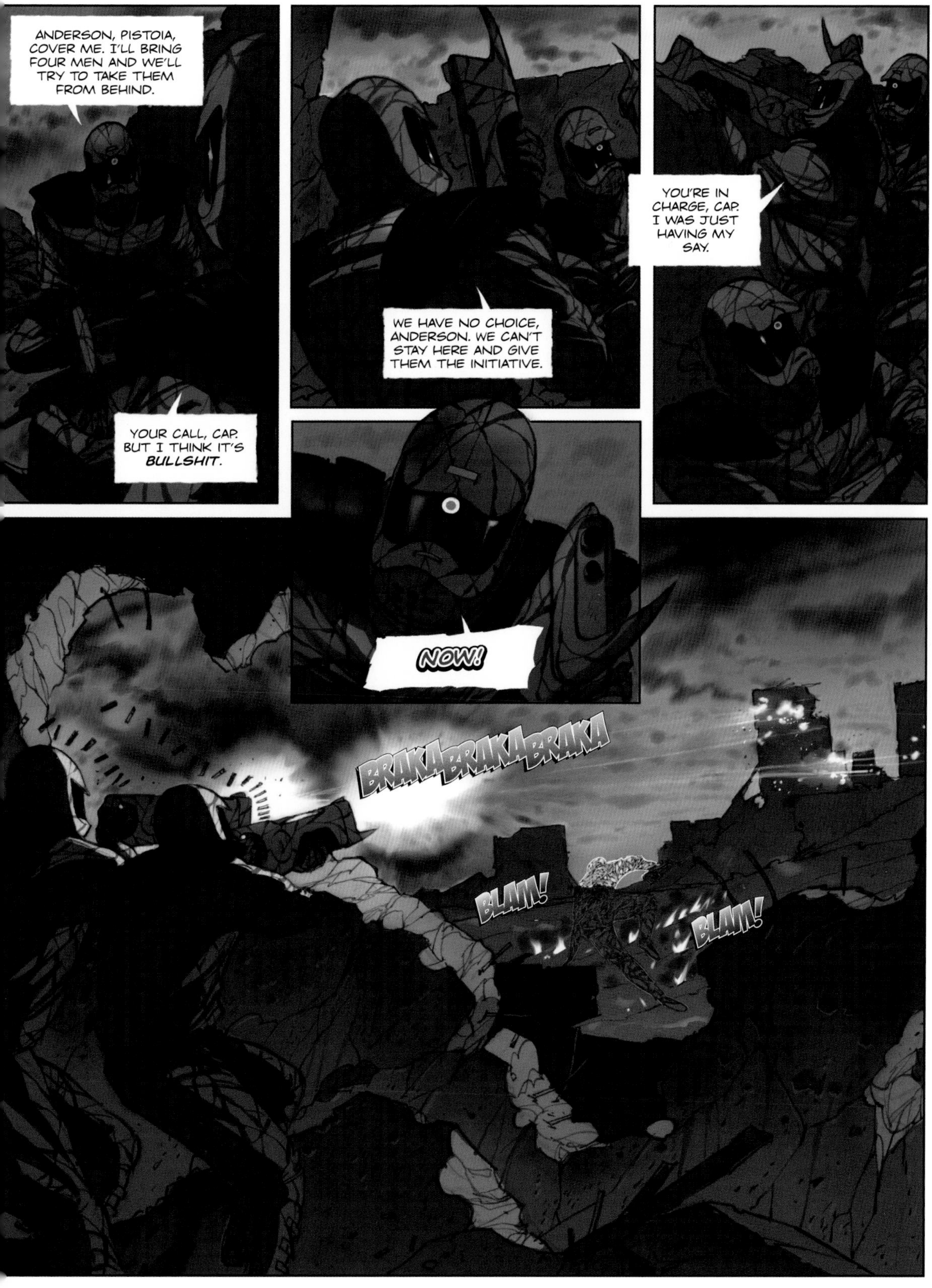
ANDERSON, PISTOIA, COVER ME. I'LL BRING FOUR MEN AND WE'LL TRY TO TAKE THEM FROM BEHIND.
YOUR CALL, CAP. BUT I THINK IT'S *BULLSHIT*.
WE HAVE NO CHOICE, ANDERSON. WE CAN'T STAY HERE AND GIVE THEM THE INITIATIVE.
YOU'RE IN CHARGE, CAP. I WAS JUST HAVING MY SAY.
NOW!
BRAKABRAKABRAKA
BLAM!
BLAM!

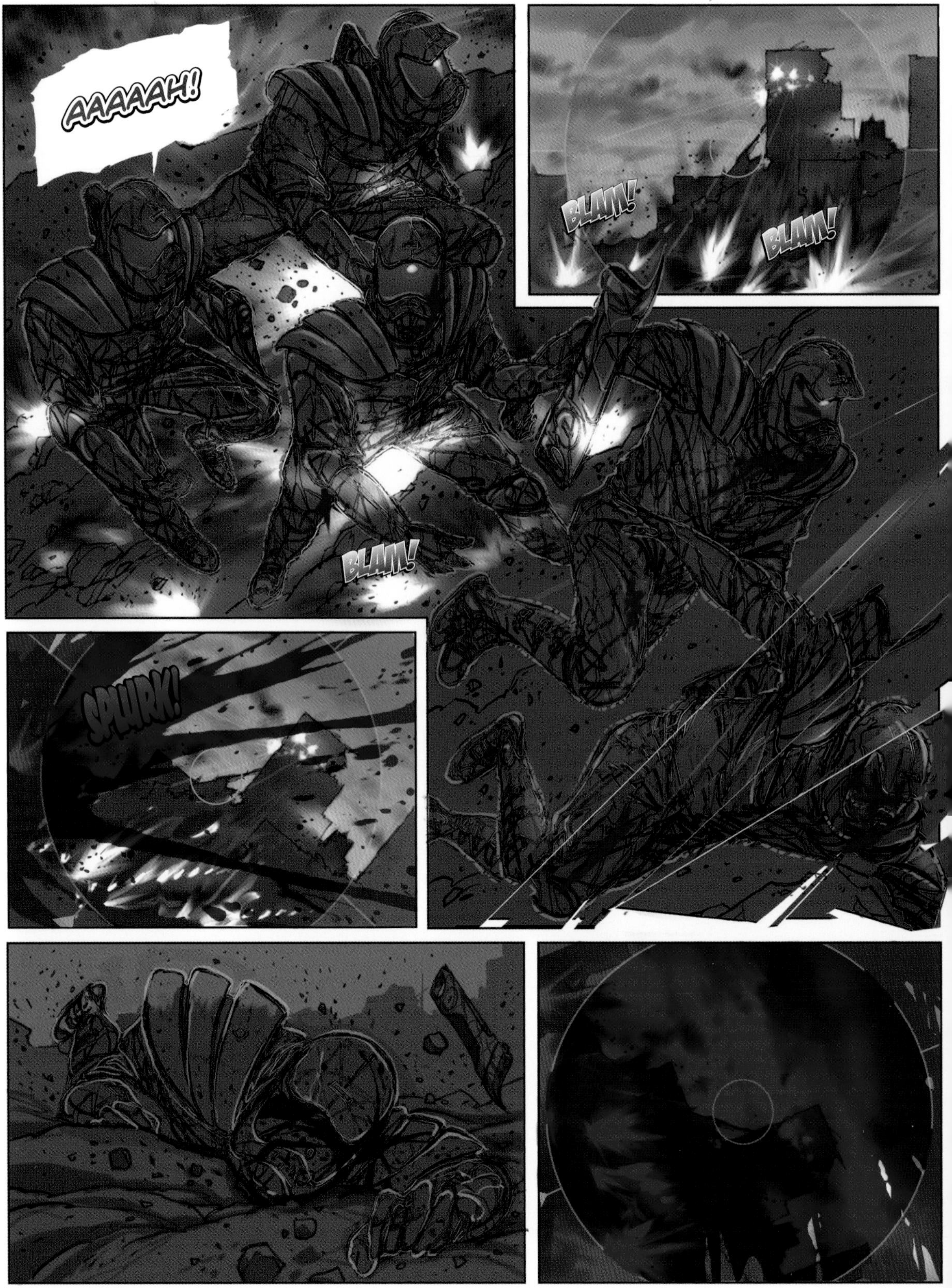
AAAAAH!
BLAM!
BLAM!
BLAM!
SPLURK!

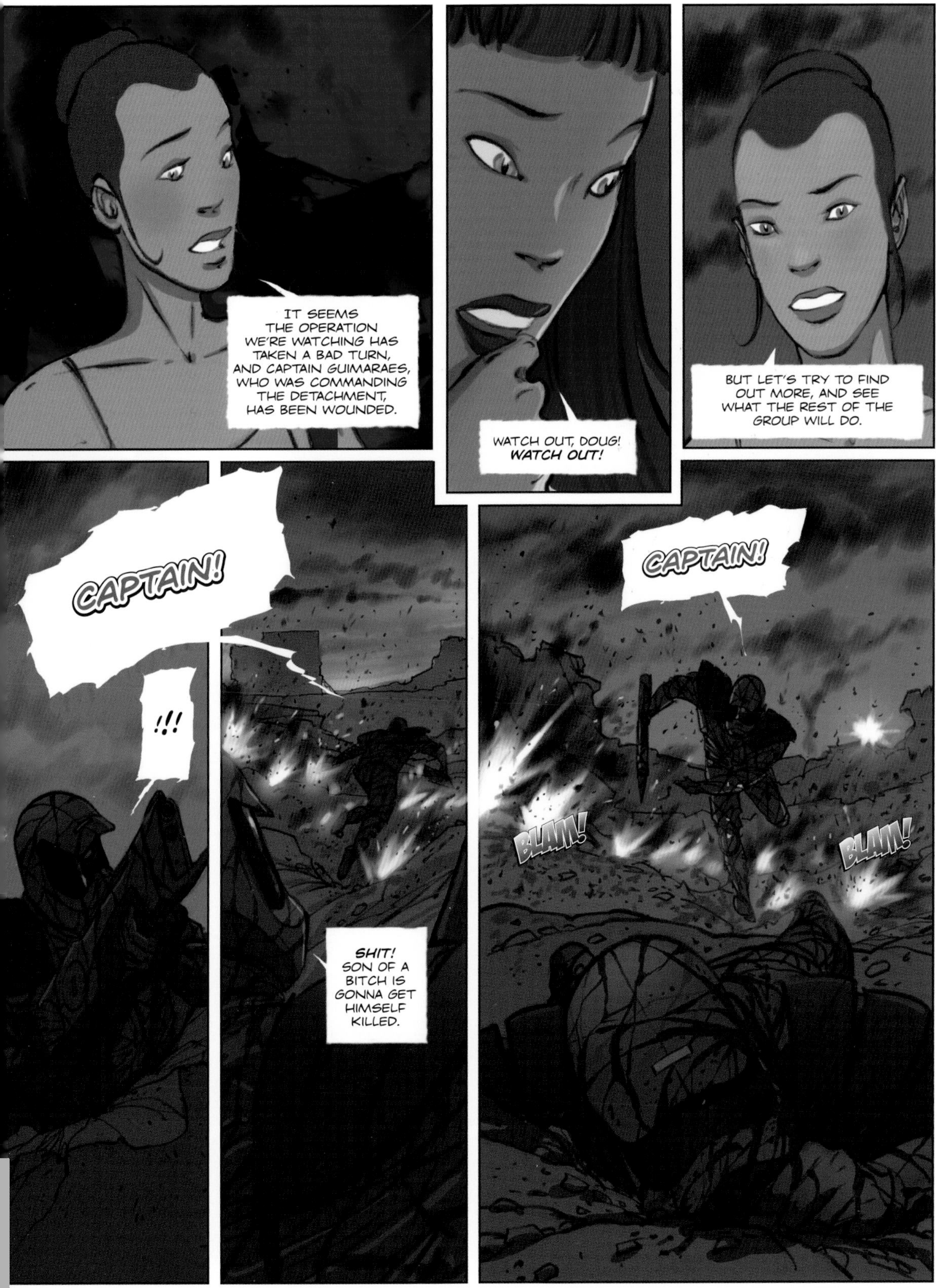
IT SEEMS THE OPERATION WE'RE WATCHING HAS TAKEN A BAD TURN, AND CAPTAIN GUIMARAES, WHO WAS COMMANDING THE DETACHMENT, HAS BEEN WOUNDED.
WATCH OUT, DOUG! WATCH OUT!
BUT LET'S TRY TO FIND OUT MORE, AND SEE WHAT THE REST OF THE GROUP WILL DO.
CAPTAIN!
!!!
SHIT! SON OF A BITCH IS GONNA GET HIMSELF KILLED.
CAPTAIN!
BLAM!
BLAM!

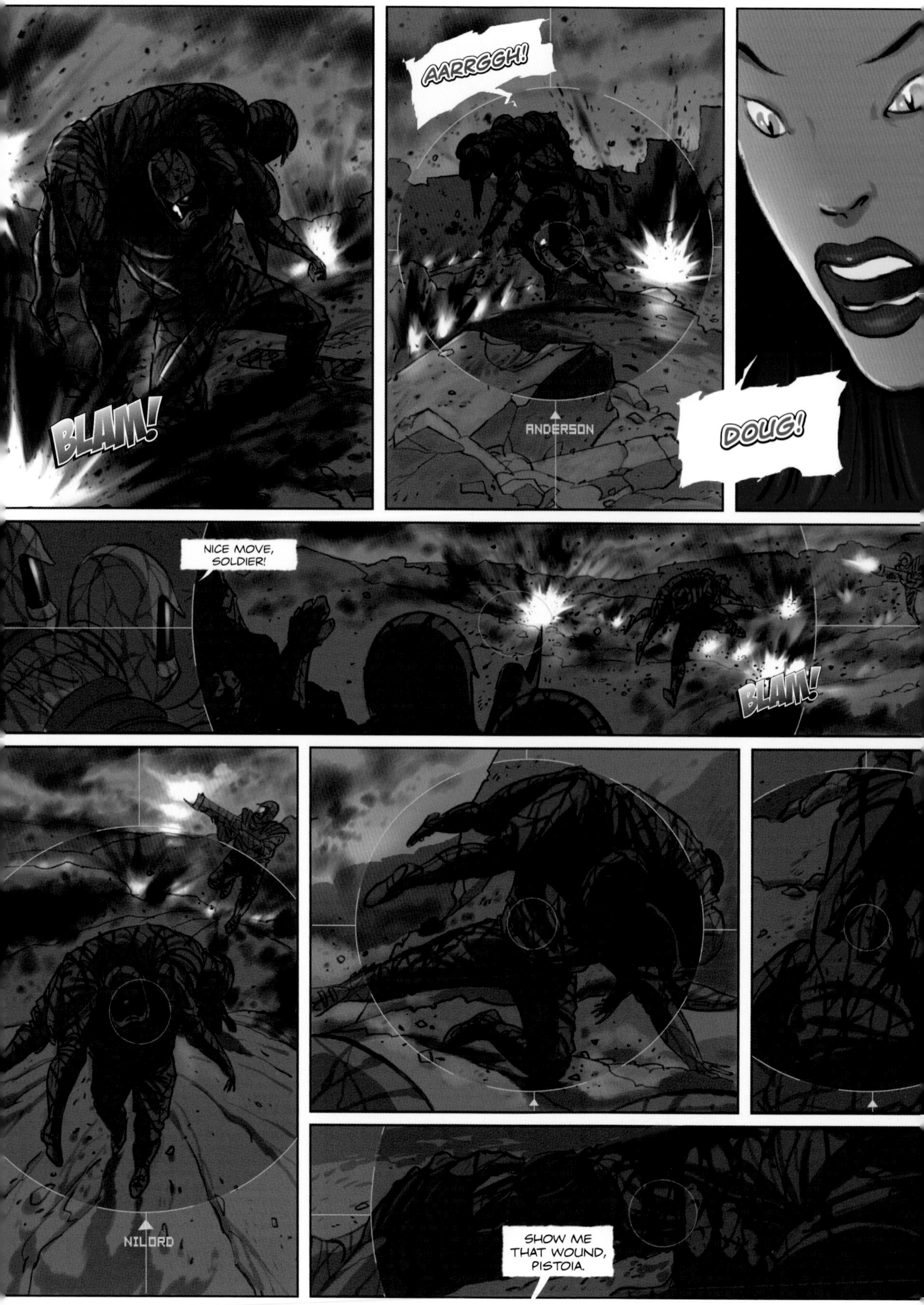
BLAM!
AARRGGH!
ANDERSON
DOUG!
NICE MOVE, SOLDIER!
BLAM!
NILORD
SHOW ME THAT WOUND, PISTOIA.

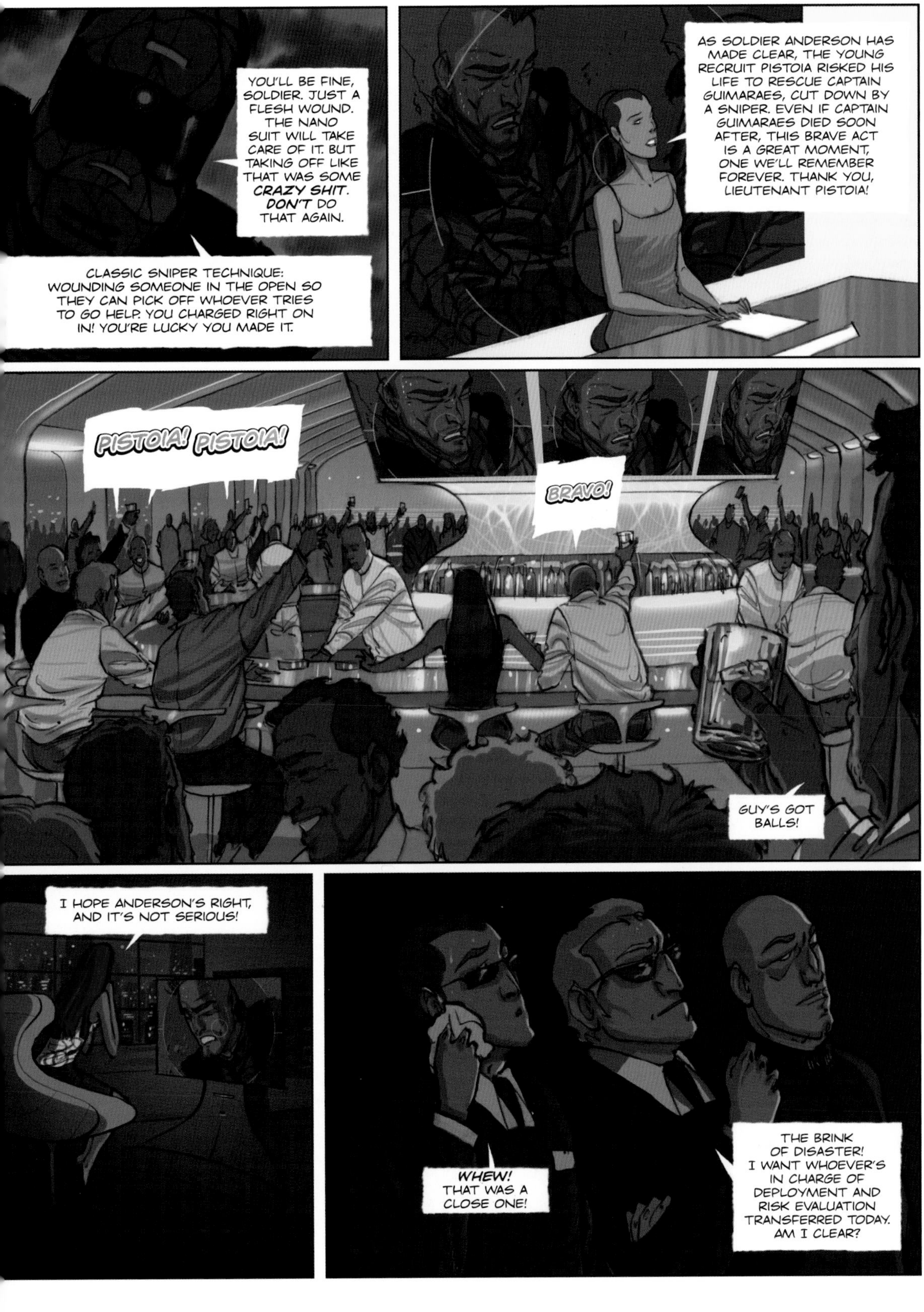
YOU'LL BE FINE, SOLDIER. JUST A FLESH WOUND. THE NANO SUIT WILL TAKE CARE OF IT. BUT TAKING OFF LIKE THAT WAS SOME CRAZY SHIT. DON'T DO THAT AGAIN.
CLASSIC SNIPER TECHNIQUE: WOUNDING SOMEONE IN THE OPEN SO THEY CAN PICK OFF WHOEVER TRIES TO GO HELP. YOU CHARGED RIGHT ON IN! YOU'RE LUCKY YOU MADE IT.
AS SOLDIER ANDERSON HAS MADE CLEAR, THE YOUNG RECRUIT PISTOIA RISKED HIS LIFE TO RESCUE CAPTAIN GUIMARAES, CUT DOWN BY A SNIPER. EVEN IF CAPTAIN GUIMARAES DIED SOON AFTER, THIS BRAVE ACT IS A GREAT MOMENT, ONE WE'LL REMEMBER FOREVER. THANK YOU, LIEUTENANT PISTOIA!
PISTOIA! PISTOIA!
BRAVO!
GUY'S GOT BALLS!
I HOPE ANDERSON'S RIGHT, AND IT'S NOT SERIOUS!
WHEW! THAT WAS A CLOSE ONE!
THE BRINK OF DISASTER! I WANT WHOEVER'S IN CHARGE OF DEPLOYMENT AND RISK EVALUATION TRANSFERRED TODAY. AM I CLEAR?

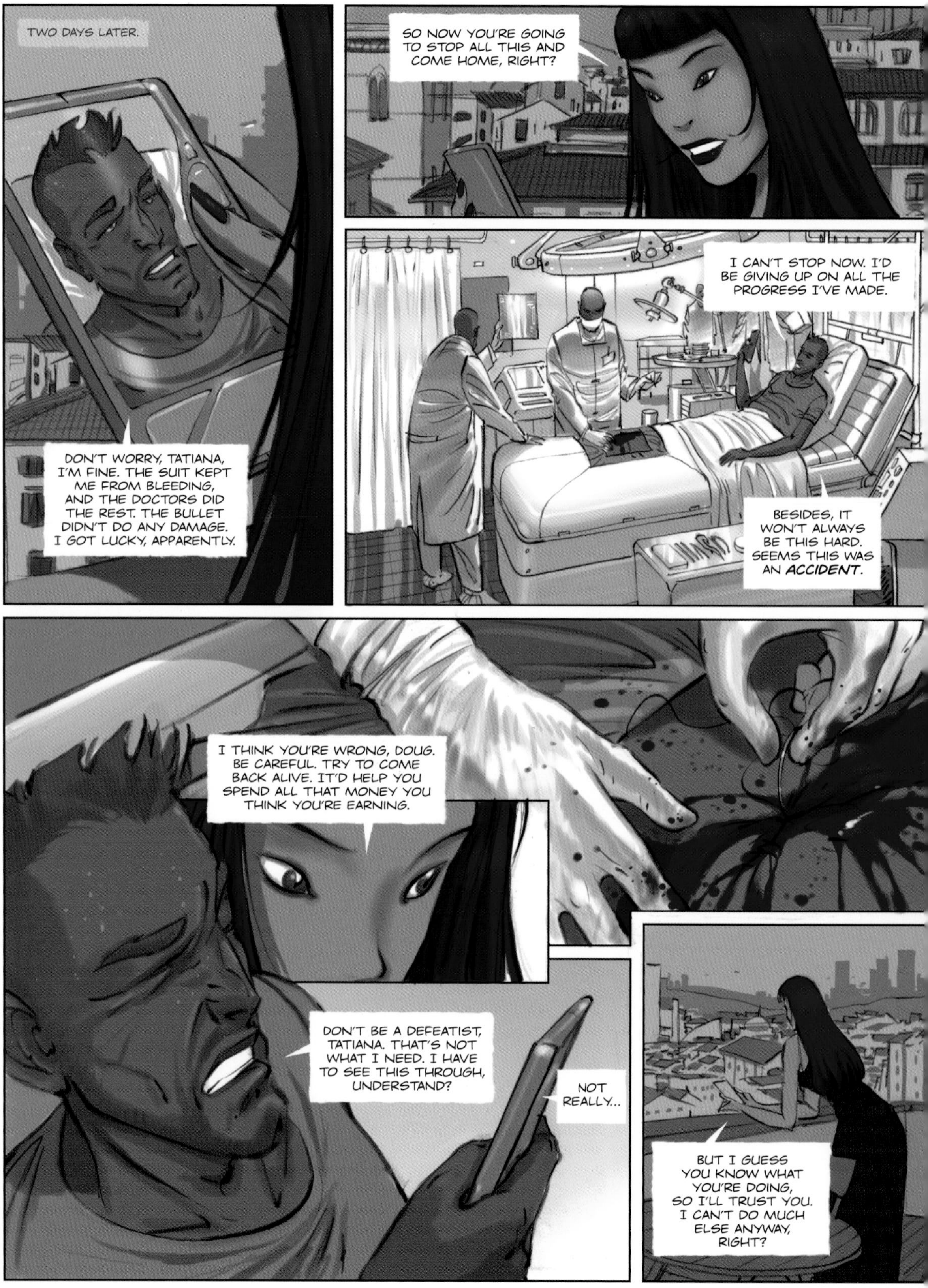
TWO DAYS LATER.
SO NOW YOU'RE GOING TO STOP ALL THIS AND COME HOME, RIGHT?
DON'T WORRY, TATIANA, I'M FINE. THE SUIT KEPT ME FROM BLEEDING, AND THE DOCTORS DID THE REST. THE BULLET DIDN'T DO ANY DAMAGE. I GOT LUCKY, APPARENTLY.
I CAN'T STOP NOW. I'D BE GIVING UP ON ALL THE PROGRESS I'VE MADE.
BESIDES, IT WON'T ALWAYS BE THIS HARD. SEEMS THIS WAS AN ACCIDENT.
I THINK YOU'RE WRONG, DOUG. BE CAREFUL. TRY TO COME BACK ALIVE. IT'D HELP YOU SPEND ALL THAT MONEY YOU THINK YOU'RE EARNING.
DON'T BE A DEFEATIST, TATIANA. THAT'S NOT WHAT I NEED. I HAVE TO SEE THIS THROUGH, UNDERSTAND?
NOT REALLY...
BUT I GUESS YOU KNOW WHAT YOU'RE DOING, SO I'LL TRUST YOU. I CAN'T DO MUCH ELSE ANYWAY, RIGHT?

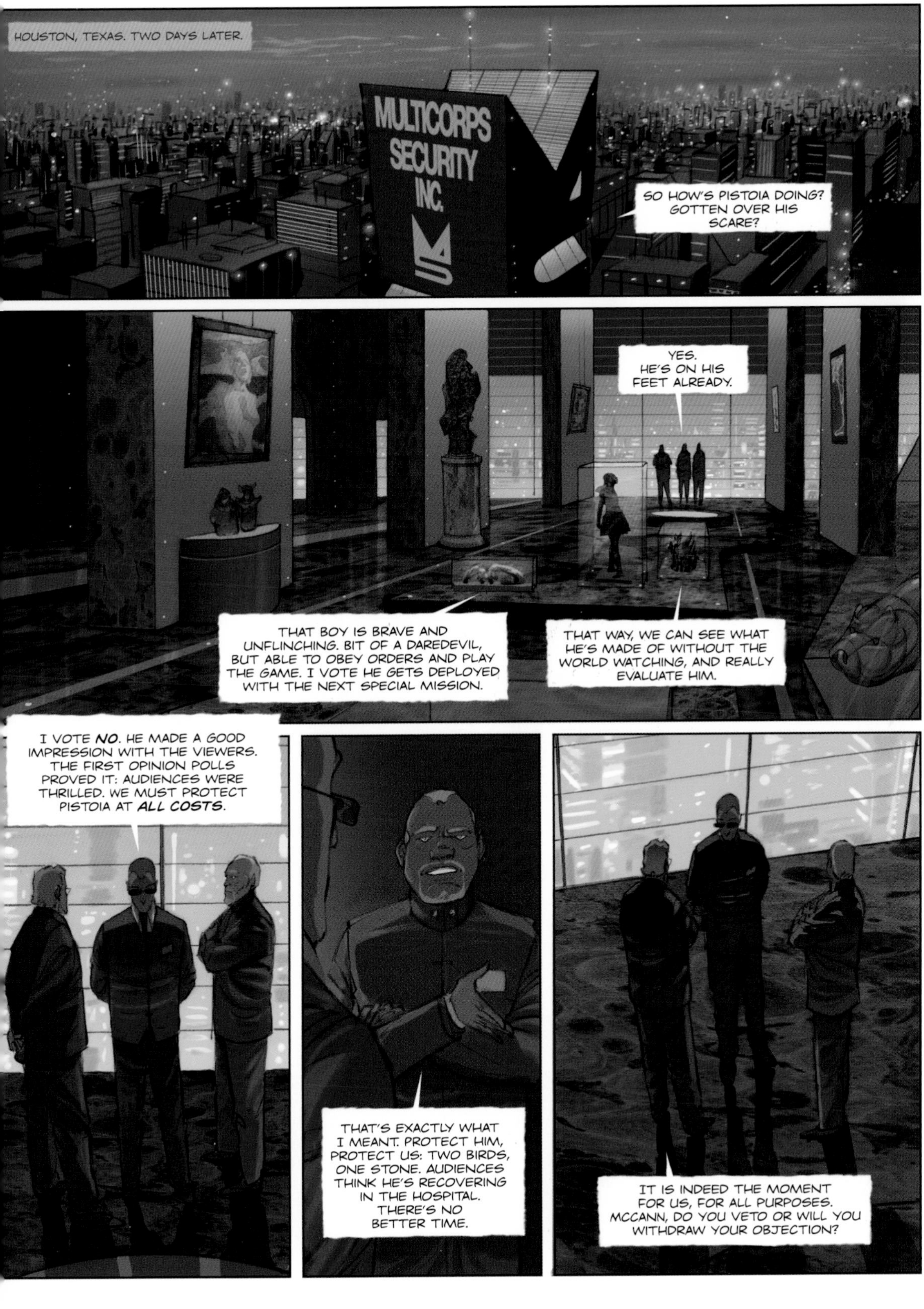
HOUSTON, TEXAS. TWO DAYS LATER.
MULTICORPS SECURITY INC.
SO HOW'S PISTOIA DOING? GOTTEN OVER HIS SCARE?
YES. HE'S ON HIS FEET ALREADY.
THAT BOY IS BRAVE AND UNFLINCHING. BIT OF A DAREDEVIL, BUT ABLE TO OBEY ORDERS AND PLAY THE GAME. I VOTE HE GETS DEPLOYED WITH THE NEXT SPECIAL MISSION.
THAT WAY, WE CAN SEE WHAT HE'S MADE OF WITHOUT THE WORLD WATCHING, AND REALLY EVALUATE HIM.
I VOTE **NO**. HE MADE A GOOD IMPRESSION WITH THE VIEWERS. THE FIRST OPINION POLLS PROVED IT: AUDIENCES WERE THRILLED. WE MUST PROTECT PISTOIA AT ***ALL COSTS***.
THAT'S EXACTLY WHAT I MEANT. PROTECT HIM, PROTECT US: TWO BIRDS, ONE STONE. AUDIENCES THINK HE'S RECOVERING IN THE HOSPITAL. THERE'S NO BETTER TIME.
IT IS INDEED THE MOMENT FOR US, FOR ALL PURPOSES. MCCANN, DO YOU VETO OR WILL YOU WITHDRAW YOUR OBJECTION?

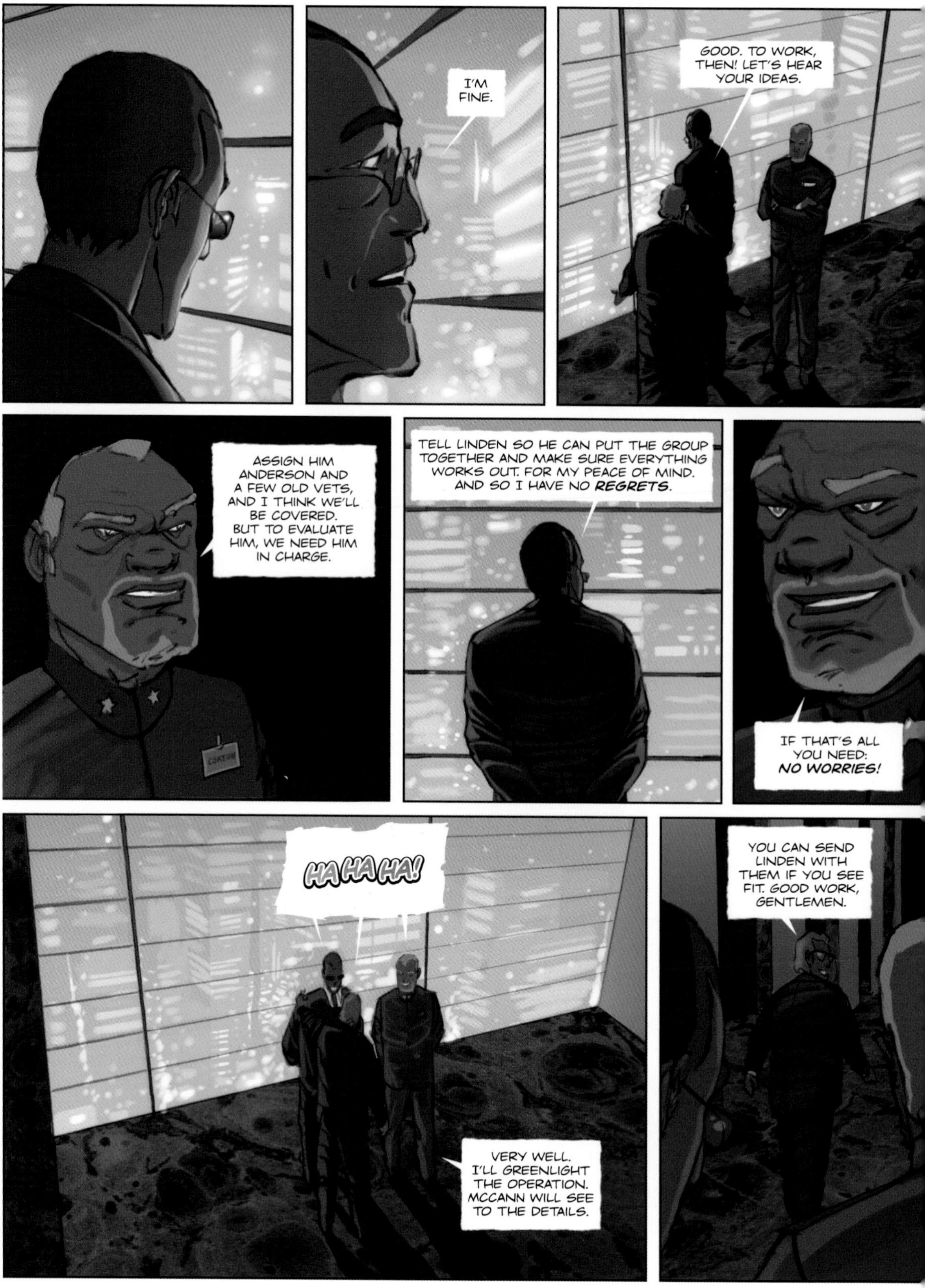
I'M FINE.
GOOD. TO WORK, THEN! LET'S HEAR YOUR IDEAS.
ASSIGN HIM ANDERSON AND A FEW OLD VETS, AND I THINK WE'LL BE COVERED. BUT TO EVALUATE HIM, WE NEED HIM IN CHARGE.
TELL LINDEN SO HE CAN PUT THE GROUP TOGETHER AND MAKE SURE EVERYTHING WORKS OUT. FOR MY PEACE OF MIND. AND SO I HAVE NO **REGRETS**.
IF THAT'S ALL YOU NEED: **NO WORRIES!**
HA HA HA!
VERY WELL. I'LL GREENLIGHT THE OPERATION. MCCANN WILL SEE TO THE DETAILS.
YOU CAN SEND LINDEN WITH THEM IF YOU SEE FIT. GOOD WORK, GENTLEMEN.

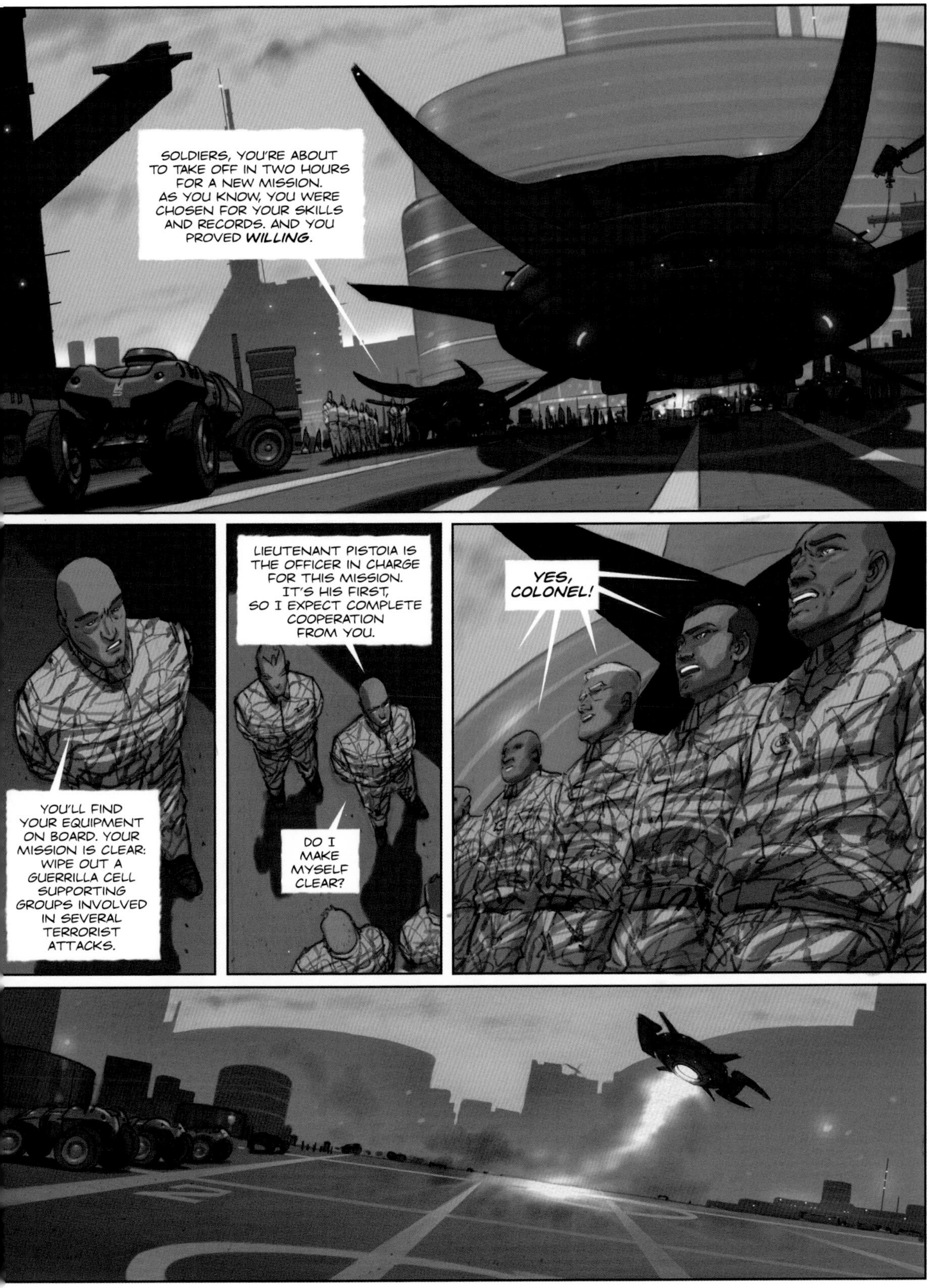
SOLDIERS, YOU'RE ABOUT TO TAKE OFF IN TWO HOURS FOR A NEW MISSION. AS YOU KNOW, YOU WERE CHOSEN FOR YOUR SKILLS AND RECORDS. AND YOU PROVED **WILLING**.
YOU'LL FIND YOUR EQUIPMENT ON BOARD. YOUR MISSION IS CLEAR: WIPE OUT A GUERRILLA CELL SUPPORTING GROUPS INVOLVED IN SEVERAL TERRORIST ATTACKS.
LIEUTENANT PISTOIA IS THE OFFICER IN CHARGE FOR THIS MISSION. IT'S HIS FIRST, SO I EXPECT COMPLETE COOPERATION FROM YOU.
DO I MAKE MYSELF CLEAR?
YES, COLONEL!

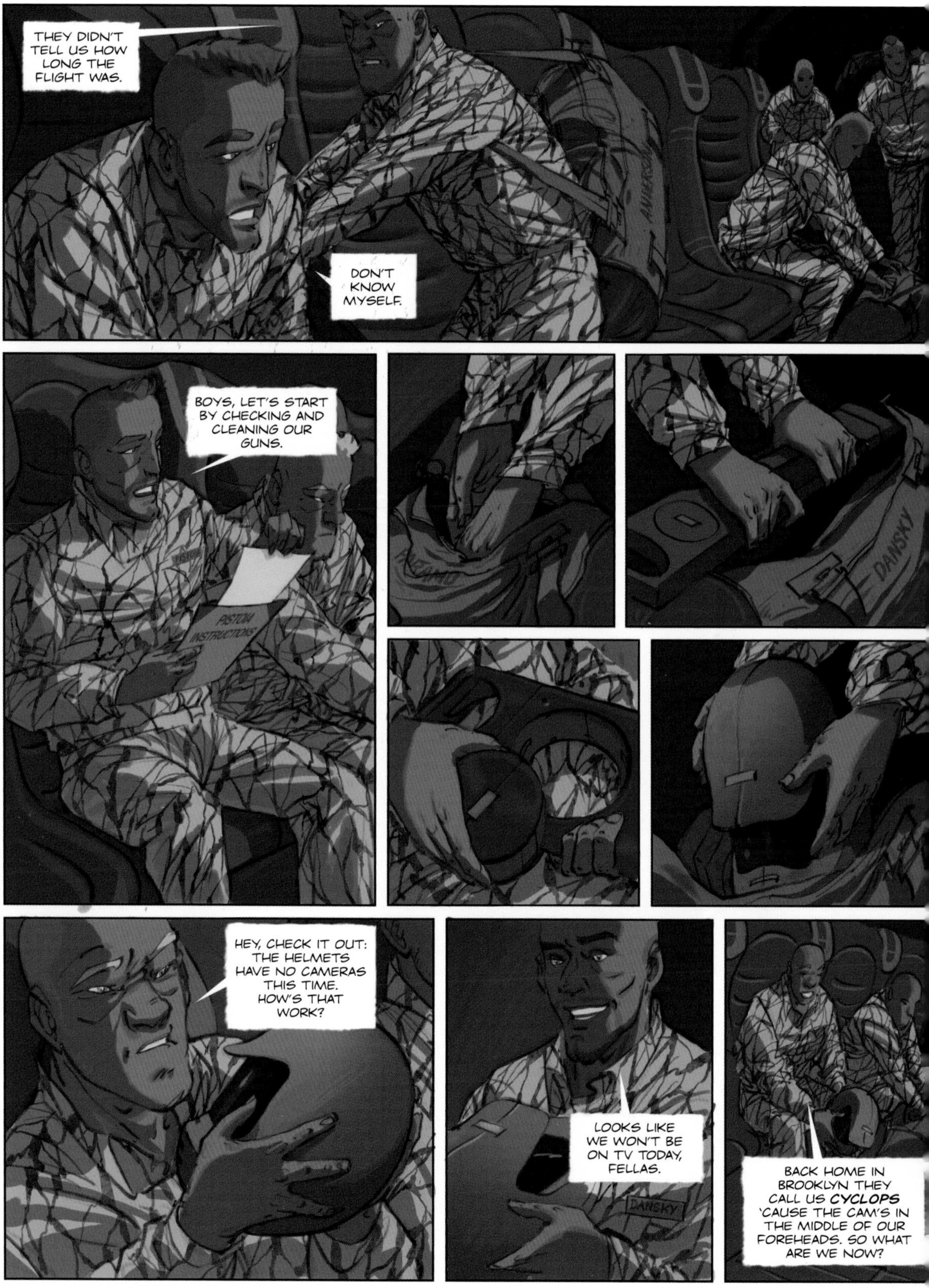
THEY DIDN'T TELL US HOW LONG THE FLIGHT WAS.
DON'T KNOW MYSELF.
BOYS, LET'S START BY CHECKING AND CLEANING OUR GUNS.
PISTOIA INSTRUCTIONS
DANSKY
HEY, CHECK IT OUT: THE HELMETS HAVE NO CAMERAS THIS TIME. HOW'S THAT WORK?
LOOKS LIKE WE WON'T BE ON TV TODAY, FELLAS.
DANSKY
BACK HOME IN BROOKLYN THEY CALL US **CYCLOPS** 'CAUSE THE CAM'S IN THE MIDDLE OF OUR FOREHEADS. SO WHAT ARE WE NOW?

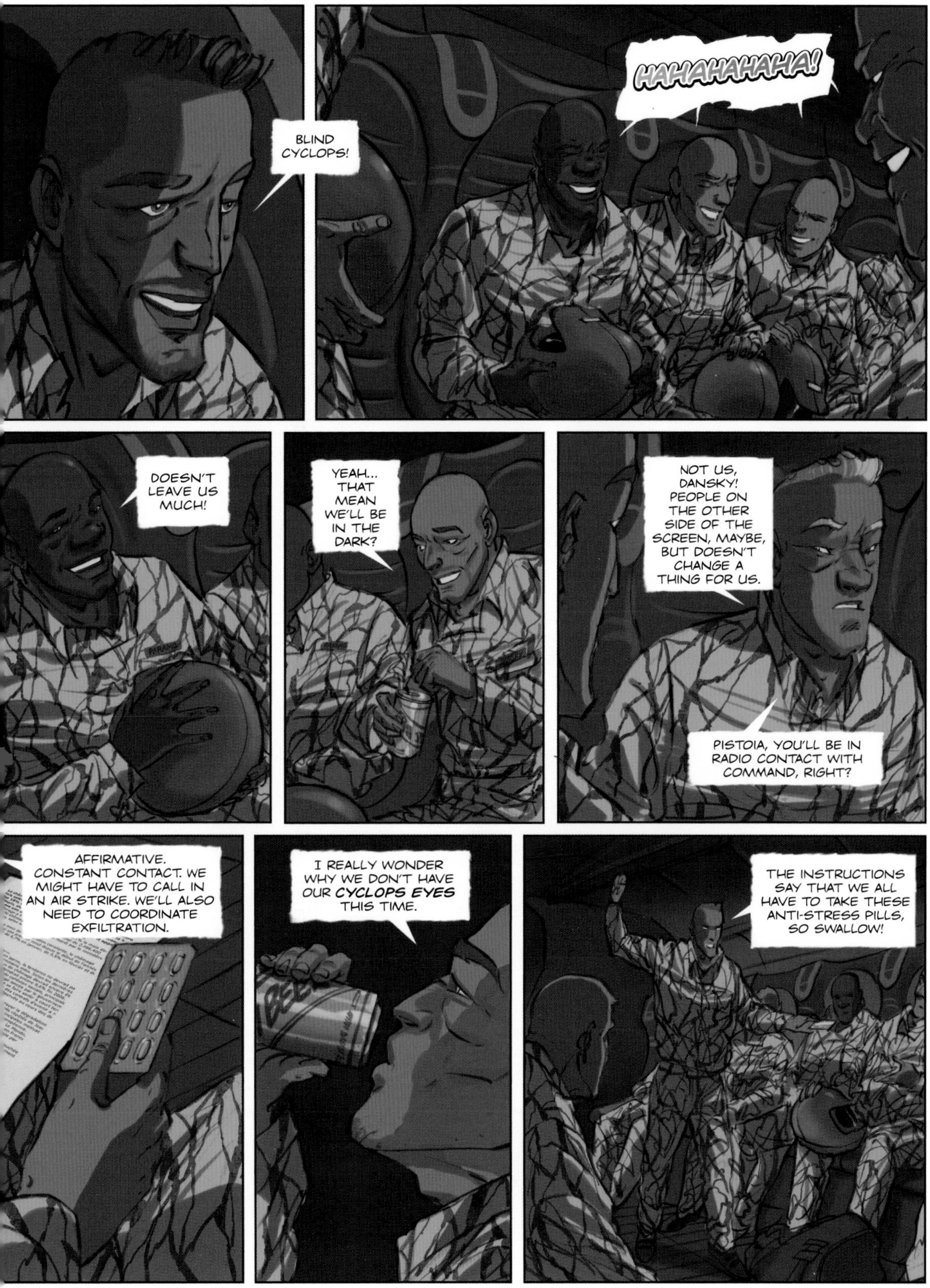
BLIND CYCLOPS!
HAHAHAHAHAHA!
DOESN'T LEAVE US MUCH!
YEAH... THAT MEAN WE'LL BE IN THE DARK?
NOT US, DANSKY! PEOPLE ON THE OTHER SIDE OF THE SCREEN, MAYBE, BUT DOESN'T CHANGE A THING FOR US.
PISTOIA, YOU'LL BE IN RADIO CONTACT WITH COMMAND, RIGHT?
AFFIRMATIVE. CONSTANT CONTACT. WE MIGHT HAVE TO CALL IN AN AIR STRIKE. WE'LL ALSO NEED TO COORDINATE EXFILTRATION.
I REALLY WONDER WHY WE DON'T HAVE OUR **CYCLOPS EYES** THIS TIME.
THE INSTRUCTIONS SAY THAT WE ALL HAVE TO TAKE THESE ANTI-STRESS PILLS, SO SWALLOW!

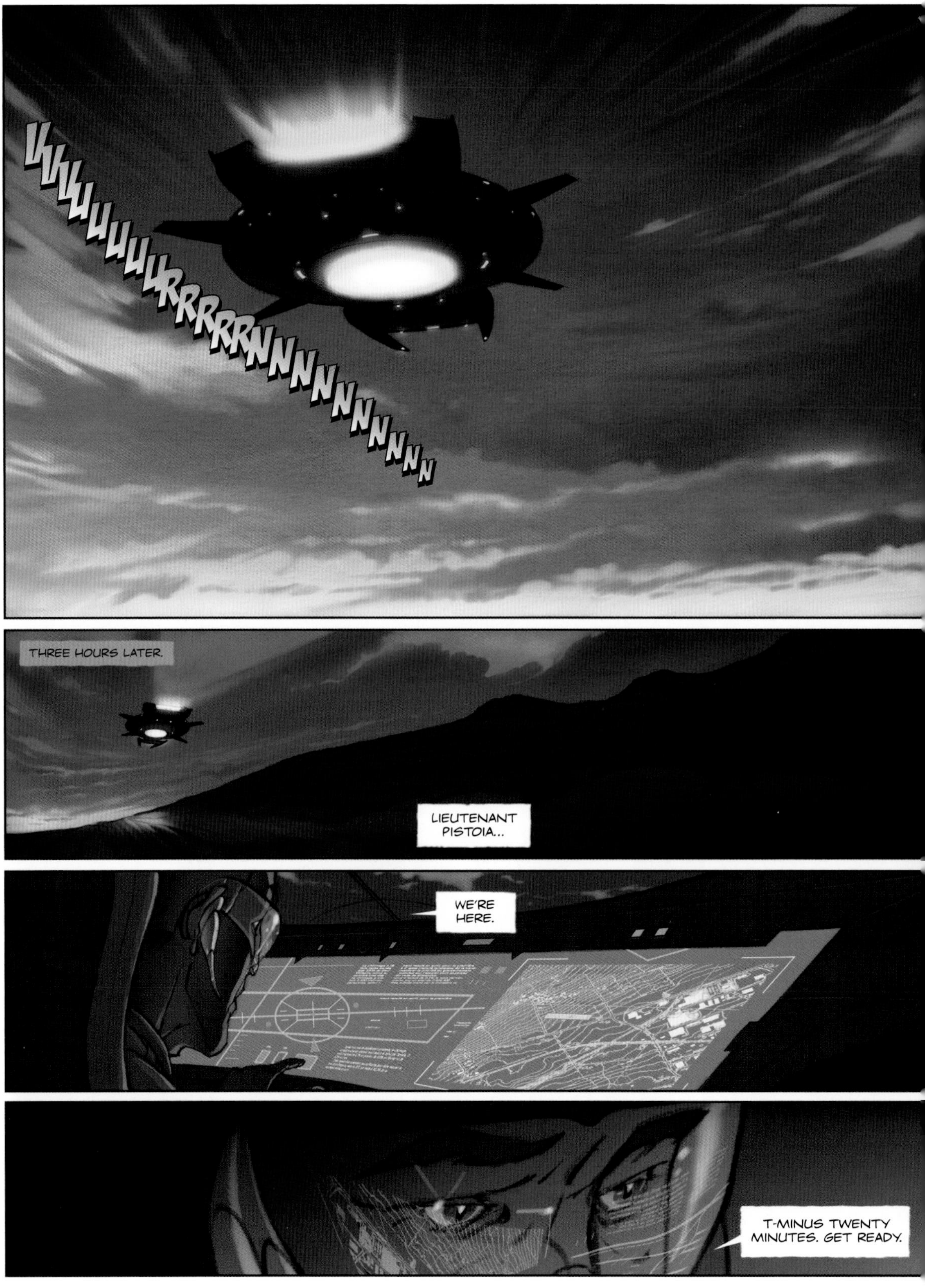
VVVUUUUURRRRRNNNNNNNNNNN
THREE HOURS LATER.
LIEUTENANT PISTOIA...
WE'RE HERE.
T-MINUS TWENTY MINUTES. GET READY.

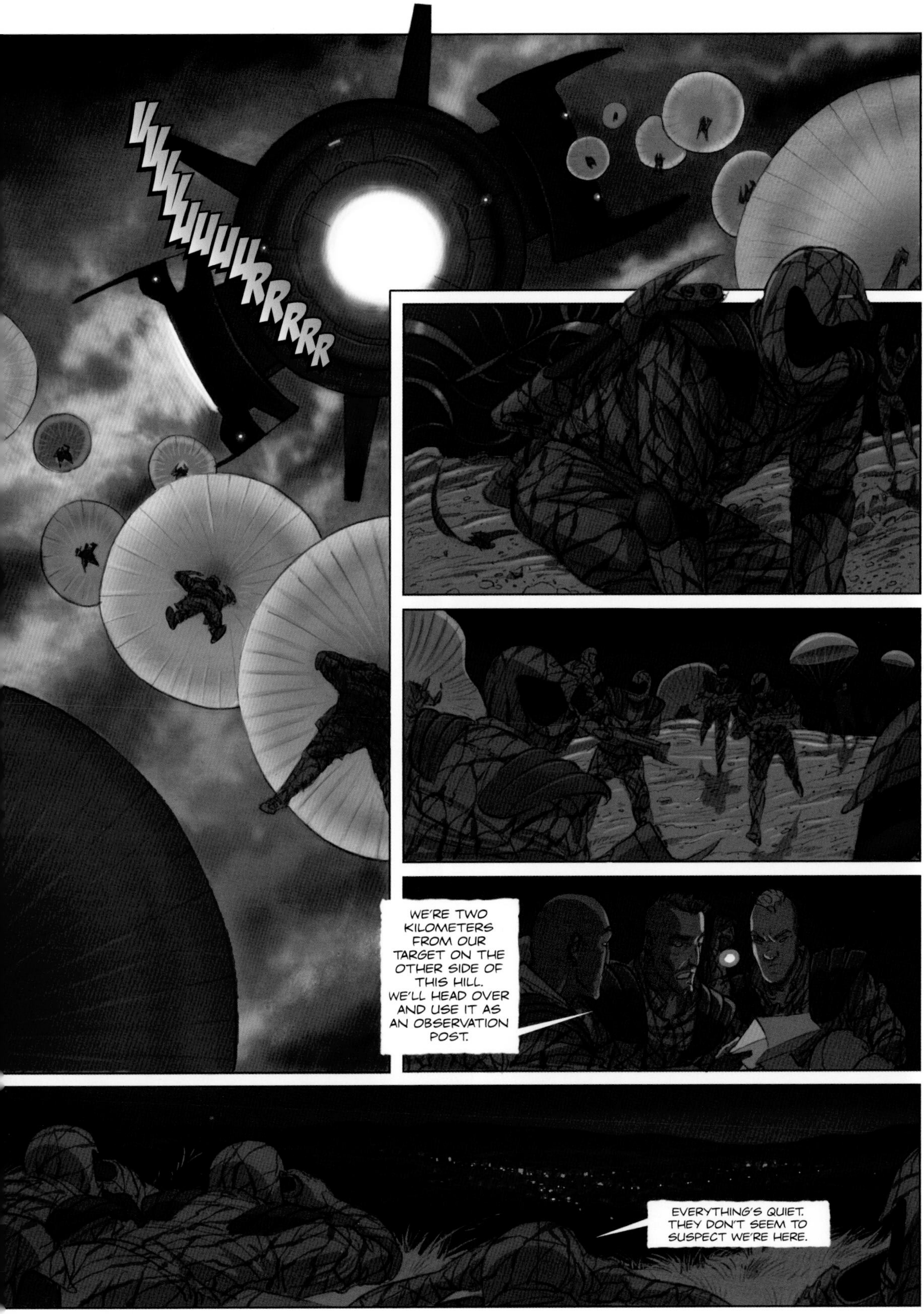
VVVVUUUUURRRRRR
WE'RE TWO KILOMETERS FROM OUR TARGET ON THE OTHER SIDE OF THIS HILL. WE'LL HEAD OVER AND USE IT AS AN OBSERVATION POST.
EVERYTHING'S QUIET. THEY DON'T SEEM TO SUSPECT WE'RE HERE.

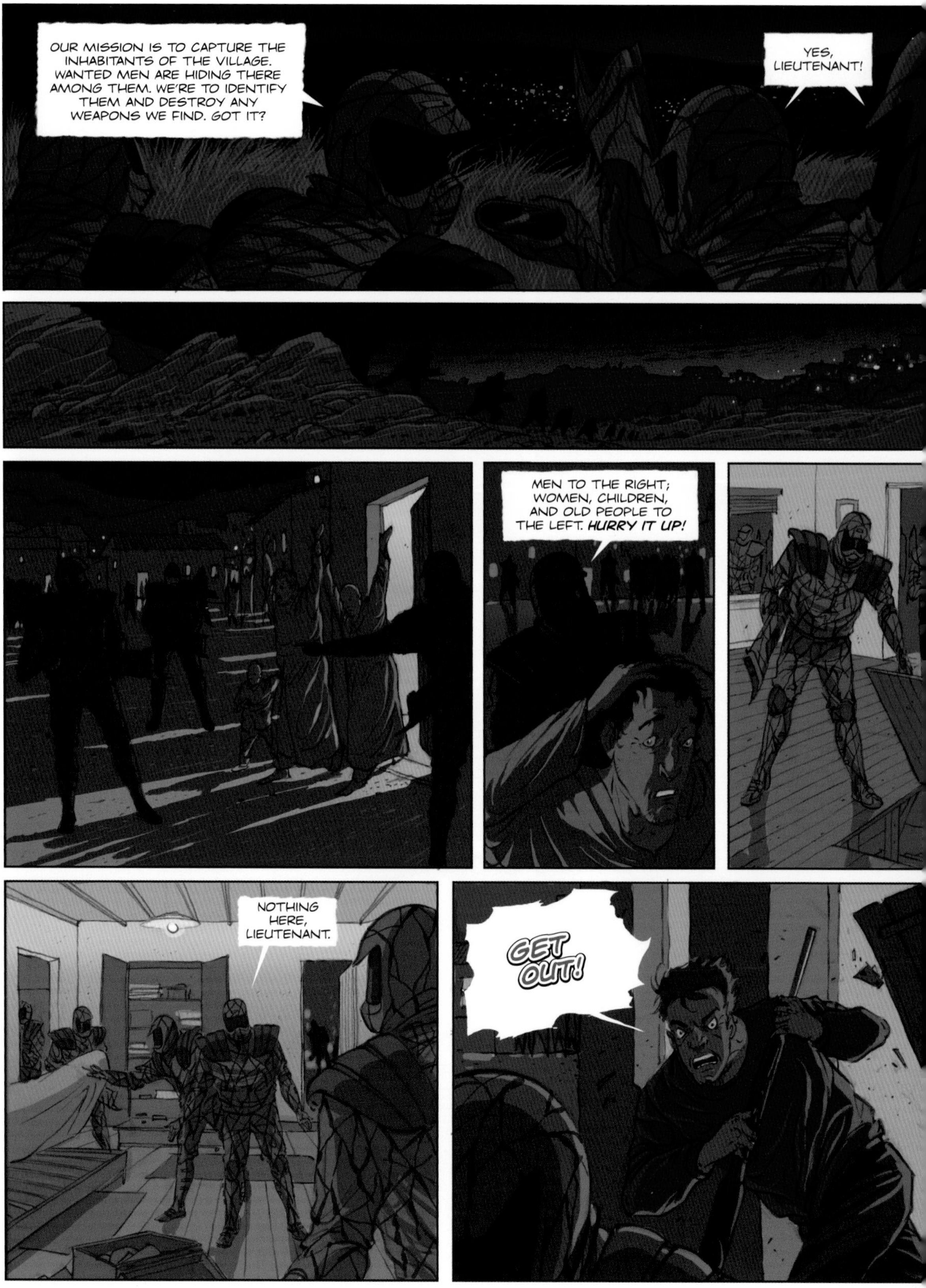
OUR MISSION IS TO CAPTURE THE INHABITANTS OF THE VILLAGE. WANTED MEN ARE HIDING THERE AMONG THEM. WE'RE TO IDENTIFY THEM AND DESTROY ANY WEAPONS WE FIND. GOT IT?
YES, LIEUTENANT!
MEN TO THE RIGHT; WOMEN, CHILDREN, AND OLD PEOPLE TO THE LEFT. *HURRY IT UP!*
NOTHING HERE, LIEUTENANT.
GET OUT!

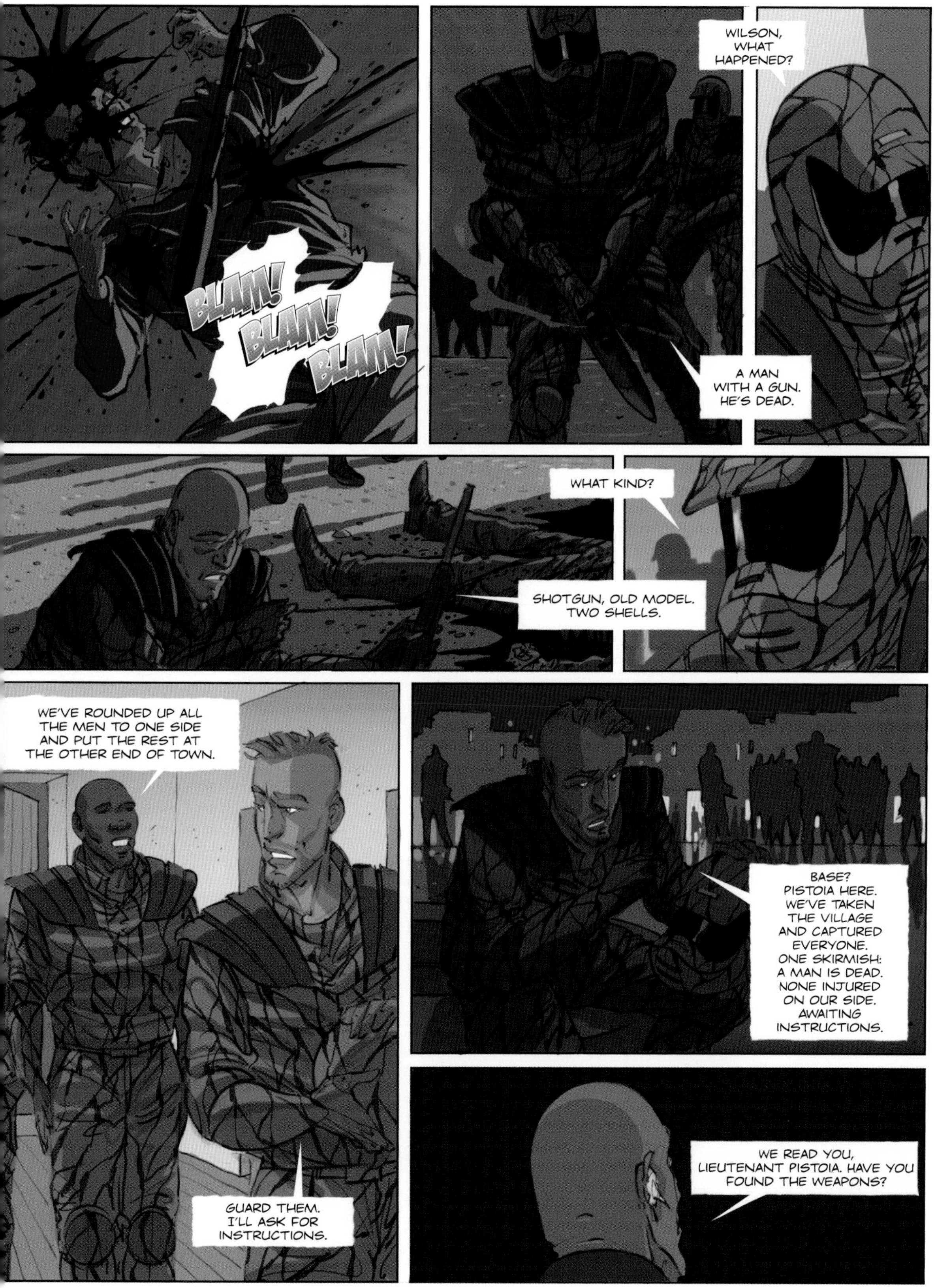
BLAM! BLAM! BLAM!
WILSON, WHAT HAPPENED?
A MAN WITH A GUN. HE'S DEAD.
WHAT KIND?
SHOTGUN, OLD MODEL. TWO SHELLS.
WE'VE ROUNDED UP ALL THE MEN TO ONE SIDE AND PUT THE REST AT THE OTHER END OF TOWN.
GUARD THEM. I'LL ASK FOR INSTRUCTIONS.
BASE? PISTOIA HERE. WE'VE TAKEN THE VILLAGE AND CAPTURED EVERYONE. ONE SKIRMISH: A MAN IS DEAD. NONE INJURED ON OUR SIDE. AWAITING INSTRUCTIONS.
WE READ YOU, LIEUTENANT PISTOIA. HAVE YOU FOUND THE WEAPONS?

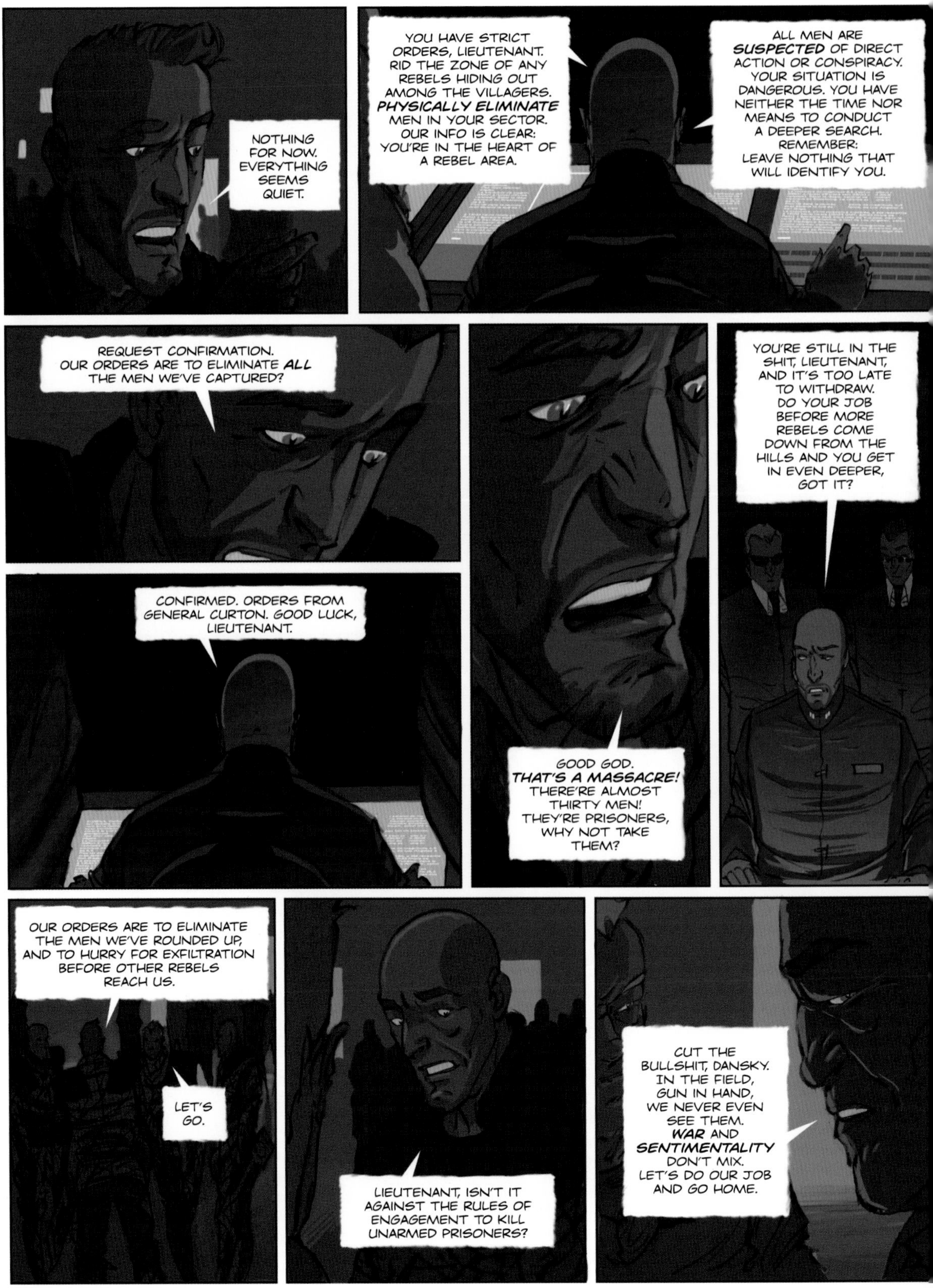
NOTHING FOR NOW. EVERYTHING SEEMS QUIET.
YOU HAVE STRICT ORDERS, LIEUTENANT. RID THE ZONE OF ANY REBELS HIDING OUT AMONG THE VILLAGERS. PHYSICALLY ELIMINATE MEN IN YOUR SECTOR. OUR INFO IS CLEAR: YOU'RE IN THE HEART OF A REBEL AREA.
ALL MEN ARE SUSPECTED OF DIRECT ACTION OR CONSPIRACY. YOUR SITUATION IS DANGEROUS. YOU HAVE NEITHER THE TIME NOR MEANS TO CONDUCT A DEEPER SEARCH. REMEMBER: LEAVE NOTHING THAT WILL IDENTIFY YOU.
REQUEST CONFIRMATION. OUR ORDERS ARE TO ELIMINATE ALL THE MEN WE'VE CAPTURED?
CONFIRMED. ORDERS FROM GENERAL CURTON. GOOD LUCK, LIEUTENANT.
GOOD GOD. THAT'S A MASSACRE! THERE'RE ALMOST THIRTY MEN! THEY'RE PRISONERS, WHY NOT TAKE THEM?
YOU'RE STILL IN THE SHIT, LIEUTENANT, AND IT'S TOO LATE TO WITHDRAW. DO YOUR JOB BEFORE MORE REBELS COME DOWN FROM THE HILLS AND YOU GET IN EVEN DEEPER, GOT IT?
OUR ORDERS ARE TO ELIMINATE THE MEN WE'VE ROUNDED UP, AND TO HURRY FOR EXFILTRATION BEFORE OTHER REBELS REACH US.
LET'S GO.
LIEUTENANT, ISN'T IT AGAINST THE RULES OF ENGAGEMENT TO KILL UNARMED PRISONERS?
CUT THE BULLSHIT, DANSKY. IN THE FIELD, GUN IN HAND, WE NEVER EVEN SEE THEM. WAR AND SENTIMENTALITY DON'T MIX. LET'S DO OUR JOB AND GO HOME.

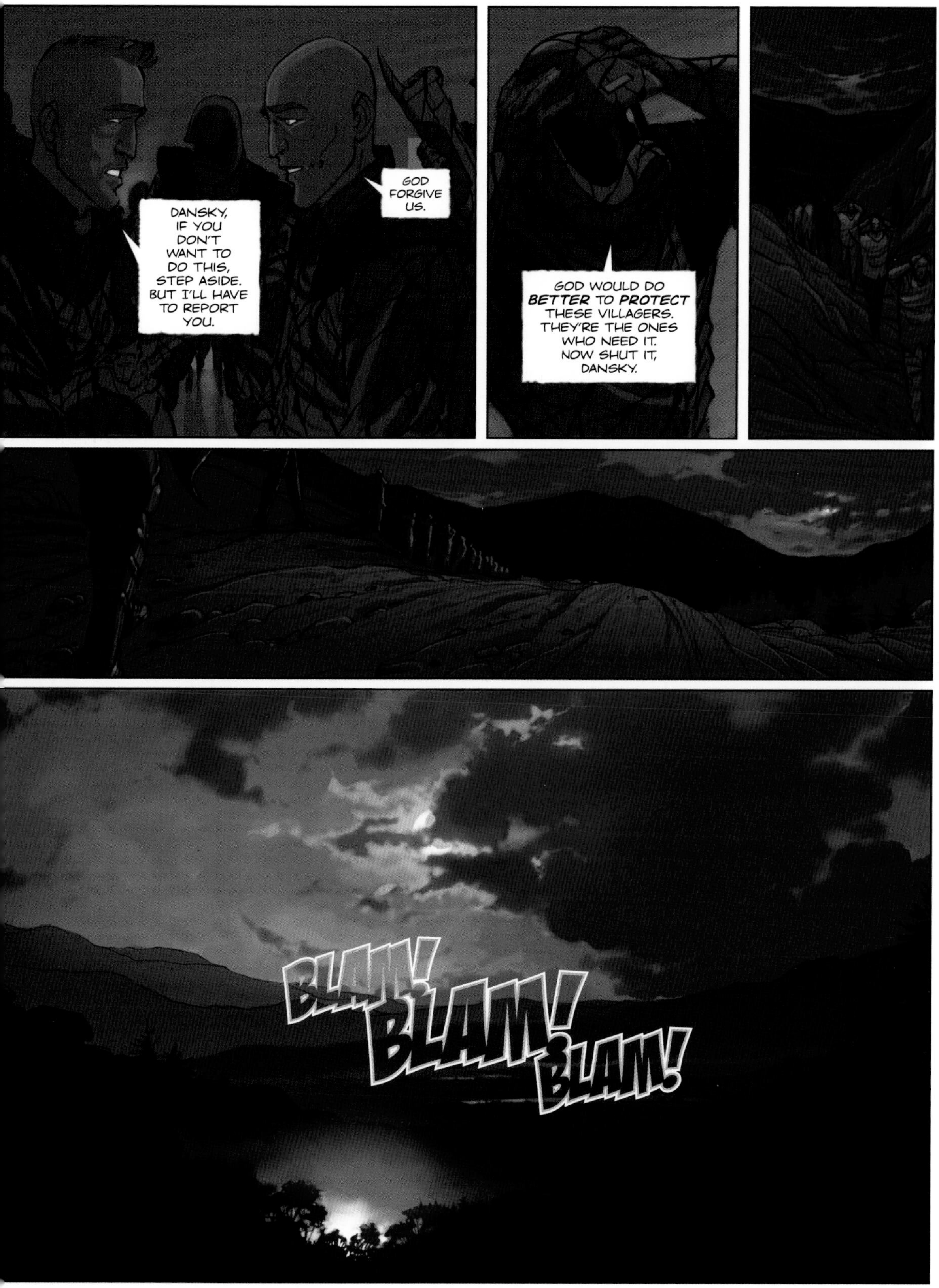
DANSKY, IF YOU DON'T WANT TO DO THIS, STEP ASIDE. BUT I'LL HAVE TO REPORT YOU.
GOD FORGIVE US.
GOD WOULD DO **BETTER** TO **PROTECT** THESE VILLAGERS. THEY'RE THE ONES WHO NEED IT. NOW SHUT IT, DANSKY.
BLAM! BLAM! BLAM!

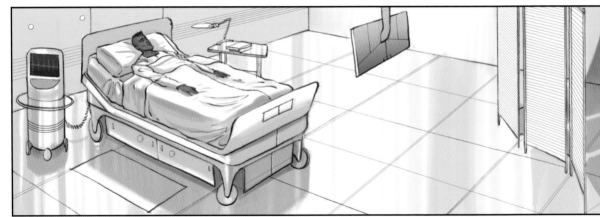

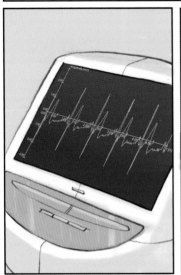

GOOD MORNING, LIEUTENANT. HOW ARE WE FEELING TODAY?

FINE, AND YOU KNOW IT. I CAN'T TAKE MUCH MORE OF THIS FARCE. I WASN'T WOUNDED. WHY HAVE I BEEN STUCK HERE FOR FIVE DAYS?

YOU NEEDED A BIT OF REST. YOUR LAST MISSION WAS TAXING. YOU HAD TO PROCESS IT. *HAVE YOU?*

I HOPE WHAT WE DID WAS *JUSTIFIED*. I ALSO HOPE I NEVER FIND MYSELF IN A SITUATION LIKE THAT AGAIN.

UNDERSTANDABLE. REMEMBER THAT YOU CAN TELL NO ONE ABOUT THIS MISSION. NOT EVEN YOUR WIFE. FOR YOUR GOOD AS WELL AS MULTICORPS'. IS THAT CLEAR?

YES.

GOOD. SOME PEOPLE WANT TO SEE YOU. ARE YOU READY?

I'M UP FOR ANYTHING THAT WILL GET ME OUT OF THIS BED AND THIS ROOM. WHO ARE THEY?

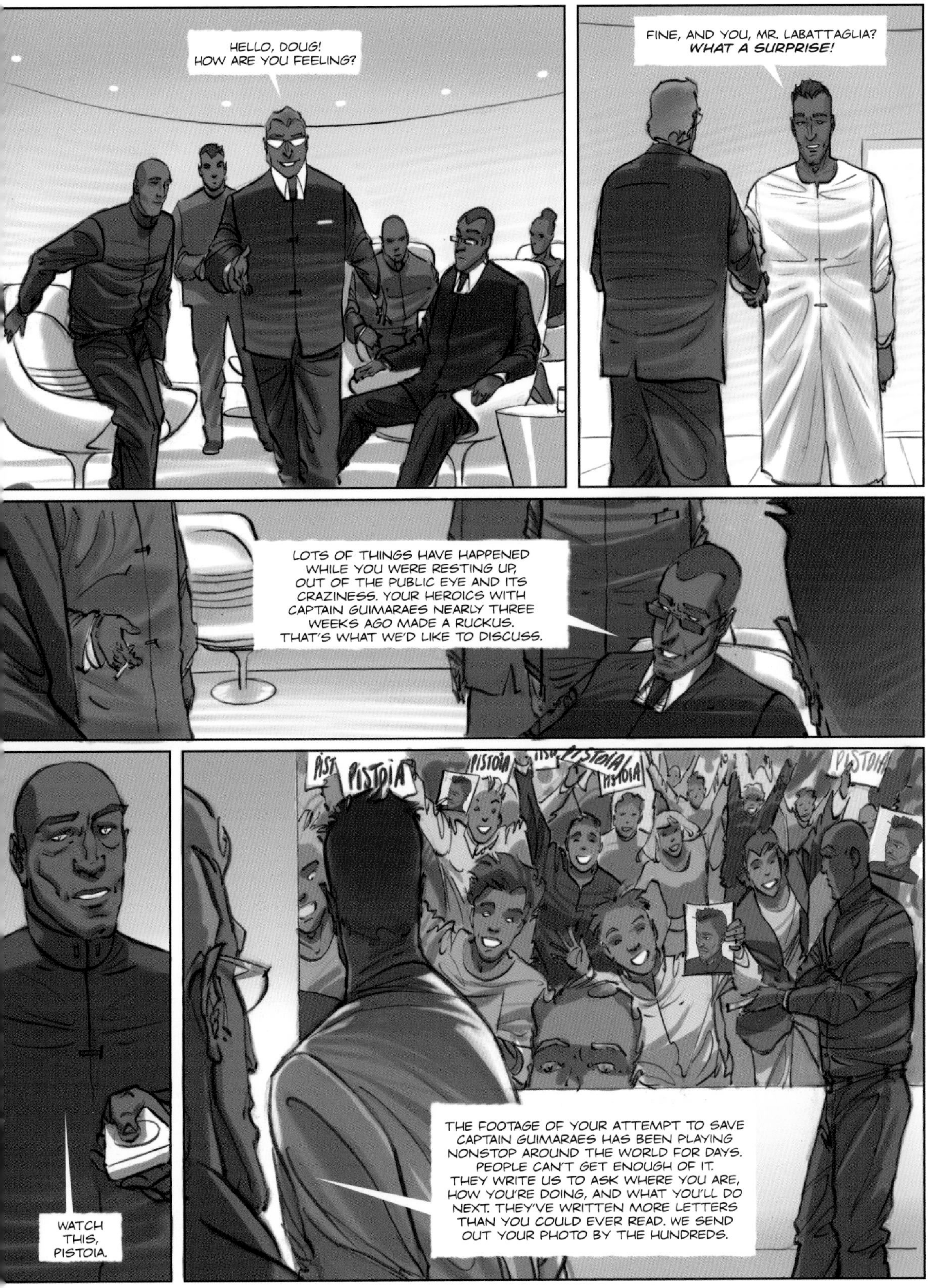
HELLO, DOUG! HOW ARE YOU FEELING?
FINE, AND YOU, MR. LABATTAGLIA? *WHAT A SURPRISE!*
LOTS OF THINGS HAVE HAPPENED WHILE YOU WERE RESTING UP, OUT OF THE PUBLIC EYE AND ITS CRAZINESS. YOUR HEROICS WITH CAPTAIN GUIMARAES NEARLY THREE WEEKS AGO MADE A RUCKUS. THAT'S WHAT WE'D LIKE TO DISCUSS.
WATCH THIS, PISTOIA.
PISTOIA
THE FOOTAGE OF YOUR ATTEMPT TO SAVE CAPTAIN GUIMARAES HAS BEEN PLAYING NONSTOP AROUND THE WORLD FOR DAYS. PEOPLE CAN'T GET ENOUGH OF IT. THEY WRITE US TO ASK WHERE YOU ARE, HOW YOU'RE DOING, AND WHAT YOU'LL DO NEXT. THEY'VE WRITTEN MORE LETTERS THAN YOU COULD EVER READ. WE SEND OUT YOUR PHOTO BY THE HUNDREDS.

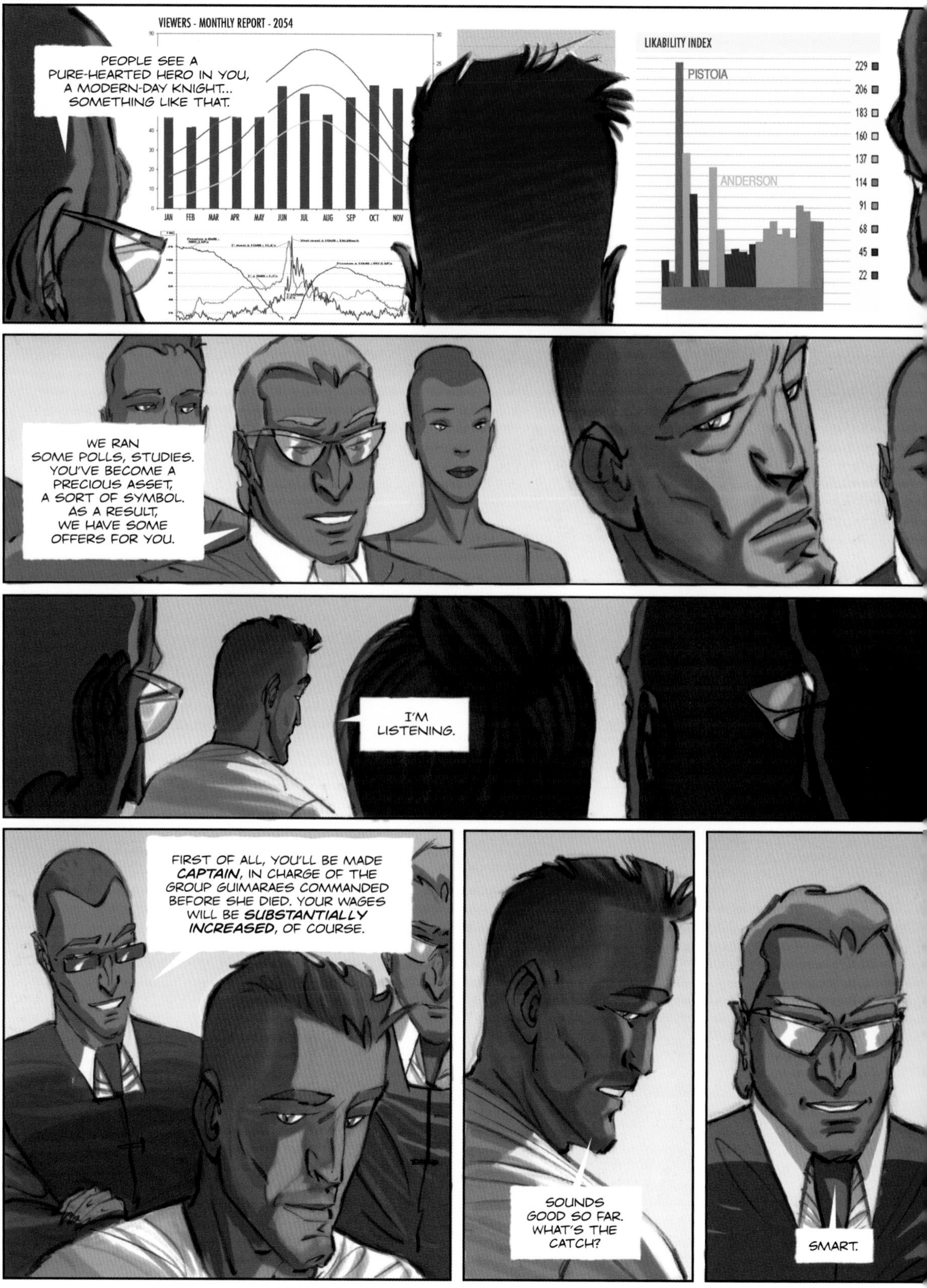
VIEWERS - MONTHLY REPORT - 2054
JAN FEB MAR APR MAY JUN JUL AUG SEP OCT NOV
PEOPLE SEE A PURE-HEARTED HERO IN YOU, A MODERN-DAY KNIGHT... SOMETHING LIKE THAT.
LIKABILITY INDEX
PISTOIA
ANDERSON
229 206 183 160 137 114 91 68 45 22
WE RAN SOME POLLS, STUDIES. YOU'VE BECOME A PRECIOUS ASSET, A SORT OF SYMBOL. AS A RESULT, WE HAVE SOME OFFERS FOR YOU.
I'M LISTENING.
FIRST OF ALL, YOU'LL BE MADE **CAPTAIN**, IN CHARGE OF THE GROUP GUIMARAES COMMANDED BEFORE SHE DIED. YOUR WAGES WILL BE **SUBSTANTIALLY INCREASED**, OF COURSE.
SOUNDS GOOD SO FAR. WHAT'S THE CATCH?
SMART.

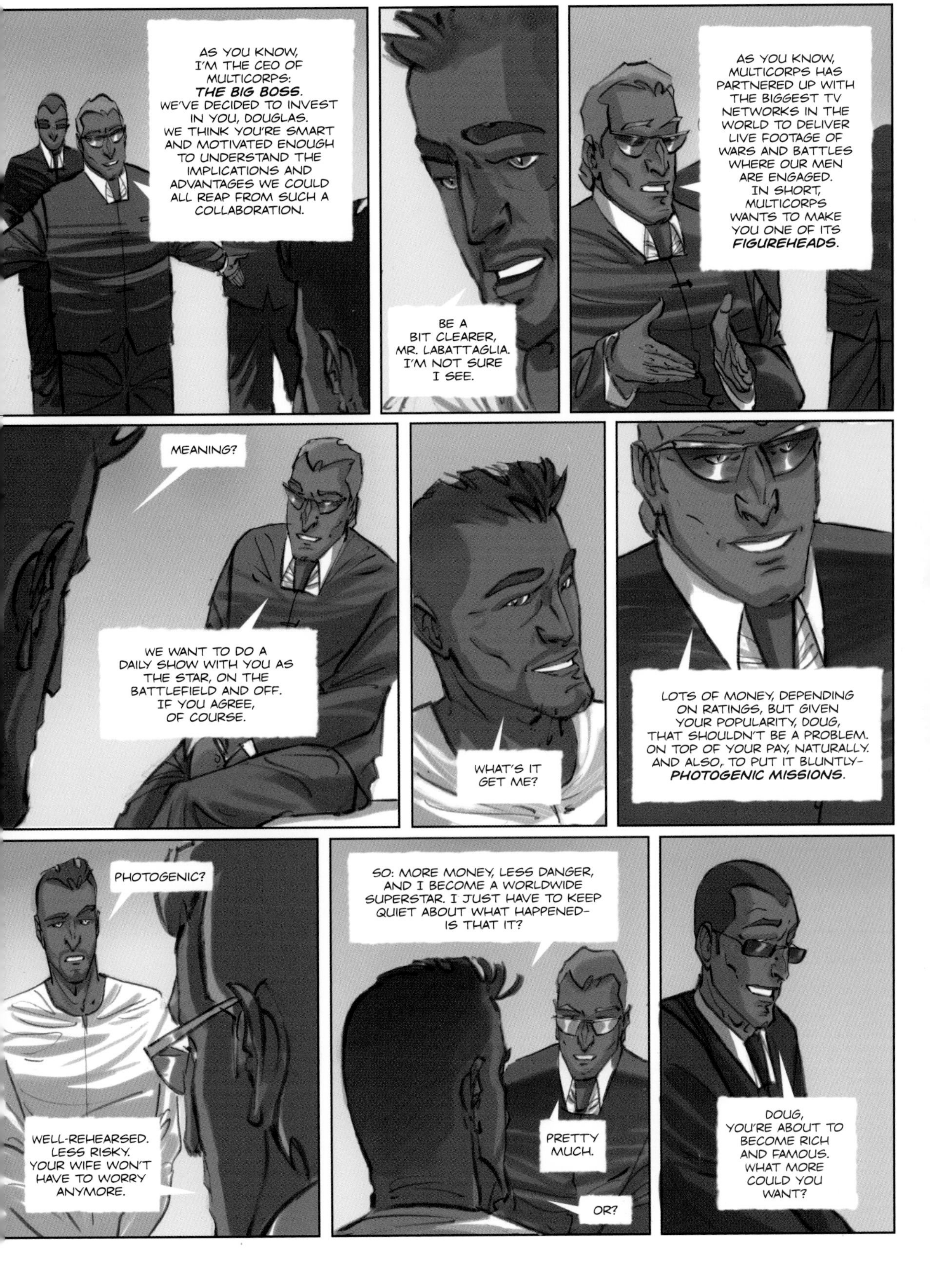
AS YOU KNOW, I'M THE CEO OF MULTICORPS: **THE BIG BOSS**. WE'VE DECIDED TO INVEST IN YOU, DOUGLAS. WE THINK YOU'RE SMART AND MOTIVATED ENOUGH TO UNDERSTAND THE IMPLICATIONS AND ADVANTAGES WE COULD ALL REAP FROM SUCH A COLLABORATION.
BE A BIT CLEARER, MR. LABATTAGLIA. I'M NOT SURE I SEE.
AS YOU KNOW, MULTICORPS HAS PARTNERED UP WITH THE BIGGEST TV NETWORKS IN THE WORLD TO DELIVER LIVE FOOTAGE OF WARS AND BATTLES WHERE OUR MEN ARE ENGAGED. IN SHORT, MULTICORPS WANTS TO MAKE YOU ONE OF ITS ***FIGUREHEADS***.
MEANING?
WE WANT TO DO A DAILY SHOW WITH YOU AS THE STAR, ON THE BATTLEFIELD AND OFF. IF YOU AGREE, OF COURSE.
WHAT'S IT GET ME?
LOTS OF MONEY, DEPENDING ON RATINGS, BUT GIVEN YOUR POPULARITY, DOUG, THAT SHOULDN'T BE A PROBLEM. ON TOP OF YOUR PAY, NATURALLY. AND ALSO, TO PUT IT BLUNTLY- ***PHOTOGENIC MISSIONS***.
PHOTOGENIC?
WELL-REHEARSED. LESS RISKY. YOUR WIFE WON'T HAVE TO WORRY ANYMORE.
SO: MORE MONEY, LESS DANGER, AND I BECOME A WORLDWIDE SUPERSTAR. I JUST HAVE TO KEEP QUIET ABOUT WHAT HAPPENED- IS THAT IT?
PRETTY MUCH.
OR?
DOUG, YOU'RE ABOUT TO BECOME RICH AND FAMOUS. WHAT MORE COULD YOU WANT?

TONIGHT, I HAVE THE PLEASURE AND HONOR OF HOSTING THE WORLD PREMIERE OF A FABULOUS NEW KIND OF DAILY PROGRAM, BROUGHT TO YOU BY THE WORLD WIDE INSTANT NEWS NETWORK.

EVERY NIGHT, WE'LL SPEND NINETY MINUTES WITH CAPTAIN DOUGLAS PISTOIA! WE ALL REMEMBER LIEUTENANT PISTOIA. HE HURTLED THROUGH THE AMBUSH HIS UNIT WAS TRAPPED IN, AND RIGHT INTO OUR LIVING ROOMS.

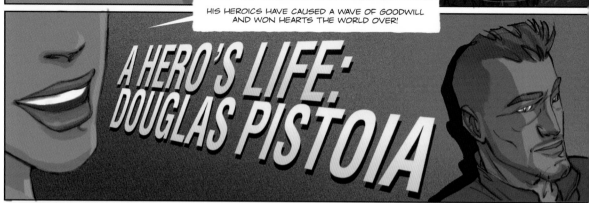

HIS HEROICS HAVE CAUSED A WAVE OF GOODWILL AND WON HEARTS THE WORLD OVER!

A HERO'S LIFE: DOUGLAS PISTOIA

TODAY, DOUGLAS PISTOIA HAS RECOVERED FROM HIS INJURIES. HE'S BEEN MADE CAPTAIN. BUT WE'RE NOT JUST GOING TO FOLLOW THE CAPTAIN INTO BATTLE.

WE'LL BE WATCHING EVERY ASPECT OF HIS LIFE... IN OUR TERRIFIC NEW SERIES, *A HERO'S LIFE*.

"Never think that war, no matter how necessary, nor how justified, is not a *crime*."

—Ernest Hemingway

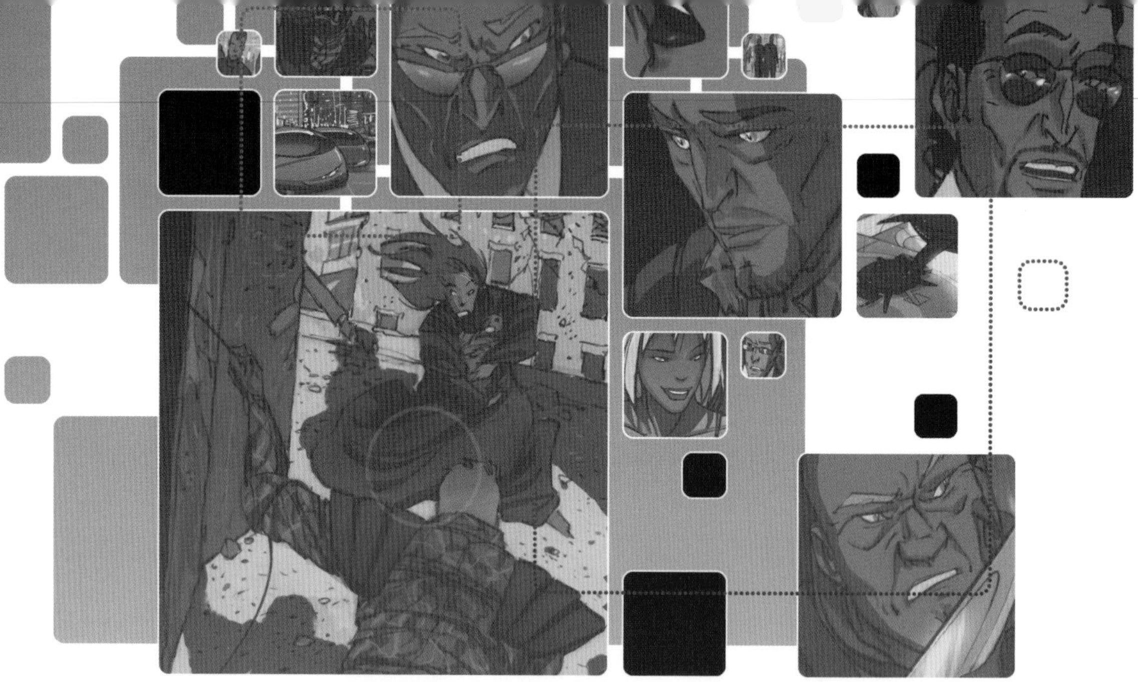

EPISODE TWO
02 THE HERO

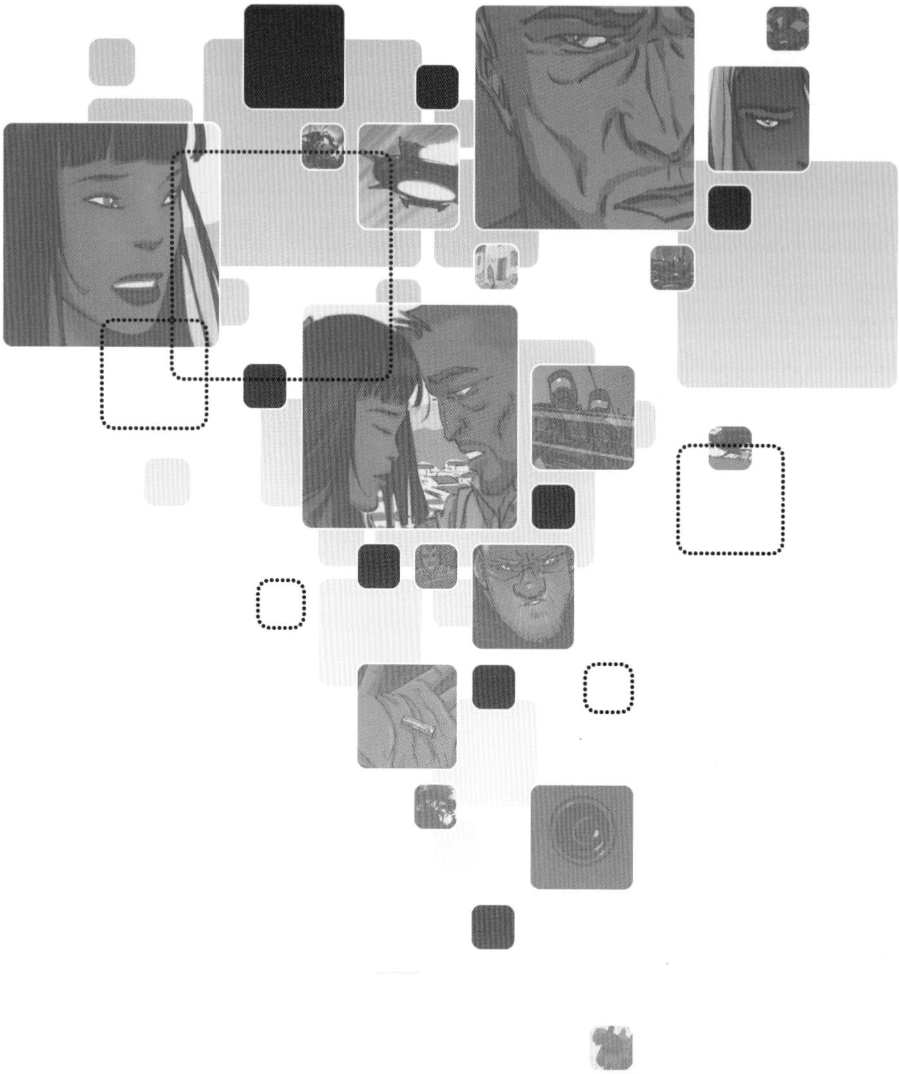

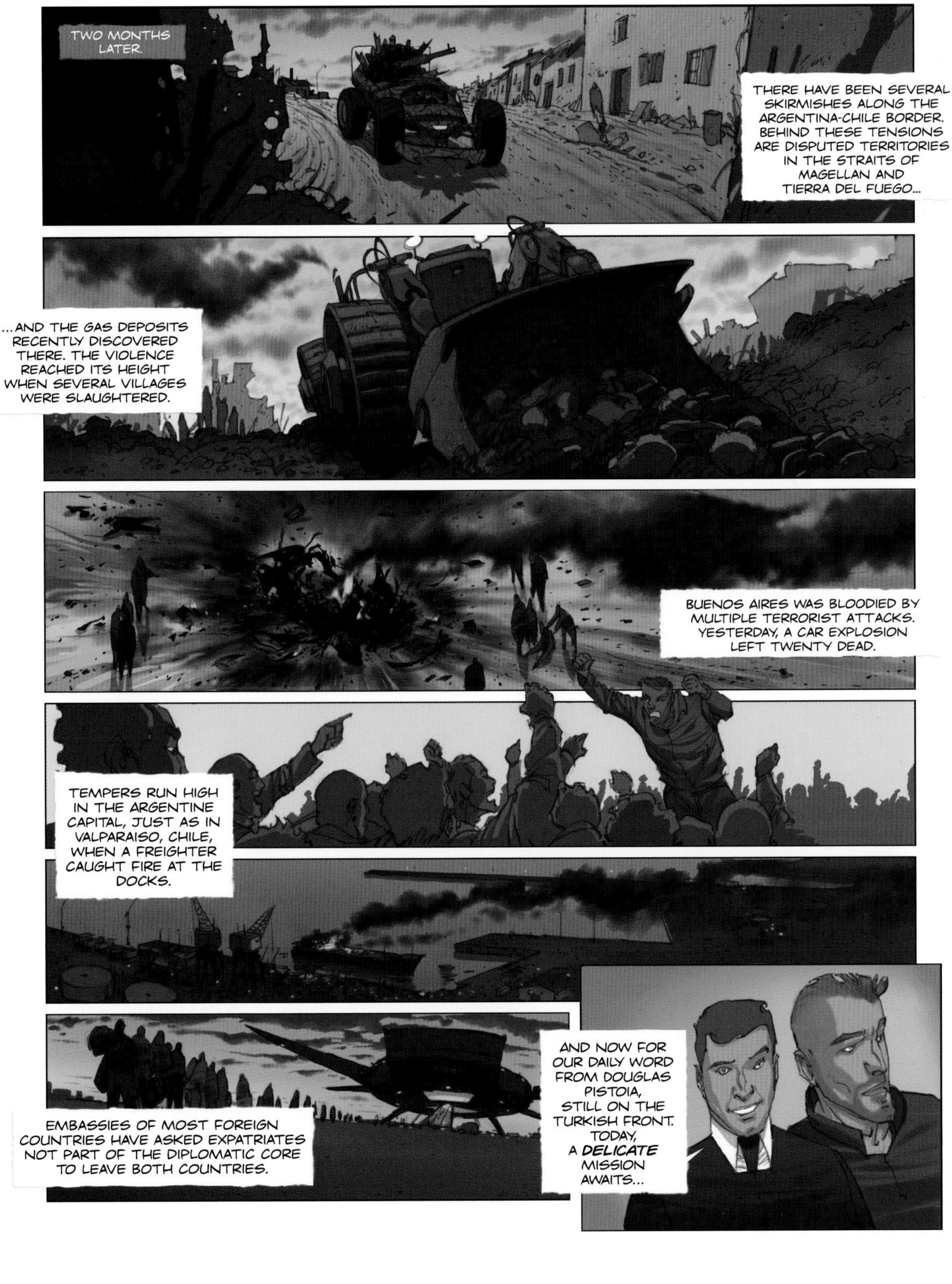
TWO MONTHS LATER.
THERE HAVE BEEN SEVERAL SKIRMISHES ALONG THE ARGENTINA-CHILE BORDER. BEHIND THESE TENSIONS ARE DISPUTED TERRITORIES IN THE STRAITS OF MAGELLAN AND TIERRA DEL FUEGO...
...AND THE GAS DEPOSITS RECENTLY DISCOVERED THERE. THE VIOLENCE REACHED ITS HEIGHT WHEN SEVERAL VILLAGES WERE SLAUGHTERED.
BUENOS AIRES WAS BLOODIED BY MULTIPLE TERRORIST ATTACKS. YESTERDAY, A CAR EXPLOSION LEFT TWENTY DEAD.
TEMPERS RUN HIGH IN THE ARGENTINE CAPITAL, JUST AS IN VALPARAISO, CHILE, WHEN A FREIGHTER CAUGHT FIRE AT THE DOCKS.
EMBASSIES OF MOST FOREIGN COUNTRIES HAVE ASKED EXPATRIATES NOT PART OF THE DIPLOMATIC CORE TO LEAVE BOTH COUNTRIES.
AND NOW FOR OUR DAILY WORD FROM DOUGLAS PISTOIA, STILL ON THE TURKISH FRONT. TODAY, A ***DELICATE*** MISSION AWAITS...

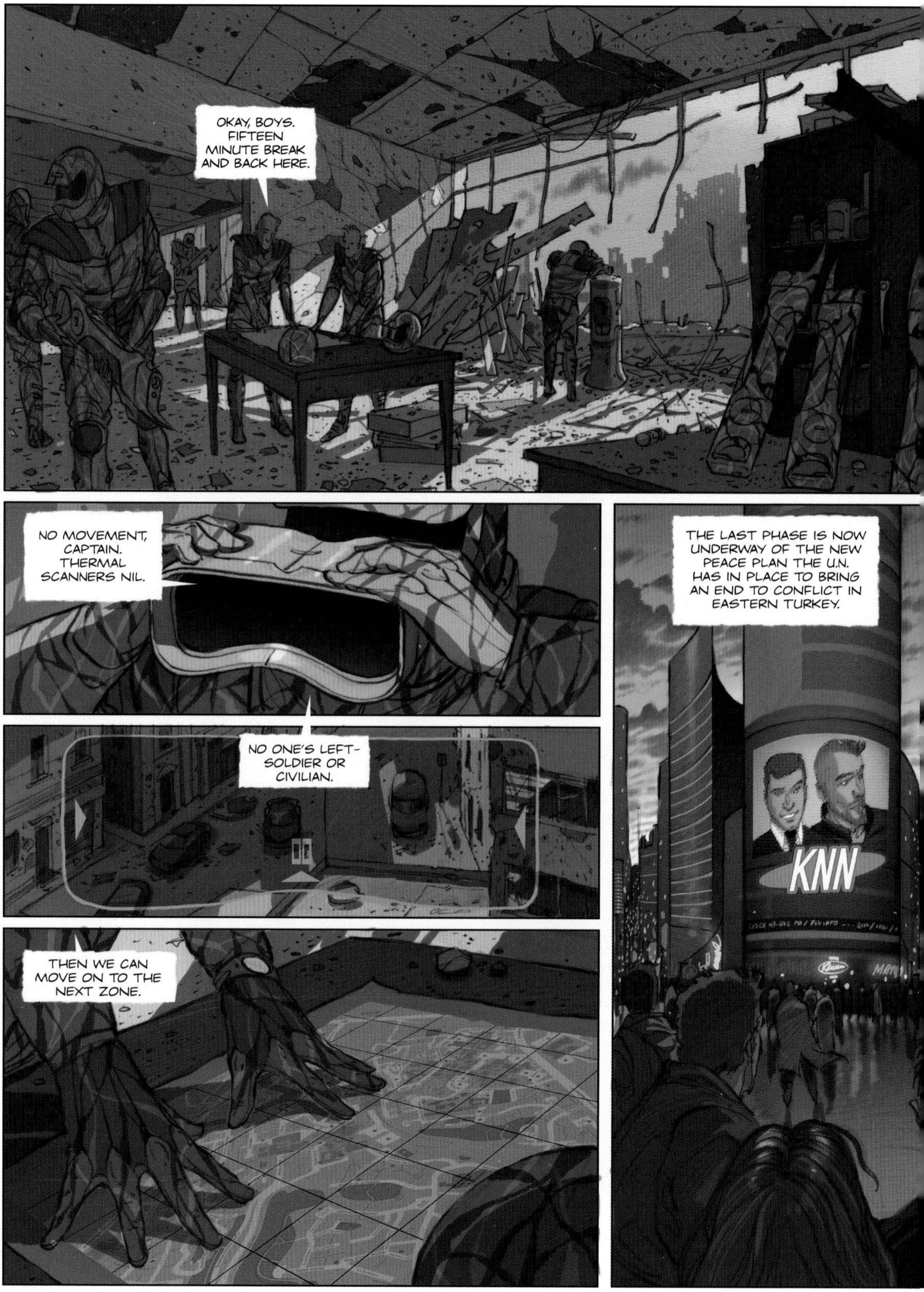
OKAY, BOYS. FIFTEEN MINUTE BREAK AND BACK HERE.
NO MOVEMENT, CAPTAIN. THERMAL SCANNERS NIL.
NO ONE'S LEFT- SOLDIER OR CIVILIAN.
THEN WE CAN MOVE ON TO THE NEXT ZONE.
THE LAST PHASE IS NOW UNDERWAY OF THE NEW PEACE PLAN THE U.N. HAS IN PLACE TO BRING AN END TO CONFLICT IN EASTERN TURKEY.
KNN

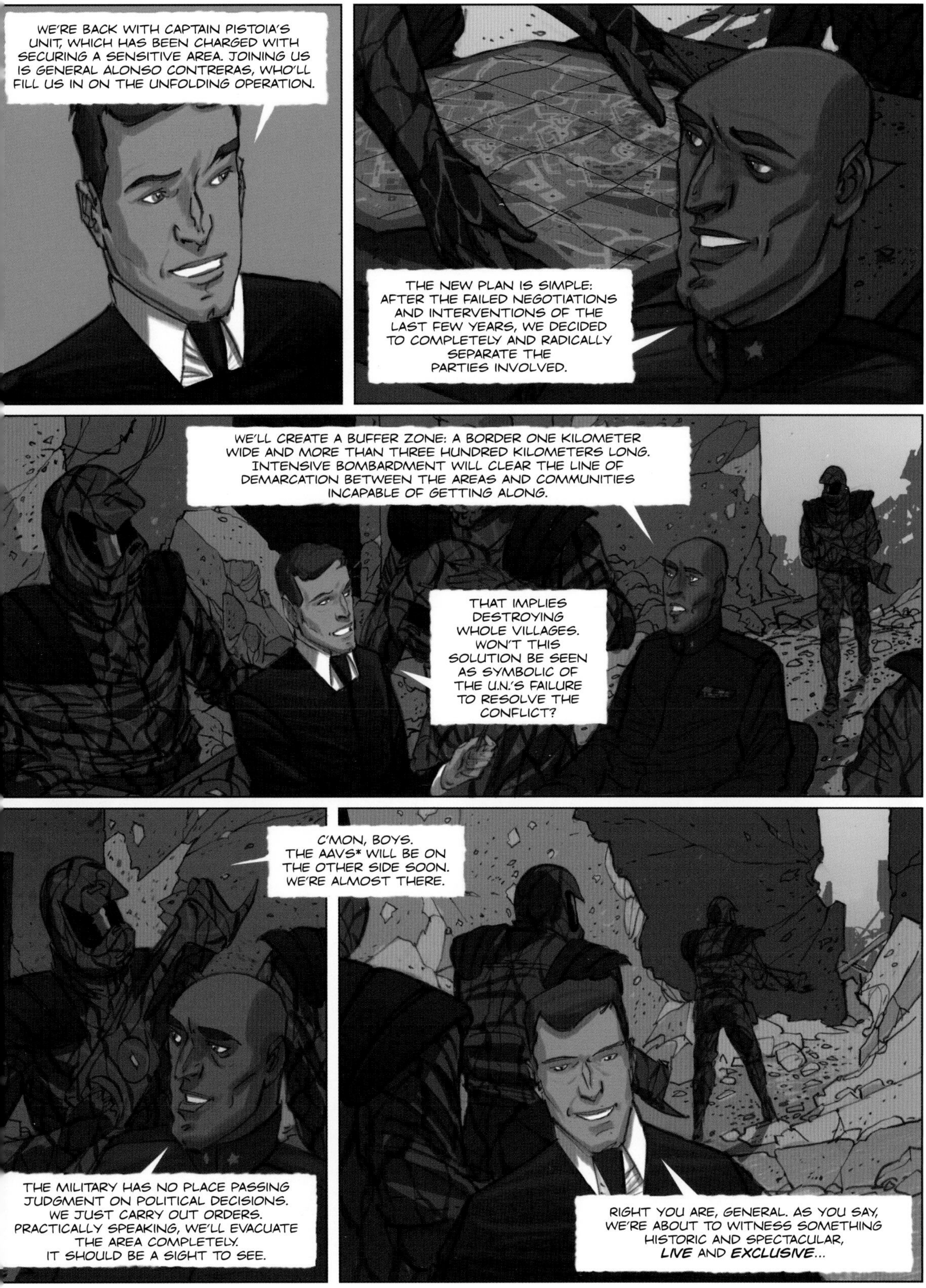
WE'RE BACK WITH CAPTAIN PISTOIA'S UNIT, WHICH HAS BEEN CHARGED WITH SECURING A SENSITIVE AREA. JOINING US IS GENERAL ALONSO CONTRERAS, WHO'LL FILL US IN ON THE UNFOLDING OPERATION.
THE NEW PLAN IS SIMPLE: AFTER THE FAILED NEGOTIATIONS AND INTERVENTIONS OF THE LAST FEW YEARS, WE DECIDED TO COMPLETELY AND RADICALLY SEPARATE THE PARTIES INVOLVED.
WE'LL CREATE A BUFFER ZONE: A BORDER ONE KILOMETER WIDE AND MORE THAN THREE HUNDRED KILOMETERS LONG. INTENSIVE BOMBARDMENT WILL CLEAR THE LINE OF DEMARCATION BETWEEN THE AREAS AND COMMUNITIES INCAPABLE OF GETTING ALONG.
THAT IMPLIES DESTROYING WHOLE VILLAGES. WON'T THIS SOLUTION BE SEEN AS SYMBOLIC OF THE U.N.'S FAILURE TO RESOLVE THE CONFLICT?
C'MON, BOYS. THE AAVS* WILL BE ON THE OTHER SIDE SOON. WE'RE ALMOST THERE.
THE MILITARY HAS NO PLACE PASSING JUDGMENT ON POLITICAL DECISIONS. WE JUST CARRY OUT ORDERS. PRACTICALLY SPEAKING, WE'LL EVACUATE THE AREA COMPLETELY. IT SHOULD BE A SIGHT TO SEE.
RIGHT YOU ARE, GENERAL. AS YOU SAY, WE'RE ABOUT TO WITNESS SOMETHING HISTORIC AND SPECTACULAR, ***LIVE*** AND ***EXCLUSIVE***...

* AIRBORNE ARMORED VEHICLES.

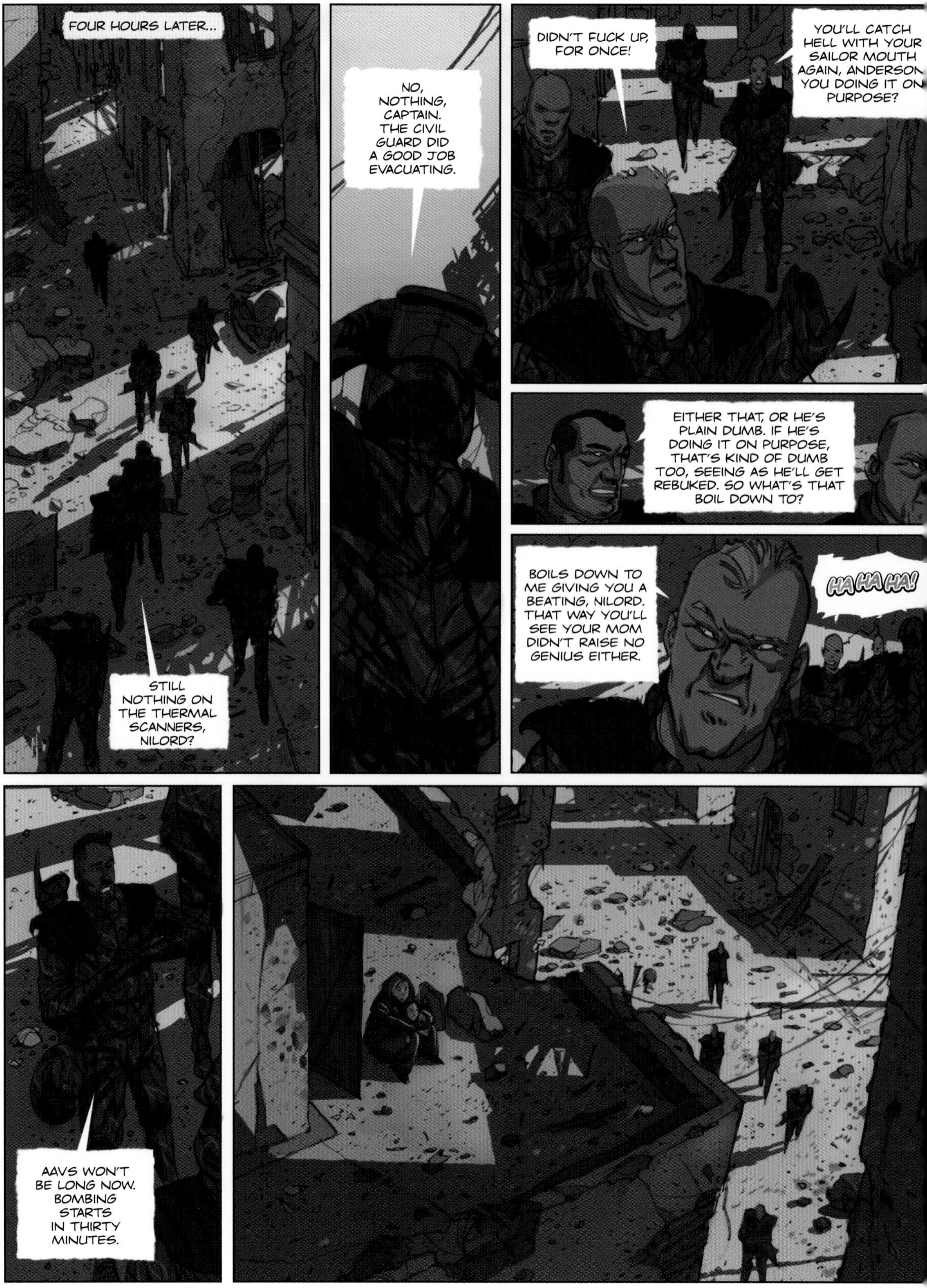
FOUR HOURS LATER...
STILL NOTHING ON THE THERMAL SCANNERS, NILORD?
NO, NOTHING, CAPTAIN. THE CIVIL GUARD DID A GOOD JOB EVACUATING.
DIDN'T FUCK UP, FOR ONCE!
YOU'LL CATCH HELL WITH YOUR SAILOR MOUTH AGAIN, ANDERSON. YOU DOING IT ON PURPOSE?
EITHER THAT, OR HE'S PLAIN DUMB. IF HE'S DOING IT ON PURPOSE, THAT'S KIND OF DUMB TOO, SEEING AS HE'LL GET REBUKED. SO WHAT'S THAT BOIL DOWN TO?
BOILS DOWN TO ME GIVING YOU A BEATING, NILORD. THAT WAY YOU'LL SEE YOUR MOM DIDN'T RAISE NO GENIUS EITHER.
HA HA HA!
AAVS WON'T BE LONG NOW. BOMBING STARTS IN THIRTY MINUTES.

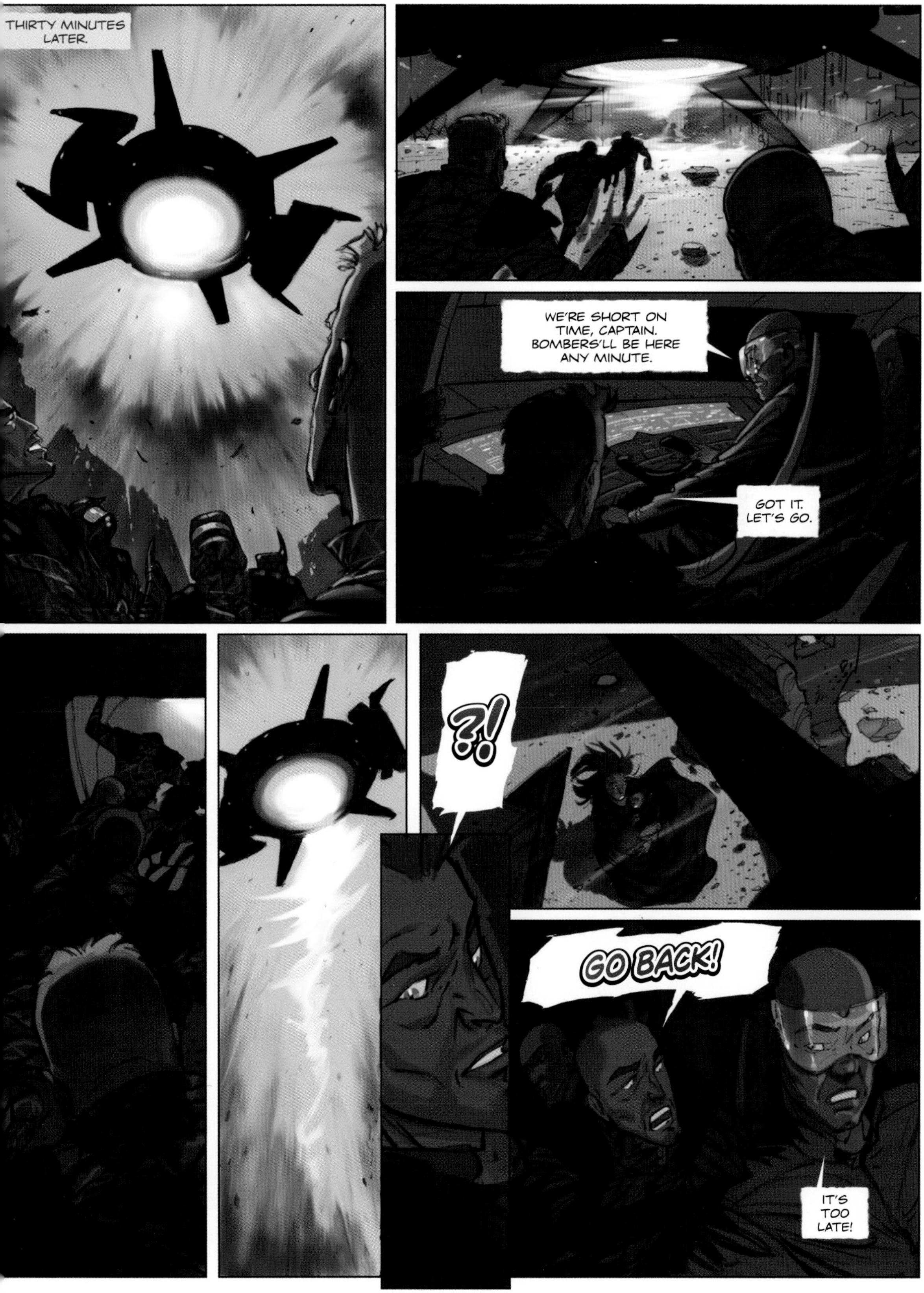
THIRTY MINUTES LATER.
WE'RE SHORT ON TIME, CAPTAIN. BOMBERS'LL BE HERE ANY MINUTE.
GOT IT. LET'S GO.
?!
GO BACK!
IT'S TOO LATE!

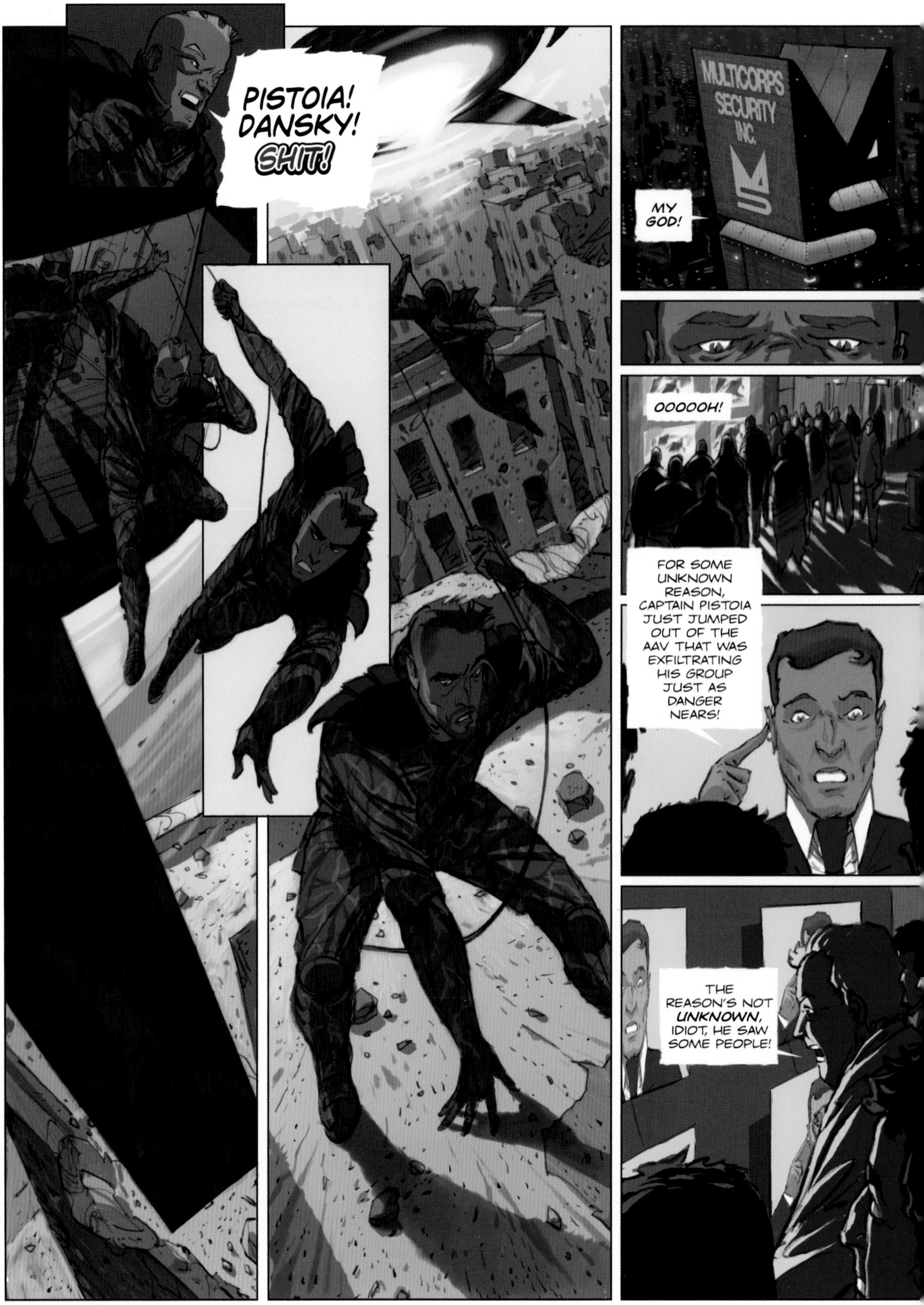
PISTOIA! DANSKY! SHIT!
MULTICORPS SECURITY INC.
MY GOD!
OOOOOH!
FOR SOME UNKNOWN REASON, CAPTAIN PISTOIA JUST JUMPED OUT OF THE AAV THAT WAS EXFILTRATING HIS GROUP JUST AS DANGER NEARS!
THE REASON'S NOT UNKNOWN, IDIOT, HE SAW SOME PEOPLE!

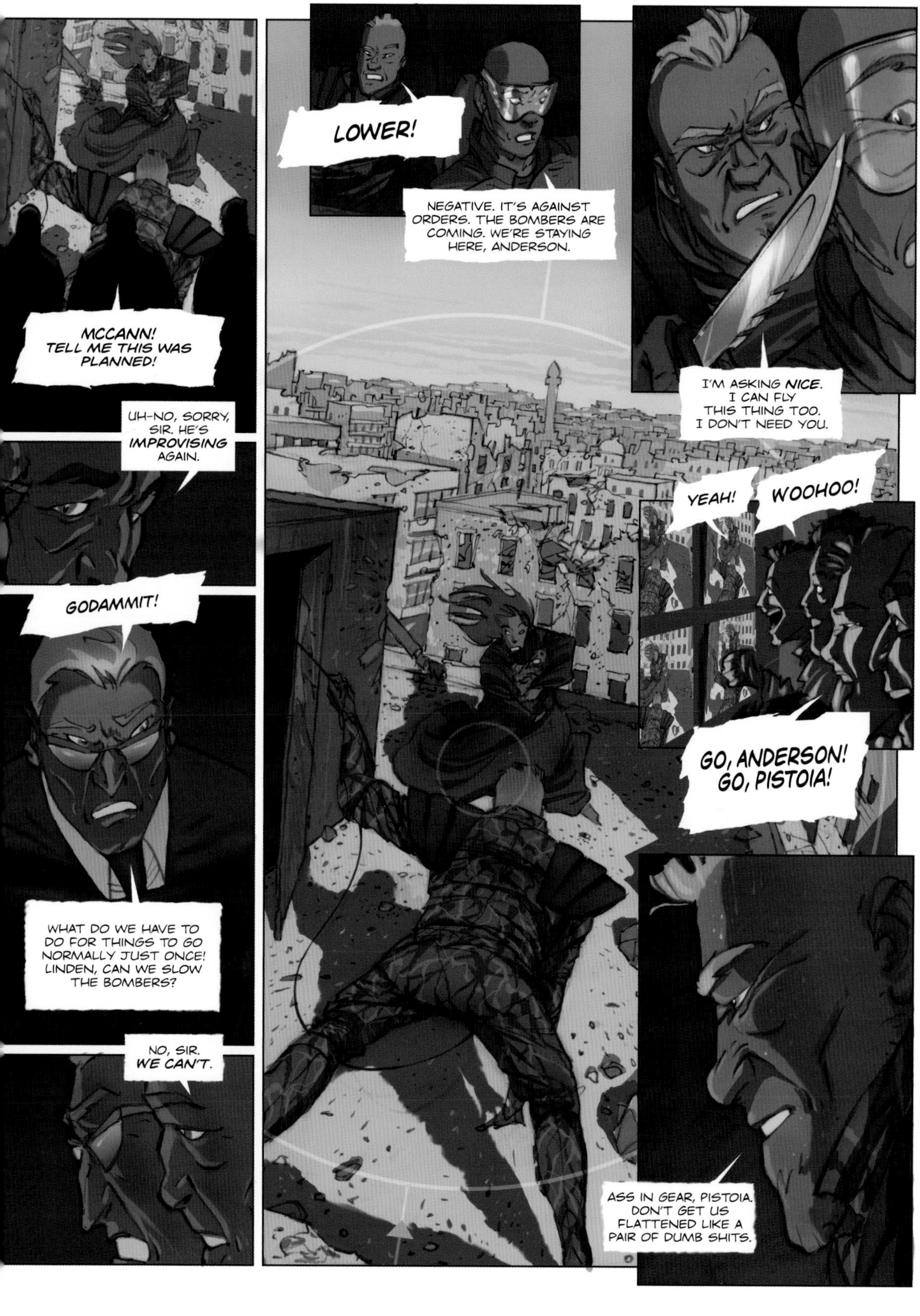
MCCANN!
TELL ME THIS WAS PLANNED!
UH-NO, SORRY, SIR. HE'S IMPROVISING AGAIN.
GODAMMIT!
WHAT DO WE HAVE TO DO FOR THINGS TO GO NORMALLY JUST ONCE! LINDEN, CAN WE SLOW THE BOMBERS?
NO, SIR. WE CAN'T.
LOWER!
NEGATIVE. IT'S AGAINST ORDERS. THE BOMBERS ARE COMING. WE'RE STAYING HERE, ANDERSON.
I'M ASKING NICE. I CAN FLY THIS THING TOO. I DON'T NEED YOU.
YEAH!
WOOHOO!
GO, ANDERSON! GO, PISTOIA!
ASS IN GEAR, PISTOIA. DON'T GET US FLATTENED LIKE A PAIR OF DUMB SHITS.

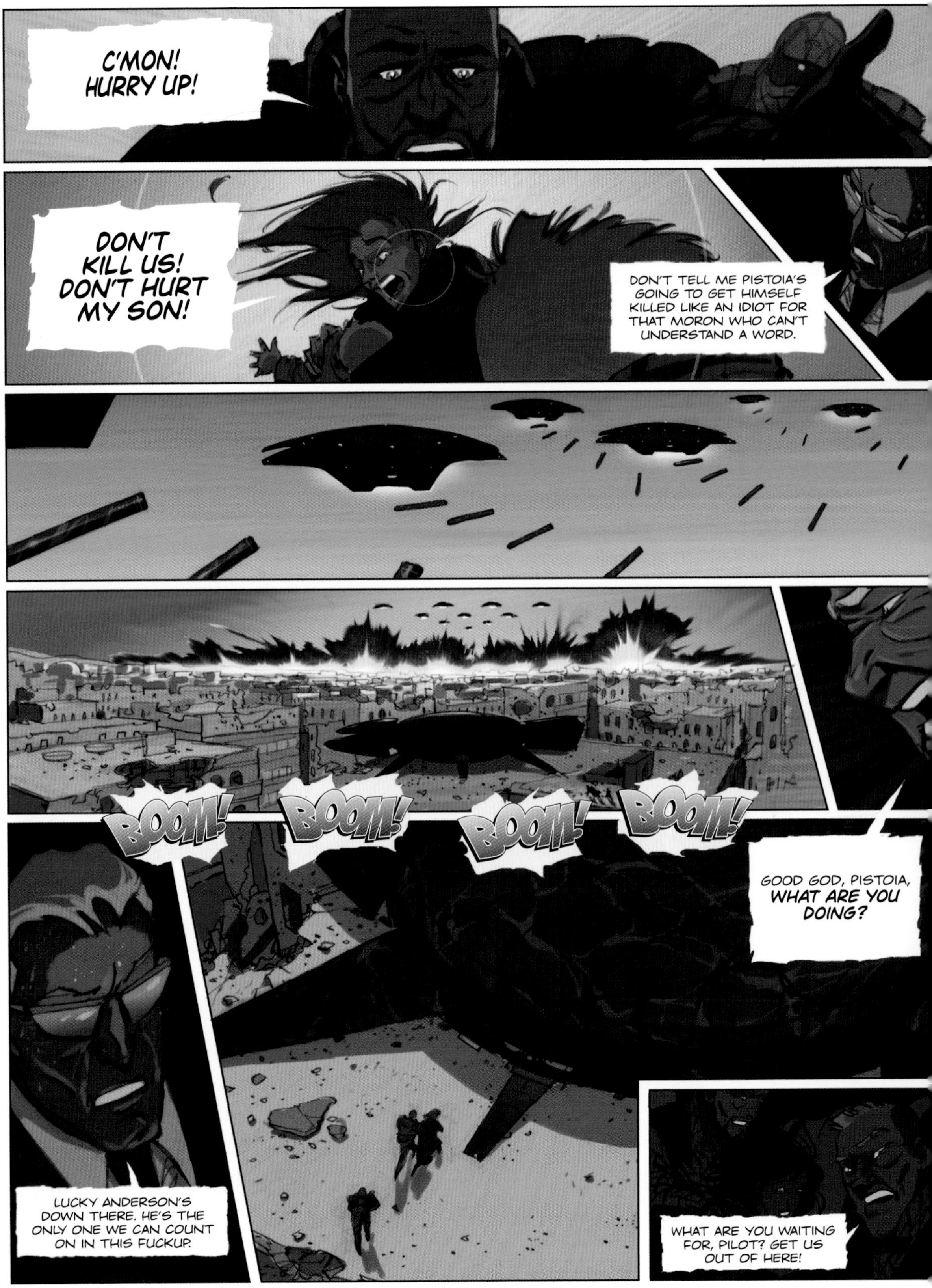
C'MON! HURRY UP!
DON'T KILL US! DON'T HURT MY SON!
DON'T TELL ME PISTOIA'S GOING TO GET HIMSELF KILLED LIKE AN IDIOT FOR THAT MORON WHO CAN'T UNDERSTAND A WORD.
BOOM!
BOOM!
BOOM!
BOOM!
GOOD GOD, PISTOIA, WHAT ARE YOU DOING?
LUCKY ANDERSON'S DOWN THERE. HE'S THE ONLY ONE WE CAN COUNT ON IN THIS FUCKUP.
WHAT ARE YOU WAITING FOR, PILOT? GET US OUT OF HERE!

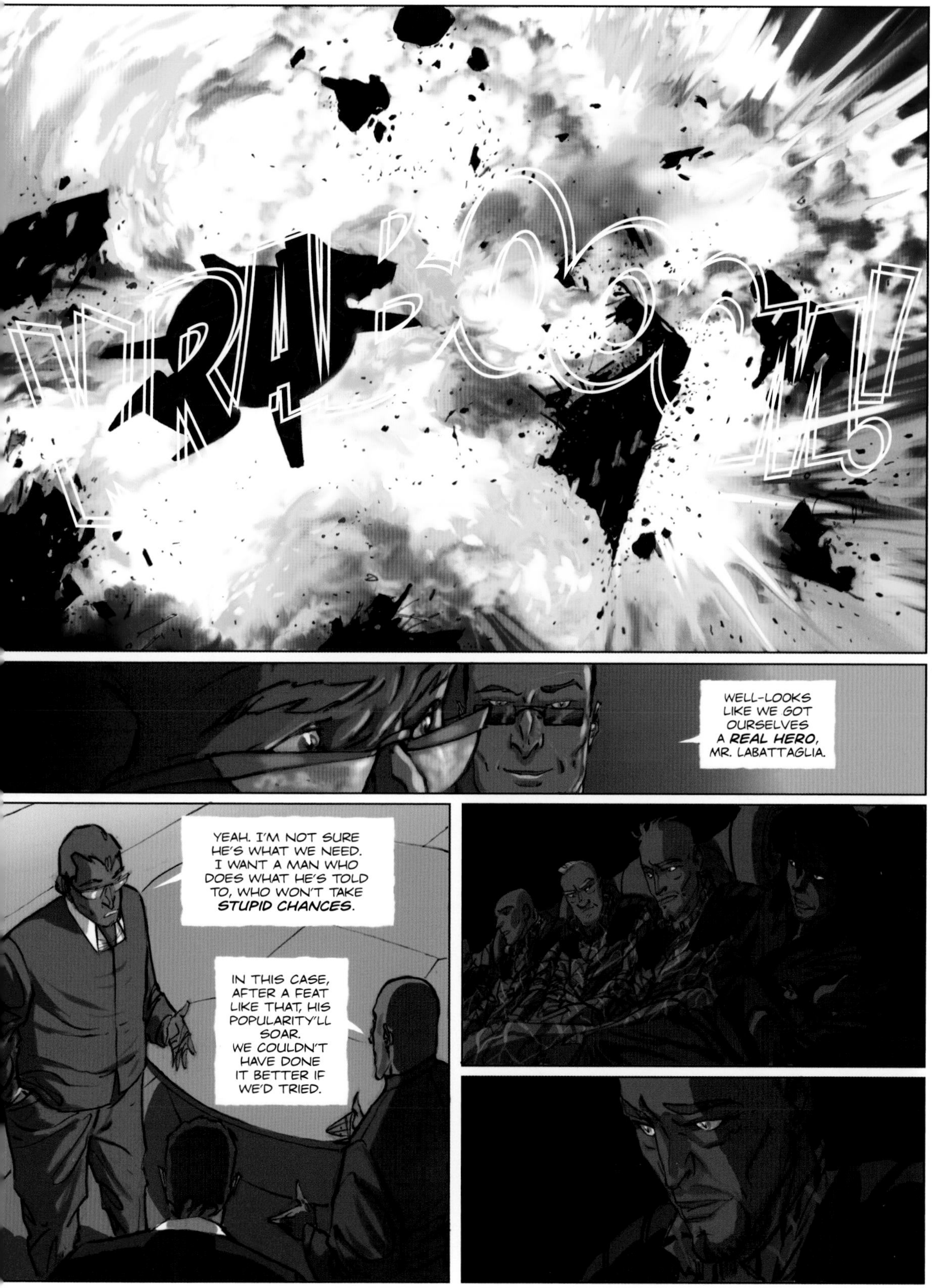
WRAW'OOOM!
WELL-LOOKS LIKE WE GOT OURSELVES A **REAL HERO**, MR. LABATTAGLIA.
YEAH. I'M NOT SURE HE'S WHAT WE NEED. I WANT A MAN WHO DOES WHAT HE'S TOLD TO, WHO WON'T TAKE **STUPID CHANCES**.
IN THIS CASE, AFTER A FEAT LIKE THAT, HIS POPULARITY'LL SOAR. WE COULDN'T HAVE DONE IT BETTER IF WE'D TRIED.

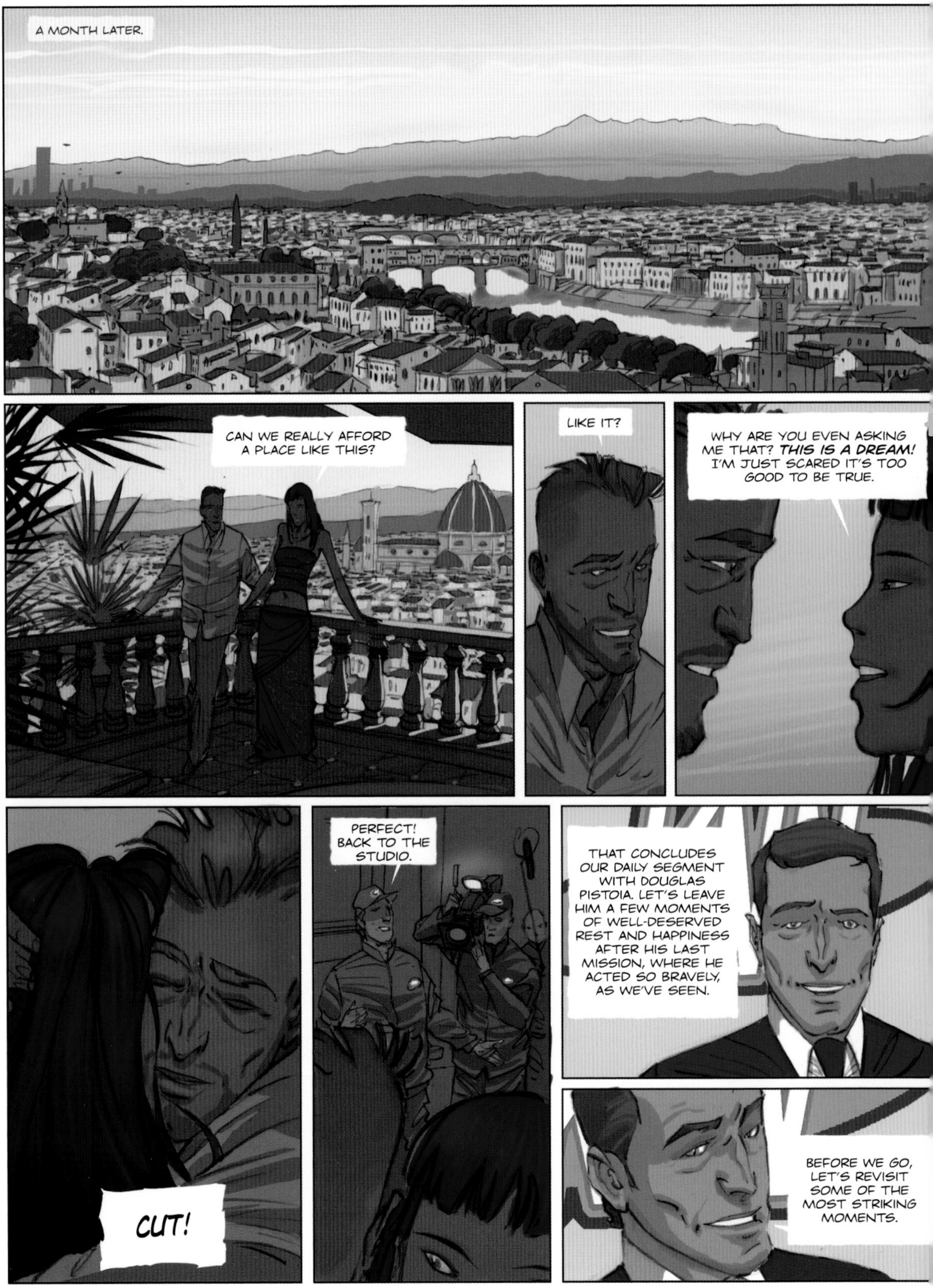
A MONTH LATER.
CAN WE REALLY AFFORD A PLACE LIKE THIS?
LIKE IT?
WHY ARE YOU EVEN ASKING ME THAT? **THIS IS A DREAM!** I'M JUST SCARED IT'S TOO GOOD TO BE TRUE.
CUT!
PERFECT! BACK TO THE STUDIO.
THAT CONCLUDES OUR DAILY SEGMENT WITH DOUGLAS PISTOIA. LET'S LEAVE HIM A FEW MOMENTS OF WELL-DESERVED REST AND HAPPINESS AFTER HIS LAST MISSION, WHERE HE ACTED SO BRAVELY, AS WE'VE SEEN.
BEFORE WE GO, LET'S REVISIT SOME OF THE MOST STRIKING MOMENTS.

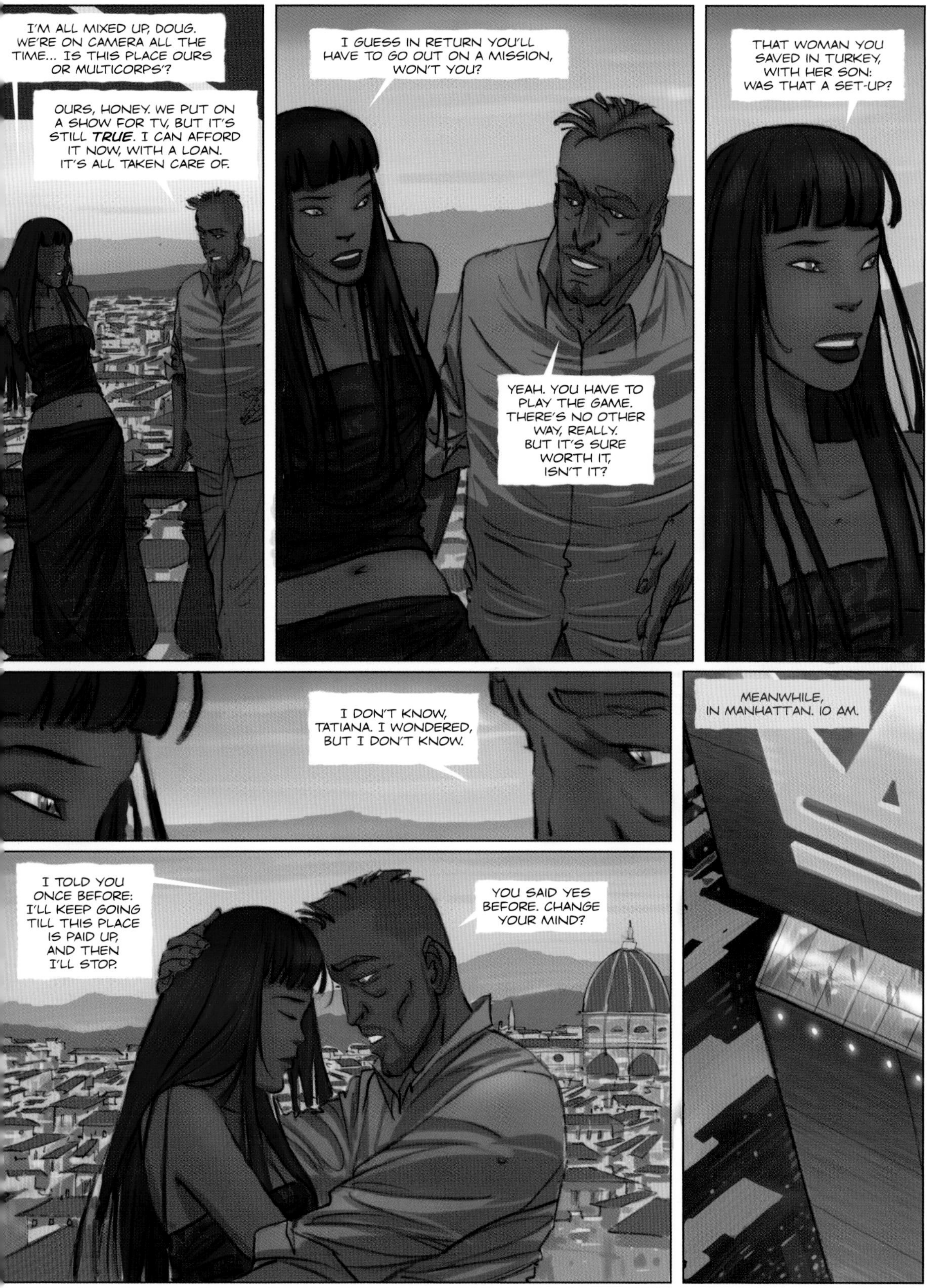
I'M ALL MIXED UP, DOUG. WE'RE ON CAMERA ALL THE TIME... IS THIS PLACE OURS OR MULTICORPS'?
OURS, HONEY. WE PUT ON A SHOW FOR TV, BUT IT'S STILL **TRUE**. I CAN AFFORD IT NOW, WITH A LOAN. IT'S ALL TAKEN CARE OF.
I GUESS IN RETURN YOU'LL HAVE TO GO OUT ON A MISSION, WON'T YOU?
YEAH. YOU HAVE TO PLAY THE GAME. THERE'S NO OTHER WAY, REALLY. BUT IT'S SURE WORTH IT, ISN'T IT?
THAT WOMAN YOU SAVED IN TURKEY, WITH HER SON: WAS THAT A SET-UP?
I DON'T KNOW, TATIANA. I WONDERED, BUT I DON'T KNOW.
I TOLD YOU ONCE BEFORE: I'LL KEEP GOING TILL THIS PLACE IS PAID UP, AND THEN I'LL STOP.
YOU SAID YES BEFORE. CHANGE YOUR MIND?
MEANWHILE, IN MANHATTAN. 10 AM.

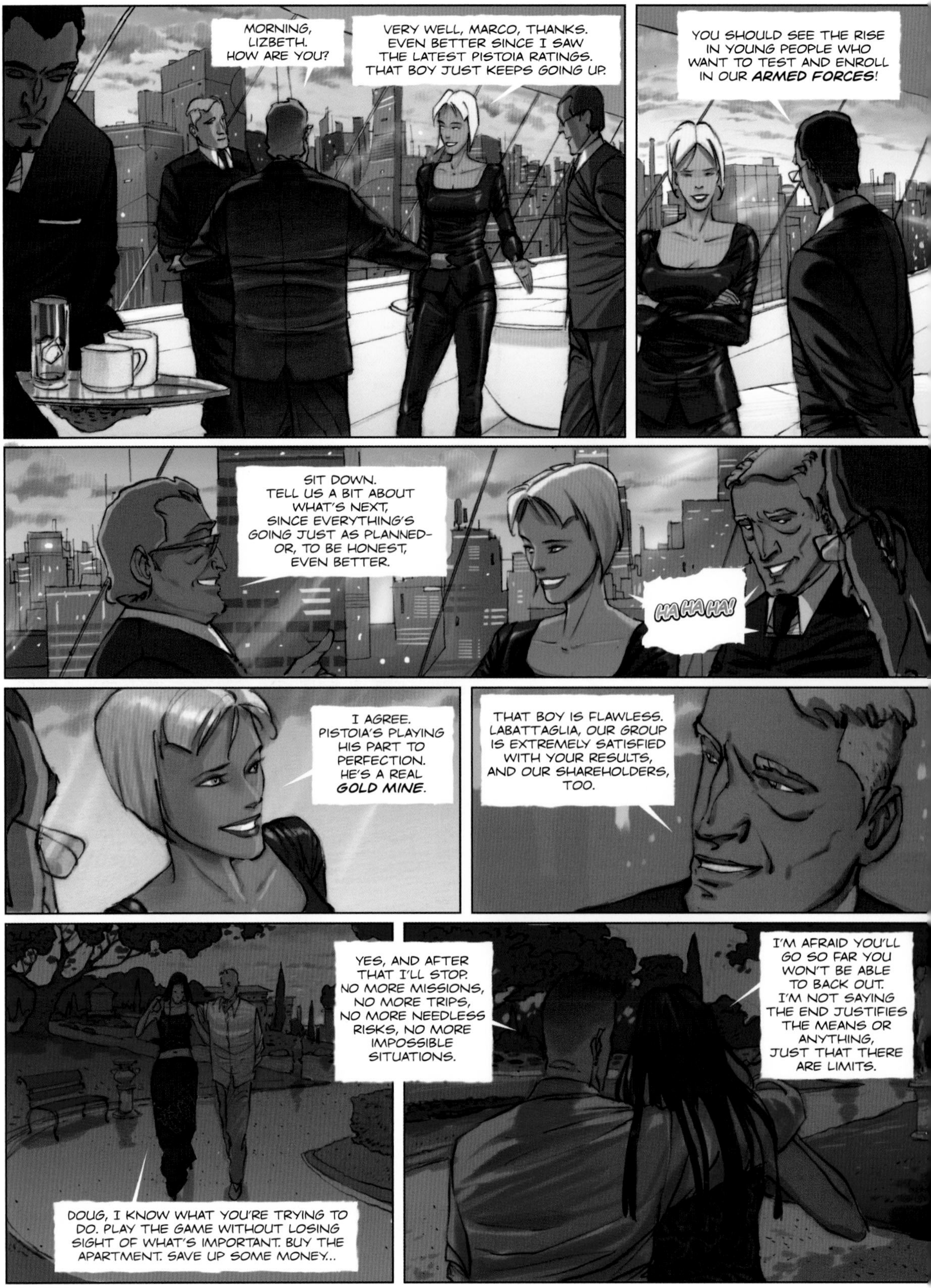
MORNING, LIZBETH. HOW ARE YOU?
VERY WELL, MARCO, THANKS. EVEN BETTER SINCE I SAW THE LATEST PISTOIA RATINGS. THAT BOY JUST KEEPS GOING UP.
YOU SHOULD SEE THE RISE IN YOUNG PEOPLE WHO WANT TO TEST AND ENROLL IN OUR ARMED FORCES!
SIT DOWN. TELL US A BIT ABOUT WHAT'S NEXT, SINCE EVERYTHING'S GOING JUST AS PLANNED- OR, TO BE HONEST, EVEN BETTER.
HA HA HA!
I AGREE. PISTOIA'S PLAYING HIS PART TO PERFECTION. HE'S A REAL GOLD MINE.
THAT BOY IS FLAWLESS. LABATTAGLIA, OUR GROUP IS EXTREMELY SATISFIED WITH YOUR RESULTS, AND OUR SHAREHOLDERS, TOO.
DOUG, I KNOW WHAT YOU'RE TRYING TO DO. PLAY THE GAME WITHOUT LOSING SIGHT OF WHAT'S IMPORTANT. BUY THE APARTMENT. SAVE UP SOME MONEY...
YES, AND AFTER THAT I'LL STOP. NO MORE MISSIONS, NO MORE TRIPS, NO MORE NEEDLESS RISKS, NO MORE IMPOSSIBLE SITUATIONS.
I'M AFRAID YOU'LL GO SO FAR YOU WON'T BE ABLE TO BACK OUT. I'M NOT SAYING THE END JUSTIFIES THE MEANS OR ANYTHING, JUST THAT THERE ARE LIMITS.

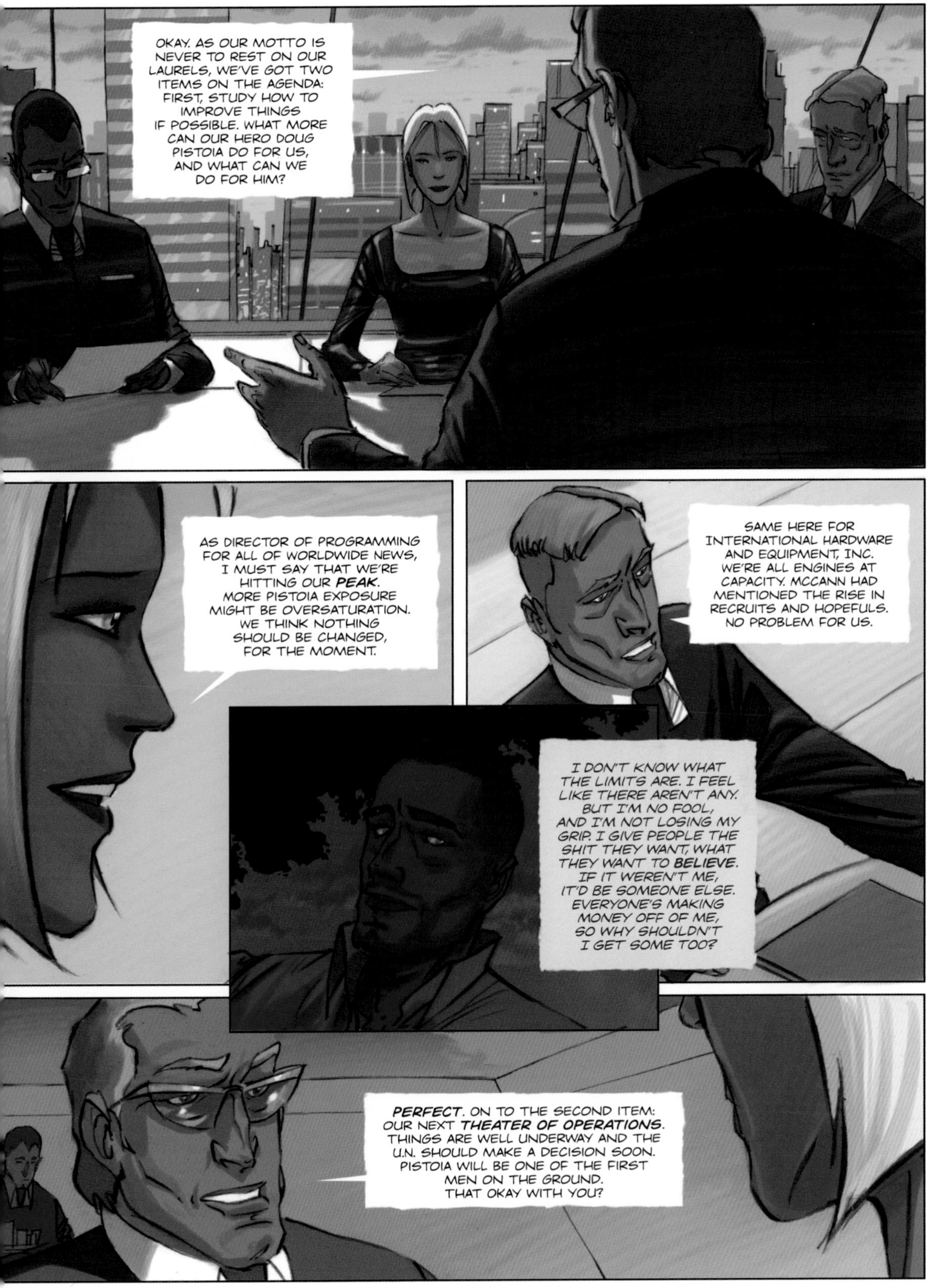
OKAY. AS OUR MOTTO IS NEVER TO REST ON OUR LAURELS, WE'VE GOT TWO ITEMS ON THE AGENDA: FIRST, STUDY HOW TO IMPROVE THINGS IF POSSIBLE. WHAT MORE CAN OUR HERO DOUG PISTOIA DO FOR US, AND WHAT CAN WE DO FOR HIM?
AS DIRECTOR OF PROGRAMMING FOR ALL OF WORLDWIDE NEWS, I MUST SAY THAT WE'RE HITTING OUR **PEAK**. MORE PISTOIA EXPOSURE MIGHT BE OVERSATURATION. WE THINK NOTHING SHOULD BE CHANGED, FOR THE MOMENT.
SAME HERE FOR INTERNATIONAL HARDWARE AND EQUIPMENT, INC. WE'RE ALL ENGINES AT CAPACITY. MCCANN HAD MENTIONED THE RISE IN RECRUITS AND HOPEFULS. NO PROBLEM FOR US.
I DON'T KNOW WHAT THE LIMITS ARE. I FEEL LIKE THERE AREN'T ANY. BUT I'M NO FOOL, AND I'M NOT LOSING MY GRIP. I GIVE PEOPLE THE SHIT THEY WANT, WHAT THEY WANT TO ***BELIEVE****. IF IT WEREN'T ME, IT'D BE SOMEONE ELSE. EVERYONE'S MAKING MONEY OFF OF ME, SO WHY SHOULDN'T I GET SOME TOO?*
PERFECT. ON TO THE SECOND ITEM: OUR NEXT ***THEATER OF OPERATIONS***. THINGS ARE WELL UNDERWAY AND THE U.N. SHOULD MAKE A DECISION SOON. PISTOIA WILL BE ONE OF THE FIRST MEN ON THE GROUND. THAT OKAY WITH YOU?

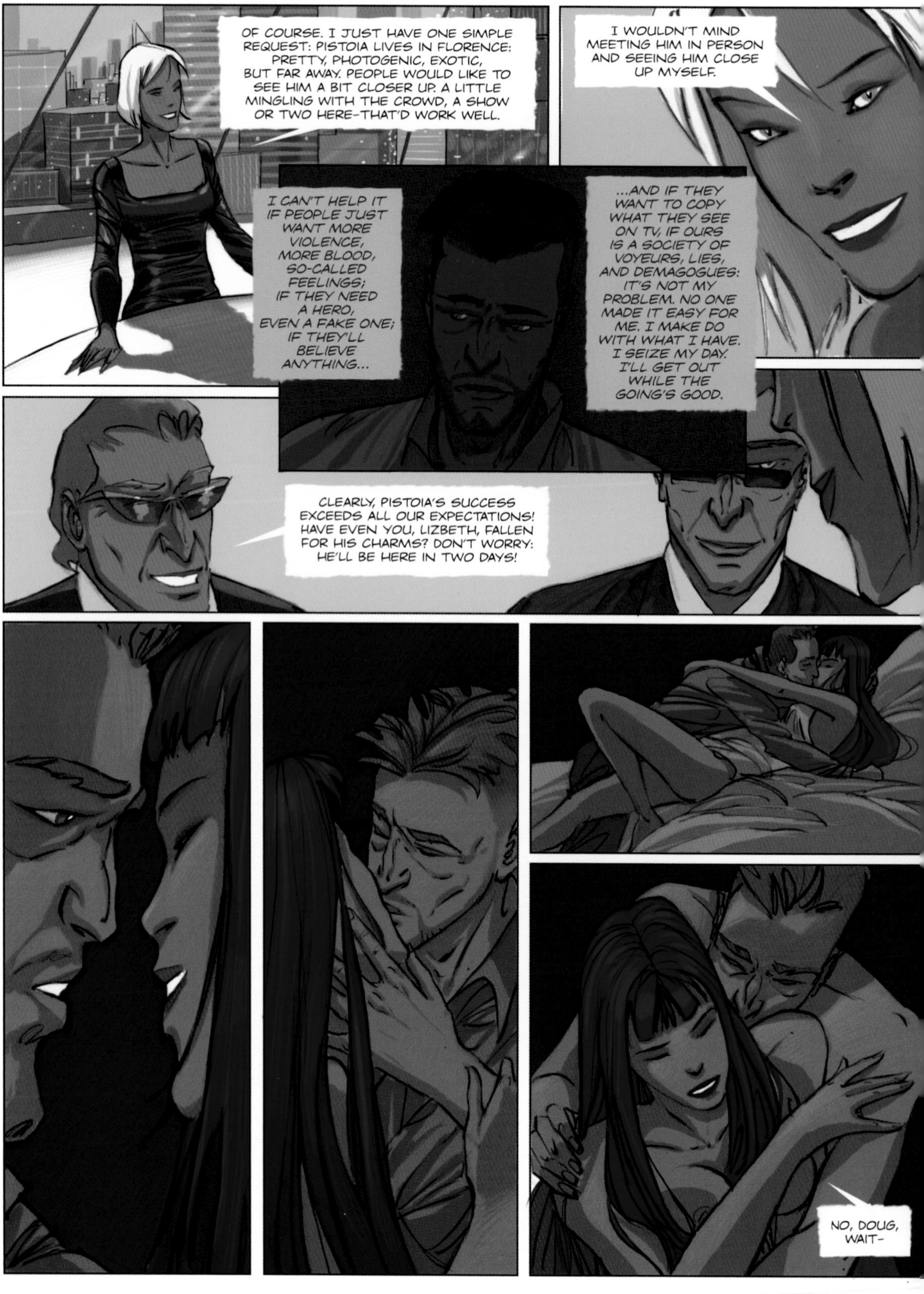
OF COURSE. I JUST HAVE ONE SIMPLE REQUEST: PISTOIA LIVES IN FLORENCE: PRETTY, PHOTOGENIC, EXOTIC, BUT FAR AWAY. PEOPLE WOULD LIKE TO SEE HIM A BIT CLOSER UP. A LITTLE MINGLING WITH THE CROWD, A SHOW OR TWO HERE-THAT'D WORK WELL.
I WOULDN'T MIND MEETING HIM IN PERSON AND SEEING HIM CLOSE UP MYSELF.
I CAN'T HELP IT IF PEOPLE JUST WANT MORE VIOLENCE, MORE BLOOD, SO-CALLED FEELINGS; IF THEY NEED A HERO, EVEN A FAKE ONE; IF THEY'LL BELIEVE ANYTHING...
...AND IF THEY WANT TO COPY WHAT THEY SEE ON TV, IF OURS IS A SOCIETY OF VOYEURS, LIES, AND DEMAGOGUES: IT'S NOT MY PROBLEM. NO ONE MADE IT EASY FOR ME. I MAKE DO WITH WHAT I HAVE. I SEIZE MY DAY. I'LL GET OUT WHILE THE GOING'S GOOD.
CLEARLY, PISTOIA'S SUCCESS EXCEEDS ALL OUR EXPECTATIONS! HAVE EVEN YOU, LIZBETH, FALLEN FOR HIS CHARMS? DON'T WORRY: HE'LL BE HERE IN TWO DAYS!
NO, DOUG, WAIT-

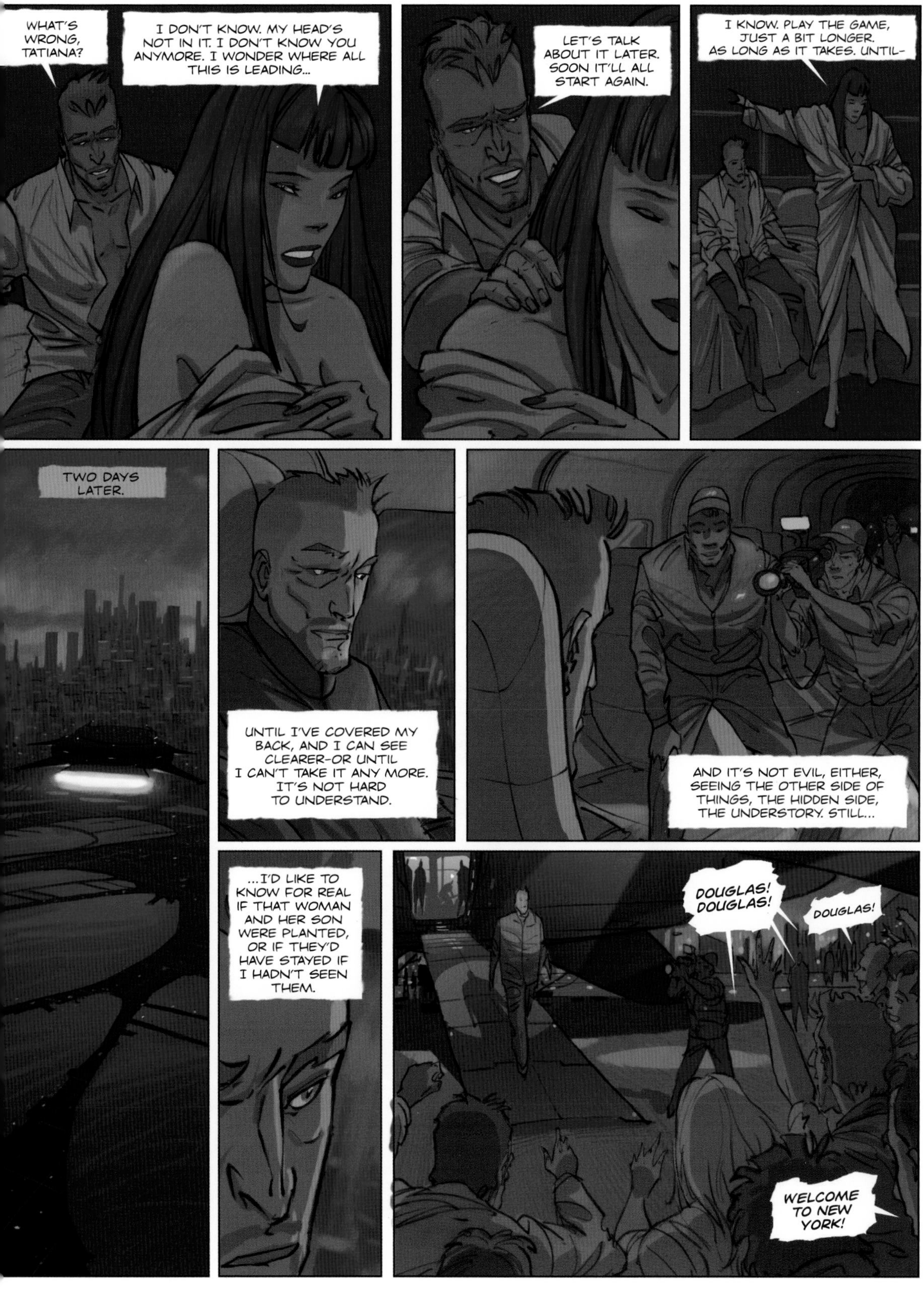
WHAT'S WRONG, TATIANA?
I DON'T KNOW. MY HEAD'S NOT IN IT. I DON'T KNOW YOU ANYMORE. I WONDER WHERE ALL THIS IS LEADING...
LET'S TALK ABOUT IT LATER. SOON IT'LL ALL START AGAIN.
I KNOW. PLAY THE GAME, JUST A BIT LONGER. AS LONG AS IT TAKES. UNTIL-
TWO DAYS LATER.
UNTIL I'VE COVERED MY BACK, AND I CAN SEE CLEARER-OR UNTIL I CAN'T TAKE IT ANY MORE. IT'S NOT HARD TO UNDERSTAND.
AND IT'S NOT EVIL, EITHER, SEEING THE OTHER SIDE OF THINGS, THE HIDDEN SIDE, THE UNDERSTORY. STILL...
...I'D LIKE TO KNOW FOR REAL IF THAT WOMAN AND HER SON WERE PLANTED, OR IF THEY'D HAVE STAYED IF I HADN'T SEEN THEM.
DOUGLAS! DOUGLAS!
DOUGLAS!
WELCOME TO NEW YORK!

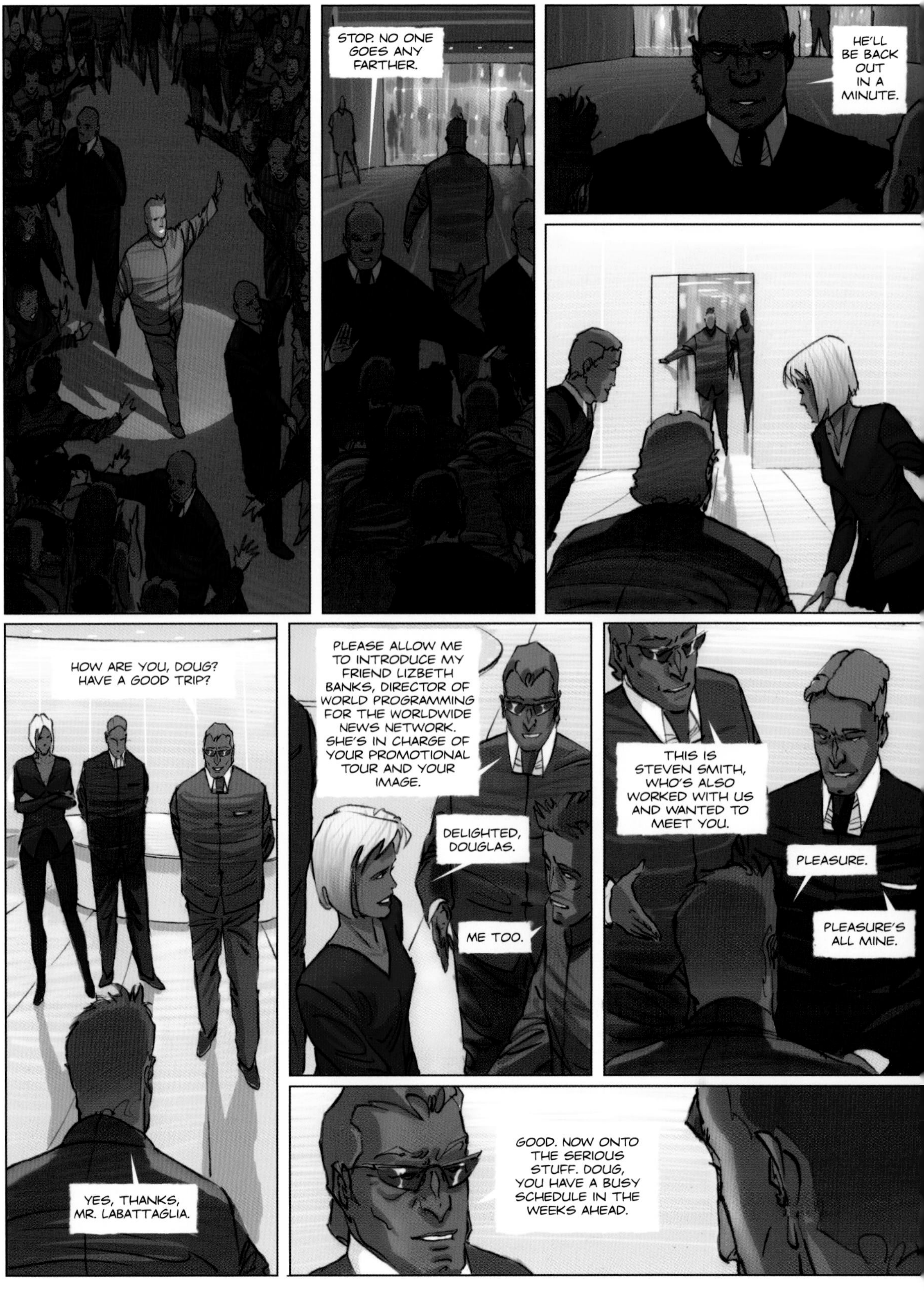
STOP. NO ONE GOES ANY FARTHER.
HE'LL BE BACK OUT IN A MINUTE.
HOW ARE YOU, DOUG? HAVE A GOOD TRIP?
YES, THANKS, MR. LABATTAGLIA.
PLEASE ALLOW ME TO INTRODUCE MY FRIEND LIZBETH BANKS, DIRECTOR OF WORLD PROGRAMMING FOR THE WORLDWIDE NEWS NETWORK. SHE'S IN CHARGE OF YOUR PROMOTIONAL TOUR AND YOUR IMAGE.
DELIGHTED, DOUGLAS.
ME TOO.
THIS IS STEVEN SMITH, WHO'S ALSO WORKED WITH US AND WANTED TO MEET YOU.
PLEASURE.
PLEASURE'S ALL MINE.
GOOD. NOW ONTO THE SERIOUS STUFF. DOUG, YOU HAVE A BUSY SCHEDULE IN THE WEEKS AHEAD.

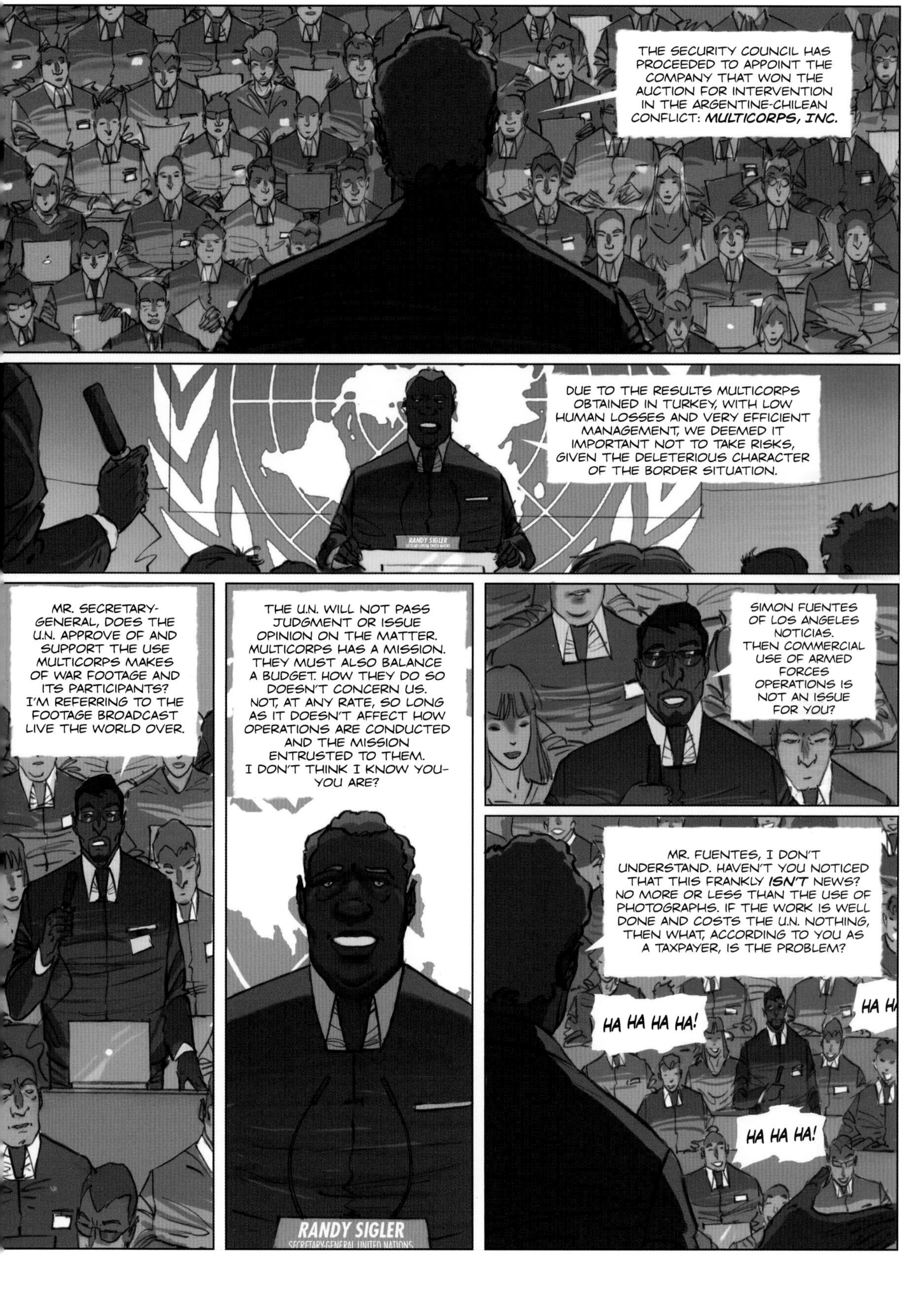
THE SECURITY COUNCIL HAS PROCEEDED TO APPOINT THE COMPANY THAT WON THE AUCTION FOR INTERVENTION IN THE ARGENTINE-CHILEAN CONFLICT: ***MULTICORPS, INC.***
DUE TO THE RESULTS MULTICORPS OBTAINED IN TURKEY, WITH LOW HUMAN LOSSES AND VERY EFFICIENT MANAGEMENT, WE DEEMED IT IMPORTANT NOT TO TAKE RISKS, GIVEN THE DELETERIOUS CHARACTER OF THE BORDER SITUATION.
RANDY SIGLER
MR. SECRETARY-GENERAL, DOES THE U.N. APPROVE OF AND SUPPORT THE USE MULTICORPS MAKES OF WAR FOOTAGE AND ITS PARTICIPANTS? I'M REFERRING TO THE FOOTAGE BROADCAST LIVE THE WORLD OVER.
THE U.N. WILL NOT PASS JUDGMENT OR ISSUE OPINION ON THE MATTER. MULTICORPS HAS A MISSION. THEY MUST ALSO BALANCE A BUDGET. HOW THEY DO SO DOESN'T CONCERN US. NOT, AT ANY RATE, SO LONG AS IT DOESN'T AFFECT HOW OPERATIONS ARE CONDUCTED AND THE MISSION ENTRUSTED TO THEM. I DON'T THINK I KNOW YOU- YOU ARE?
RANDY SIGLER
SECRETARY-GENERAL UNITED NATIONS
SIMON FUENTES OF LOS ANGELES NOTICIAS. THEN COMMERCIAL USE OF ARMED FORCES OPERATIONS IS NOT AN ISSUE FOR YOU?
MR. FUENTES, I DON'T UNDERSTAND. HAVEN'T YOU NOTICED THAT THIS FRANKLY ***ISN'T*** NEWS? NO MORE OR LESS THAN THE USE OF PHOTOGRAPHS. IF THE WORK IS WELL DONE AND COSTS THE U.N. NOTHING, THEN WHAT, ACCORDING TO YOU AS A TAXPAYER, IS THE PROBLEM?
HA HA HA HA!
HA HA
HA HA HA!

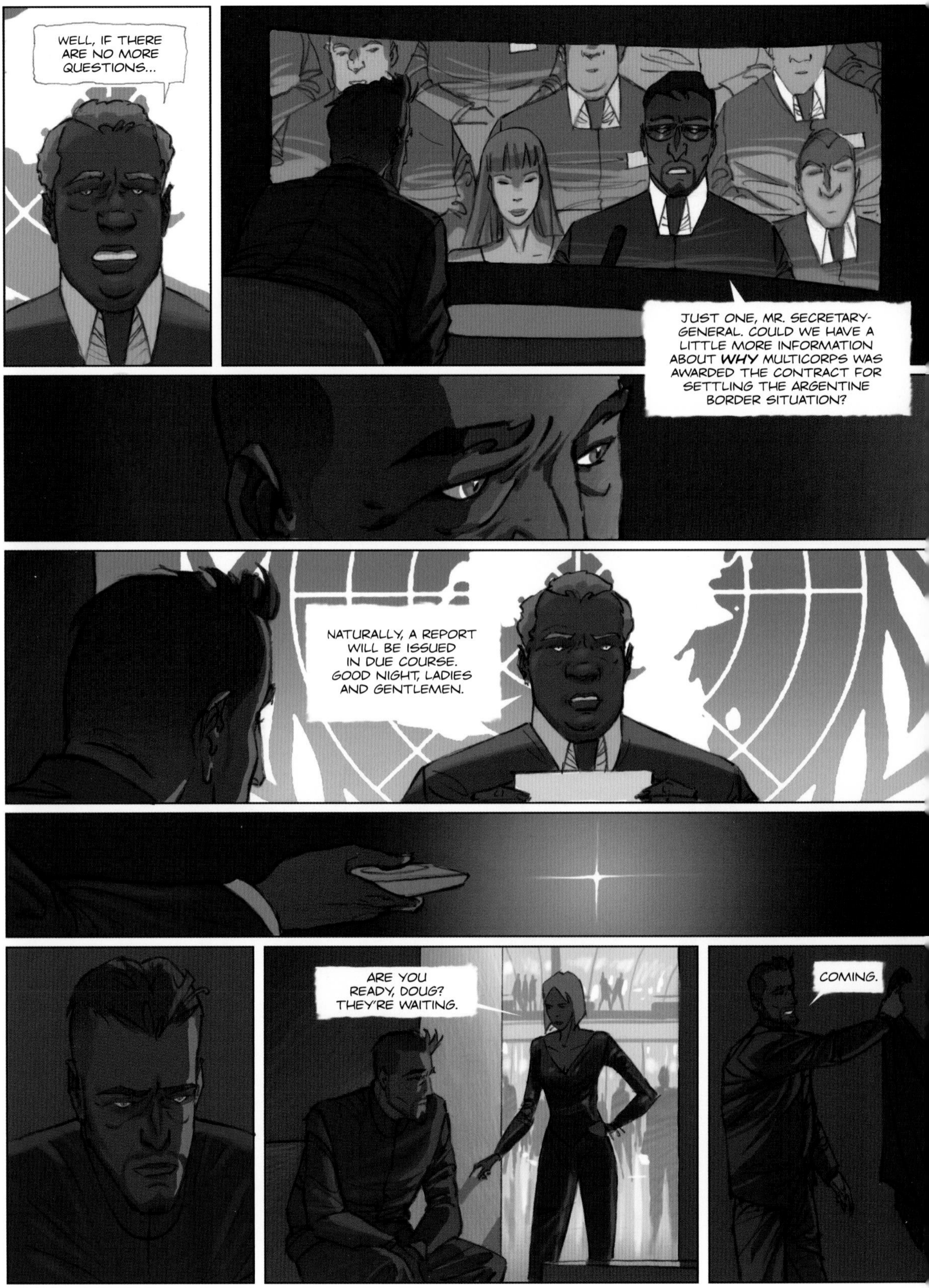
WELL, IF THERE ARE NO MORE QUESTIONS...
JUST ONE, MR. SECRETARY-GENERAL. COULD WE HAVE A LITTLE MORE INFORMATION ABOUT WHY MULTICORPS WAS AWARDED THE CONTRACT FOR SETTLING THE ARGENTINE BORDER SITUATION?
NATURALLY, A REPORT WILL BE ISSUED IN DUE COURSE. GOOD NIGHT, LADIES AND GENTLEMEN.
ARE YOU READY, DOUG? THEY'RE WAITING.
COMING.

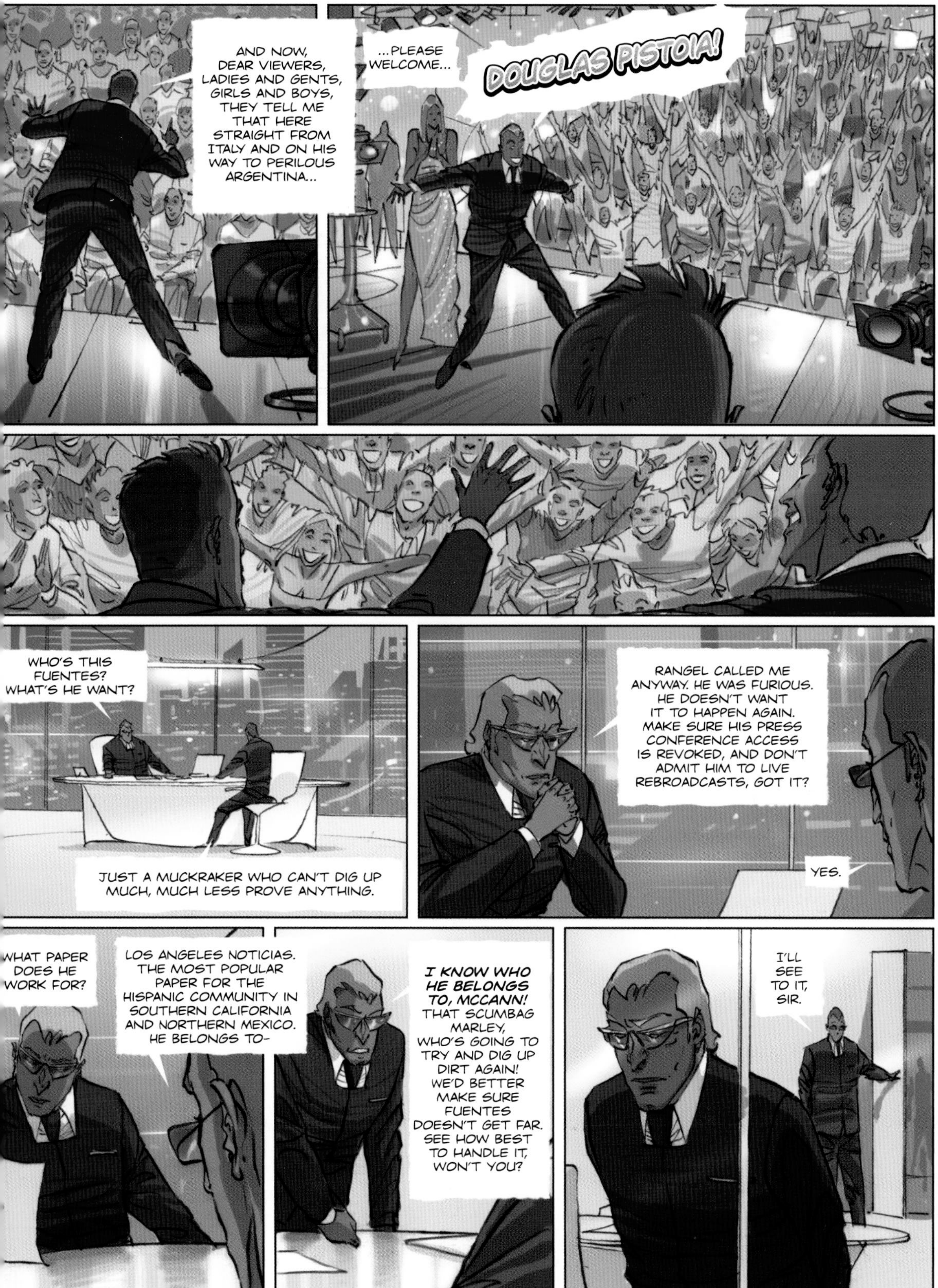
AND NOW, DEAR VIEWERS, LADIES AND GENTS, GIRLS AND BOYS, THEY TELL ME THAT HERE STRAIGHT FROM ITALY AND ON HIS WAY TO PERILOUS ARGENTINA...
...PLEASE WELCOME...
DOUGLAS PISTOIA!
WHO'S THIS FUENTES? WHAT'S HE WANT?
JUST A MUCKRAKER WHO CAN'T DIG UP MUCH, MUCH LESS PROVE ANYTHING.
RANGEL CALLED ME ANYWAY. HE WAS FURIOUS. HE DOESN'T WANT IT TO HAPPEN AGAIN. MAKE SURE HIS PRESS CONFERENCE ACCESS IS REVOKED, AND DON'T ADMIT HIM TO LIVE REBROADCASTS, GOT IT?
YES.
WHAT PAPER DOES HE WORK FOR?
LOS ANGELES NOTICIAS. THE MOST POPULAR PAPER FOR THE HISPANIC COMMUNITY IN SOUTHERN CALIFORNIA AND NORTHERN MEXICO. HE BELONGS TO-
I KNOW WHO HE BELONGS TO, MCCANN! THAT SCUMBAG MARLEY, WHO'S GOING TO TRY AND DIG UP DIRT AGAIN! WE'D BETTER MAKE SURE FUENTES DOESN'T GET FAR. SEE HOW BEST TO HANDLE IT, WON'T YOU?
I'LL SEE TO IT, SIR.

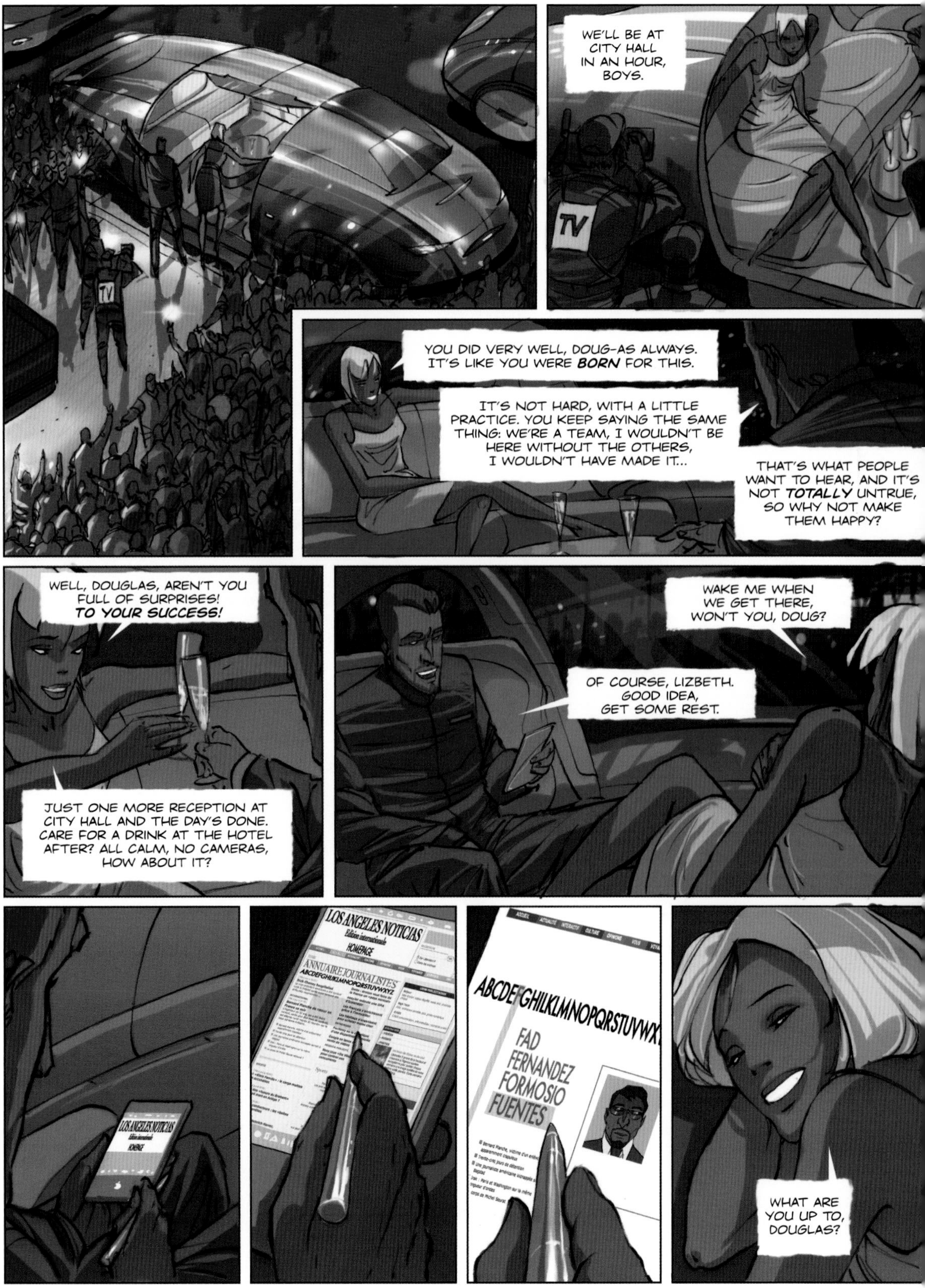
WE'LL BE AT CITY HALL IN AN HOUR, BOYS.
YOU DID VERY WELL, DOUG-AS ALWAYS. IT'S LIKE YOU WERE **BORN** FOR THIS.
IT'S NOT HARD, WITH A LITTLE PRACTICE. YOU KEEP SAYING THE SAME THING: WE'RE A TEAM, I WOULDN'T BE HERE WITHOUT THE OTHERS, I WOULDN'T HAVE MADE IT...
THAT'S WHAT PEOPLE WANT TO HEAR, AND IT'S NOT **TOTALLY** UNTRUE, SO WHY NOT MAKE THEM HAPPY?
WELL, DOUGLAS, AREN'T YOU FULL OF SURPRISES! **TO YOUR SUCCESS!**
JUST ONE MORE RECEPTION AT CITY HALL AND THE DAY'S DONE. CARE FOR A DRINK AT THE HOTEL AFTER? ALL CALM, NO CAMERAS, HOW ABOUT IT?
WAKE ME WHEN WE GET THERE, WON'T YOU, DOUG?
OF COURSE, LIZBETH. GOOD IDEA, GET SOME REST.
LOS ANGELES NOTICIAS
ANNUAIRE JOURNALISTES
ABCDEFGHILKLMNOPQRSTUVWXY
FAD
FERNANDEZ
FORMOSIO
FUENTES
WHAT ARE YOU UP TO, DOUGLAS?

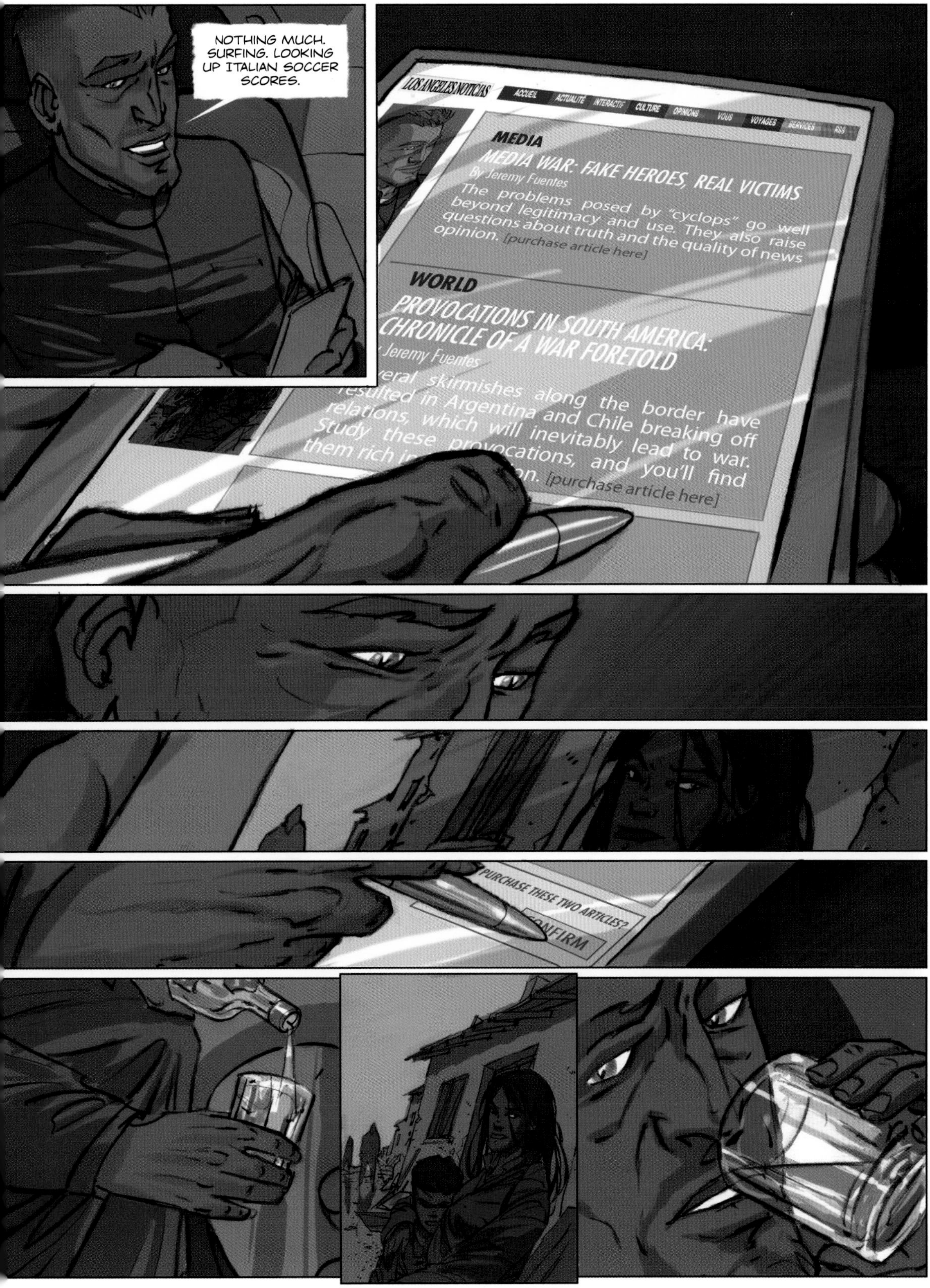
NOTHING MUCH. SURFING. LOOKING UP ITALIAN SOCCER SCORES.
LOS ANGELES NOTICIAS
ACCUEIL ACTUALITÉ INTERACTIF CULTURE OPINIONS VOUS VOYAGES SERVICES RSS
MEDIA
MEDIA WAR: FAKE HEROES, REAL VICTIMS
By Jeremy Fuentes
The problems posed by "cyclops" go well beyond legitimacy and use. They also raise questions about truth and the quality of news opinion. [purchase article here]
WORLD
PROVOCATIONS IN SOUTH AMERICA: CHRONICLE OF A WAR FORETOLD
Jeremy Fuentes
resulted in Argentina and Chile breaking off relations, which will inevitably lead to war. Study these provocations, and you'll find
[purchase article here]
PURCHASE THESE TWO ARTICLES?
CONFIRM

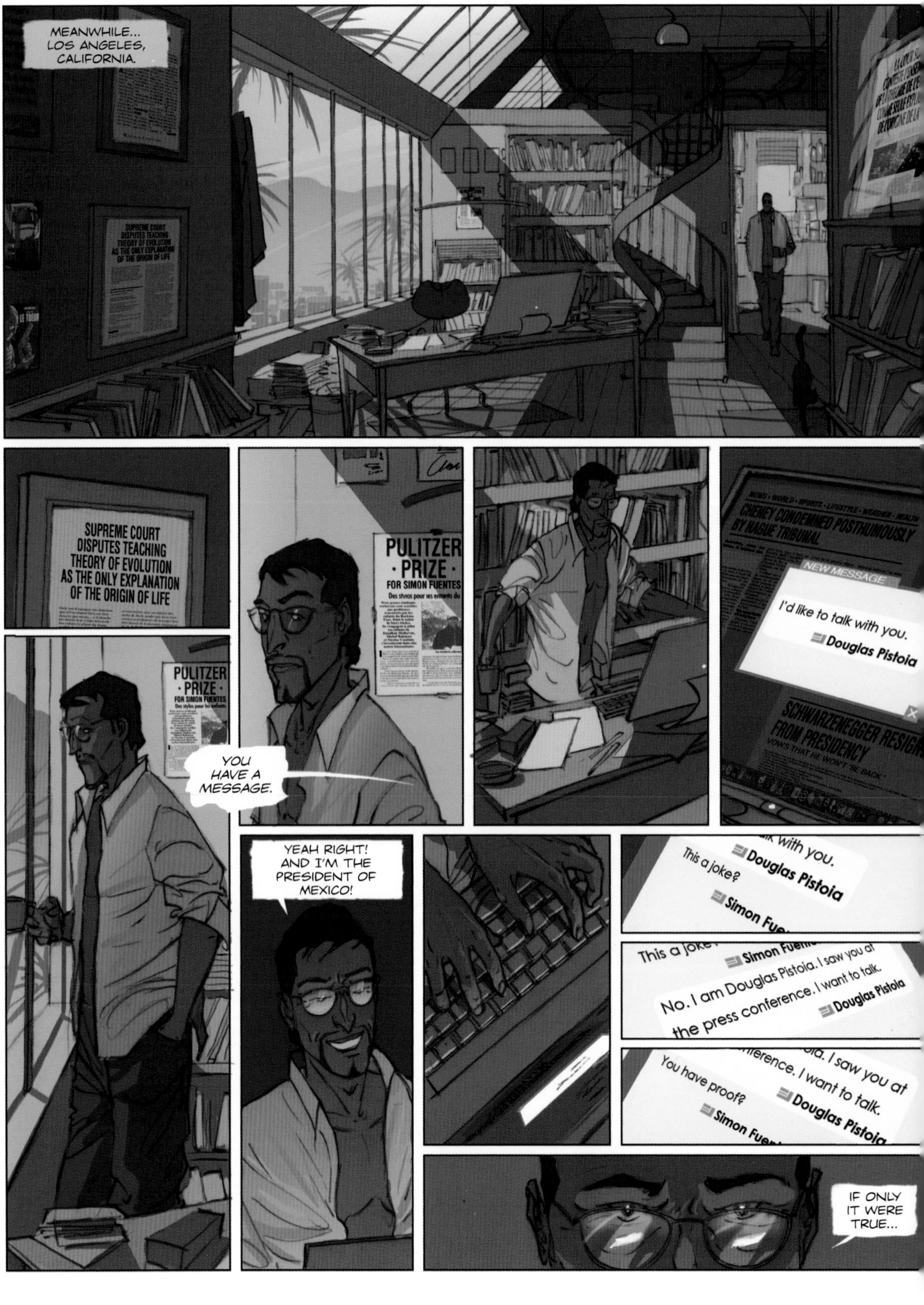
MEANWHILE... LOS ANGELES, CALIFORNIA.
SUPREME COURT DISPUTES TEACHING THEORY OF EVOLUTION AS THE ONLY EXPLANATION OF THE ORIGIN OF LIFE
SUPREME COURT DISPUTES TEACHING THEORY OF EVOLUTION AS THE ONLY EXPLANATION OF THE ORIGIN OF LIFE
PULITZER PRIZE FOR SIMON FUENTES
PULITZER PRIZE FOR SIMON FUENTES
YOU HAVE A MESSAGE.
CHENEY CONDEMNED POSTHUMOUSLY BY HAGUE TRIBUNAL
NEW MESSAGE
I'd like to talk with you.
Douglas Pistoia
SCHWARZENEGGER RESIGNS FROM PRESIDENCY
VOWS THAT HE WON'T 'BE BACK'
YEAH RIGHT! AND I'M THE PRESIDENT OF MEXICO!
Douglas Pistoia
This a joke?
Simon Fuentes
This a joke?
Simon Fuentes
No. I am Douglas Pistoia. I saw you at the press conference. I want to talk.
Douglas Pistoia
I saw you at the press conference. I want to talk.
Douglas Pistoia
You have proof?
Simon Fuentes
IF ONLY IT WERE TRUE...

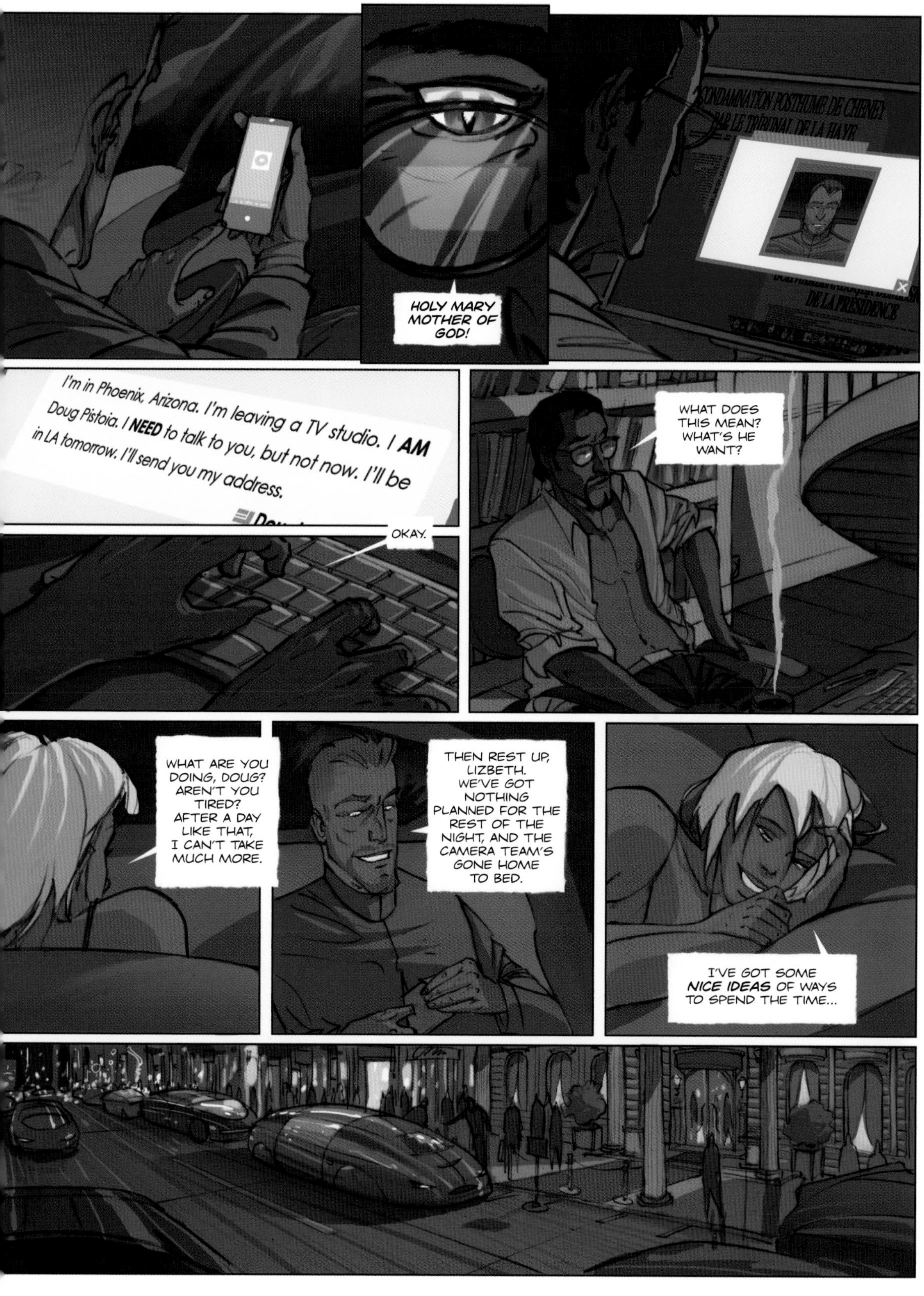
HOLY MARY MOTHER OF GOD!
CONDAMNATION POSTHUME DE CHENEY PAR LE TRIBUNAL DE LA HAYE
DE LA PRESIDENCE
I'm in Phoenix, Arizona. I'm leaving a TV studio. I **AM** Doug Pistoia. I **NEED** to talk to you, but not now. I'll be in LA tomorrow. I'll send you my address.
WHAT DOES THIS MEAN? WHAT'S HE WANT?
OKAY.
WHAT ARE YOU DOING, DOUG? AREN'T YOU TIRED? AFTER A DAY LIKE THAT, I CAN'T TAKE MUCH MORE.
THEN REST UP, LIZBETH. WE'VE GOT NOTHING PLANNED FOR THE REST OF THE NIGHT, AND THE CAMERA TEAM'S GONE HOME TO BED.
I'VE GOT SOME **NICE IDEAS** OF WAYS TO SPEND THE TIME...

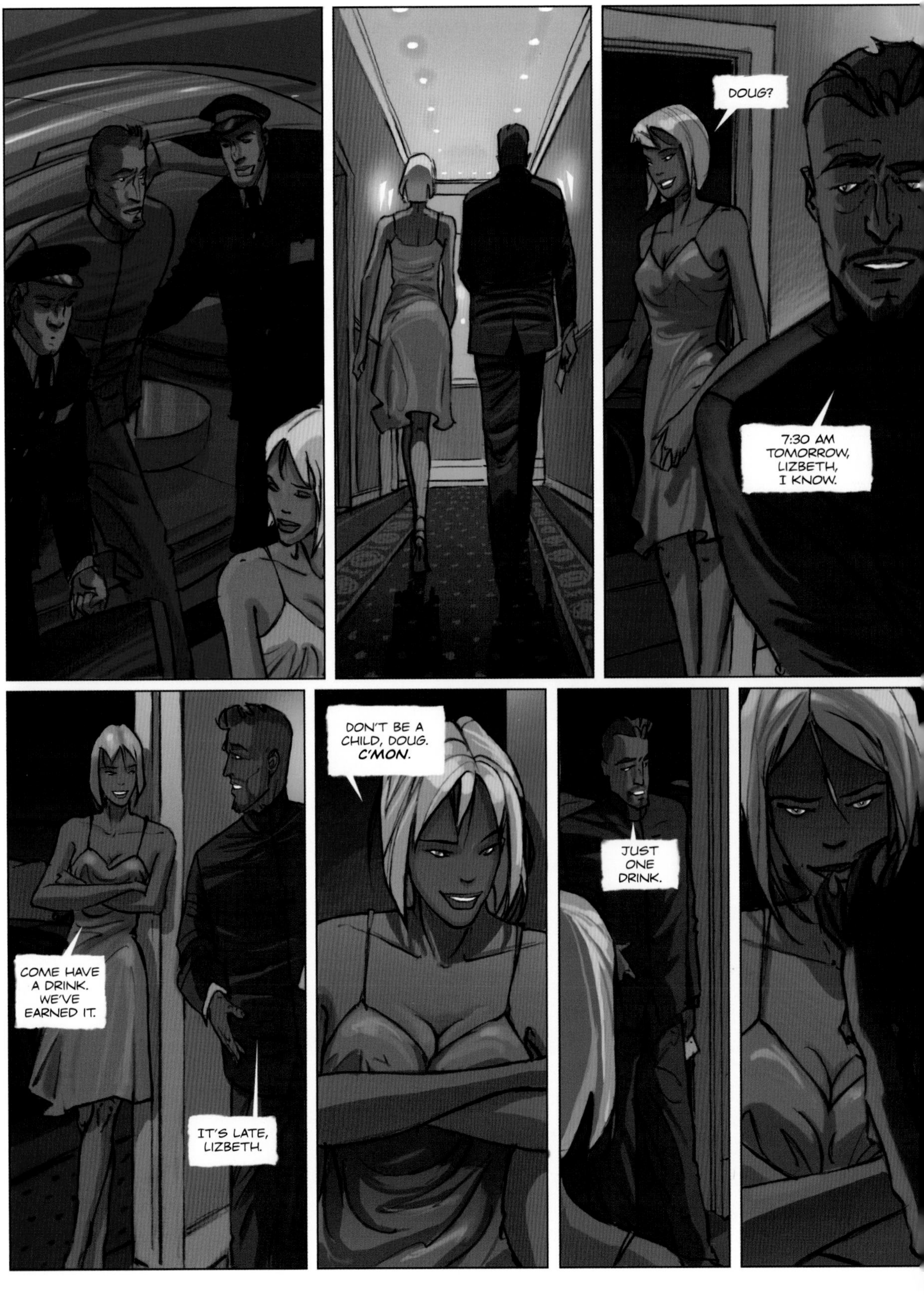
DOUG?
7:30 AM TOMORROW, LIZBETH, I KNOW.
COME HAVE A DRINK. WE'VE EARNED IT.
IT'S LATE, LIZBETH.
DON'T BE A CHILD, DOUG. C'MON.
JUST ONE DRINK.

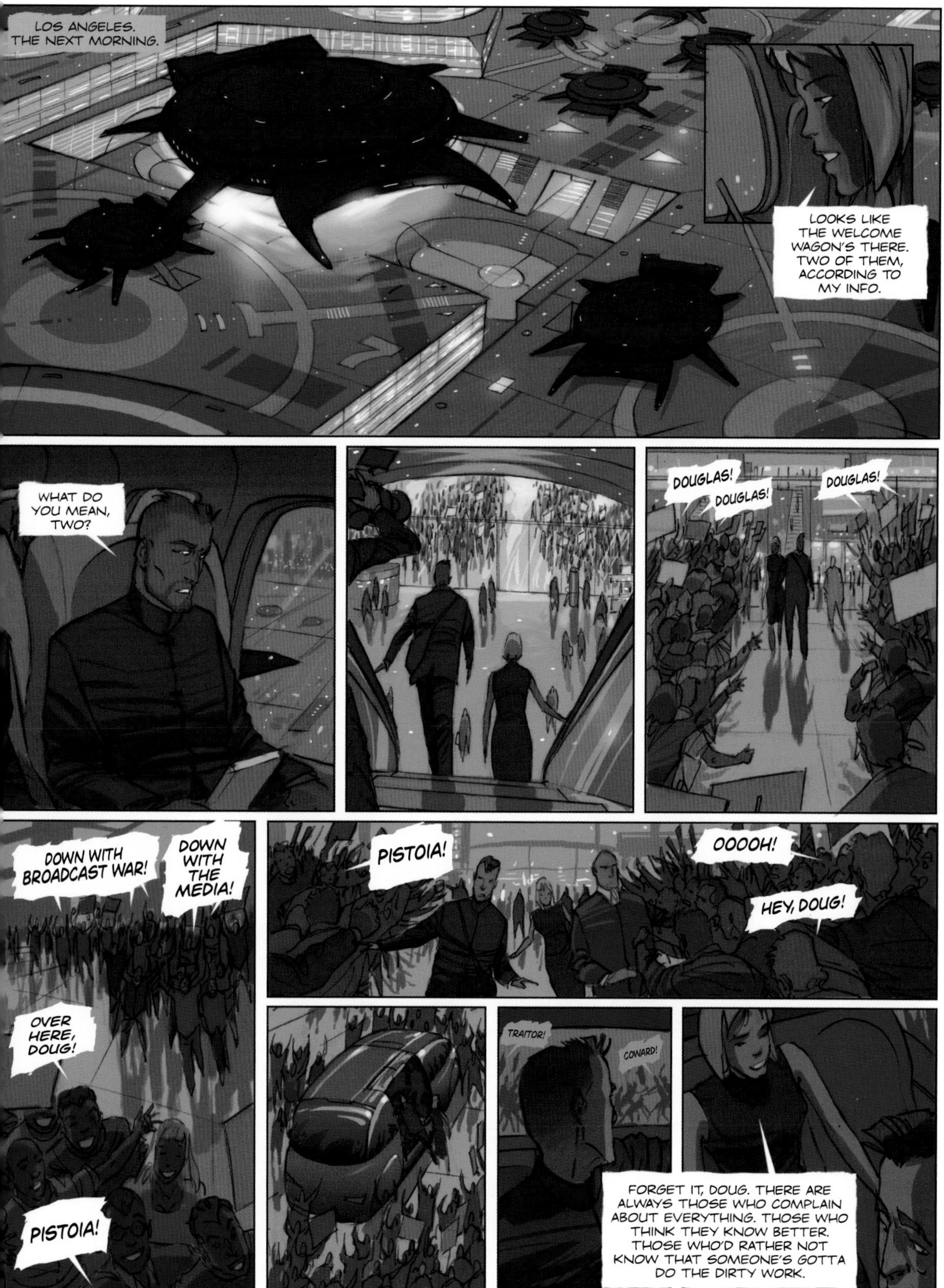
LOS ANGELES.
THE NEXT MORNING.
LOOKS LIKE THE WELCOME WAGON'S THERE. TWO OF THEM, ACCORDING TO MY INFO.
WHAT DO YOU MEAN, TWO?
DOUGLAS!
DOUGLAS!
DOUGLAS!
DOWN WITH BROADCAST WAR!
DOWN WITH THE MEDIA!
OVER HERE, DOUG!
PISTOIA!
PISTOIA!
OOOOH!
HEY, DOUG!
TRAITOR!
COWARD!
FORGET IT, DOUG. THERE ARE ALWAYS THOSE WHO COMPLAIN ABOUT EVERYTHING. THOSE WHO THINK THEY KNOW BETTER. THOSE WHO'D RATHER NOT KNOW THAT SOMEONE'S GOTTA DO THE DIRTY WORK.

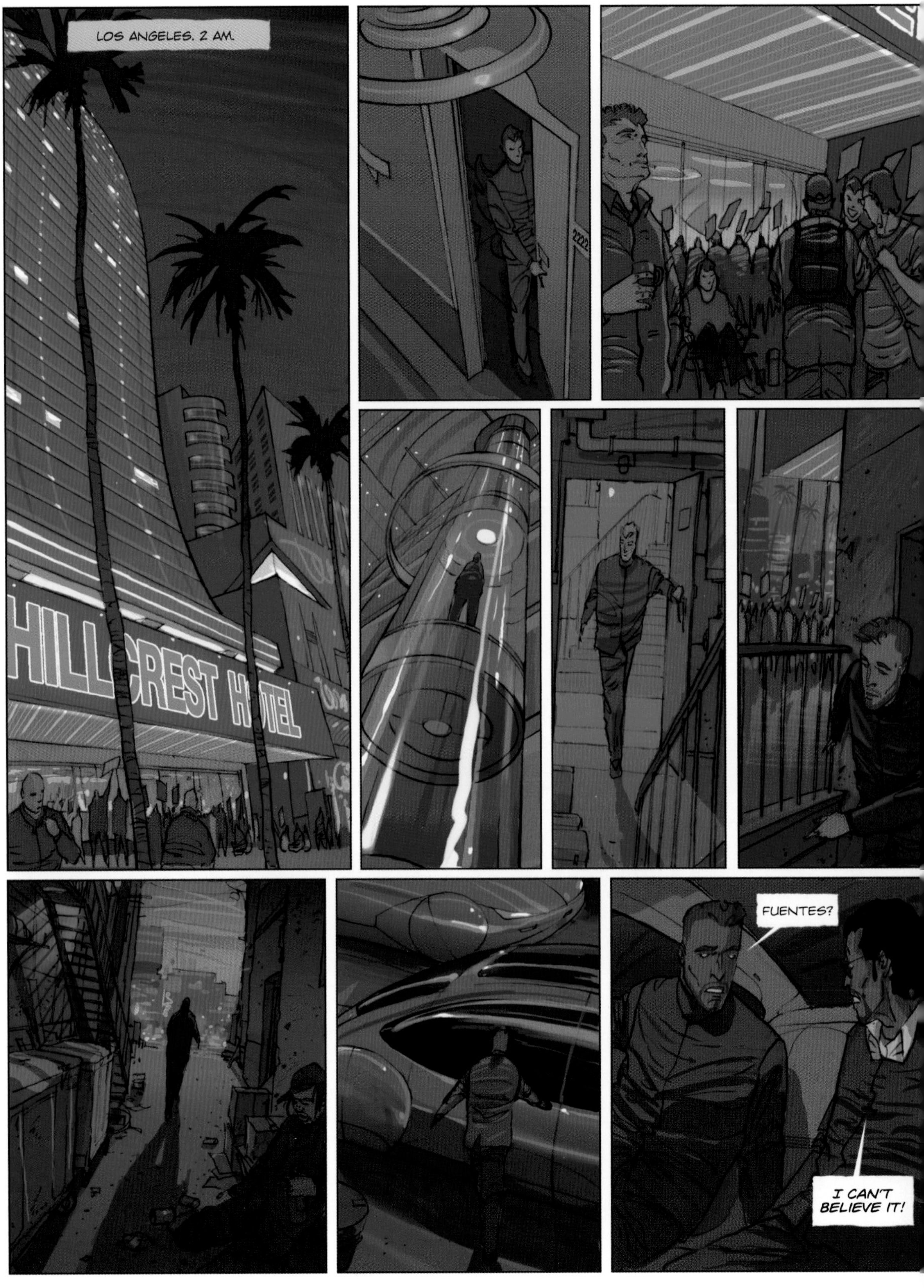
LOS ANGELES. 2 AM.
HILLCREST HOTEL
2222
FUENTES?
I CAN'T BELIEVE IT!

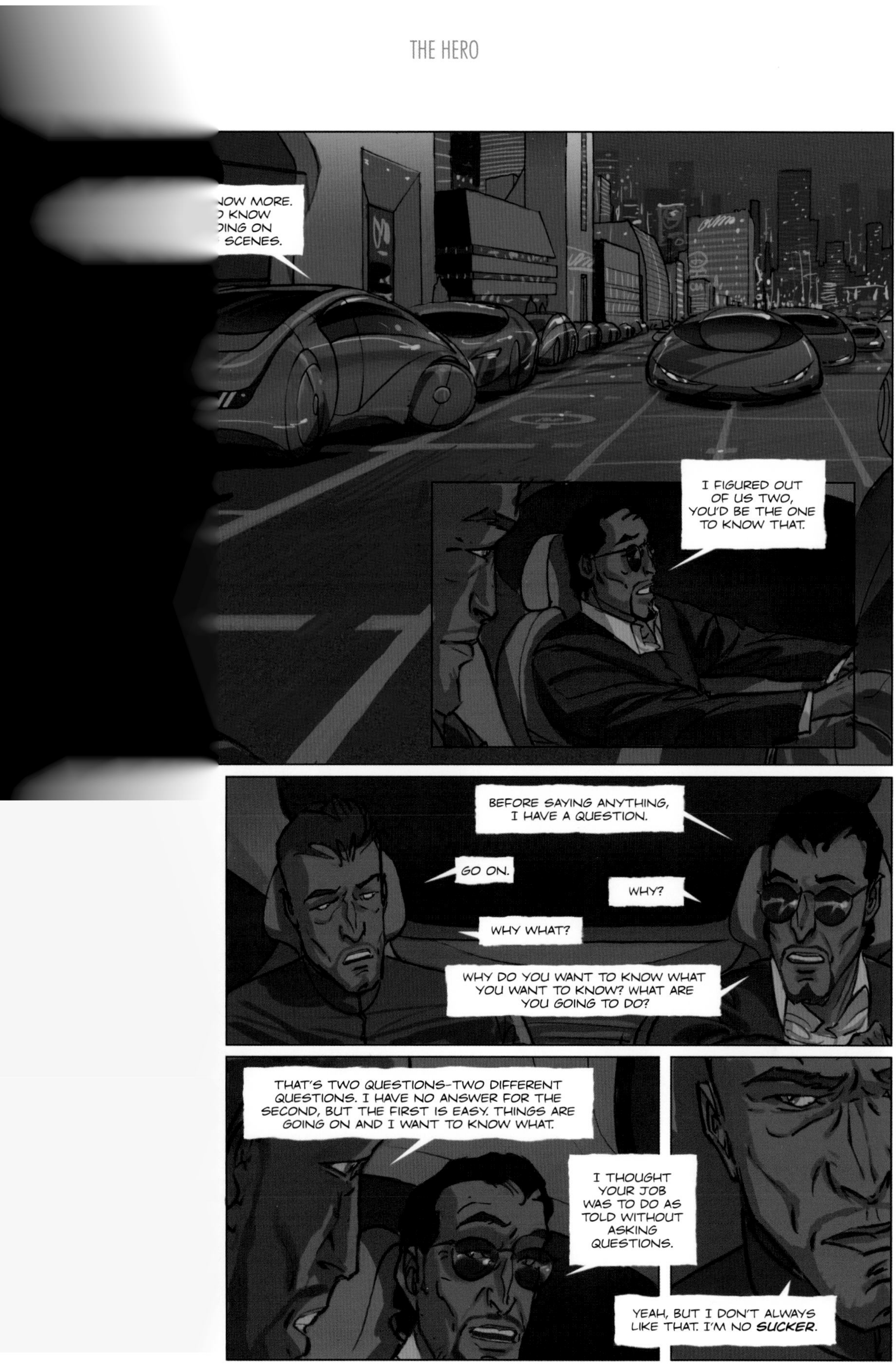
NOW MORE.
KNOW
SCENES.
I FIGURED OUT OF US TWO, YOU'D BE THE ONE TO KNOW THAT.
BEFORE SAYING ANYTHING, I HAVE A QUESTION.
GO ON.
WHY?
WHY WHAT?
WHY DO YOU WANT TO KNOW WHAT YOU WANT TO KNOW? WHAT ARE YOU GOING TO DO?
THAT'S TWO QUESTIONS–TWO DIFFERENT QUESTIONS. I HAVE NO ANSWER FOR THE SECOND, BUT THE FIRST IS EASY. THINGS ARE GOING ON AND I WANT TO KNOW WHAT.
I THOUGHT YOUR JOB WAS TO DO AS TOLD WITHOUT ASKING QUESTIONS.
YEAH, BUT I DON'T ALWAYS LIKE THAT. I'M NO **SUCKER**.

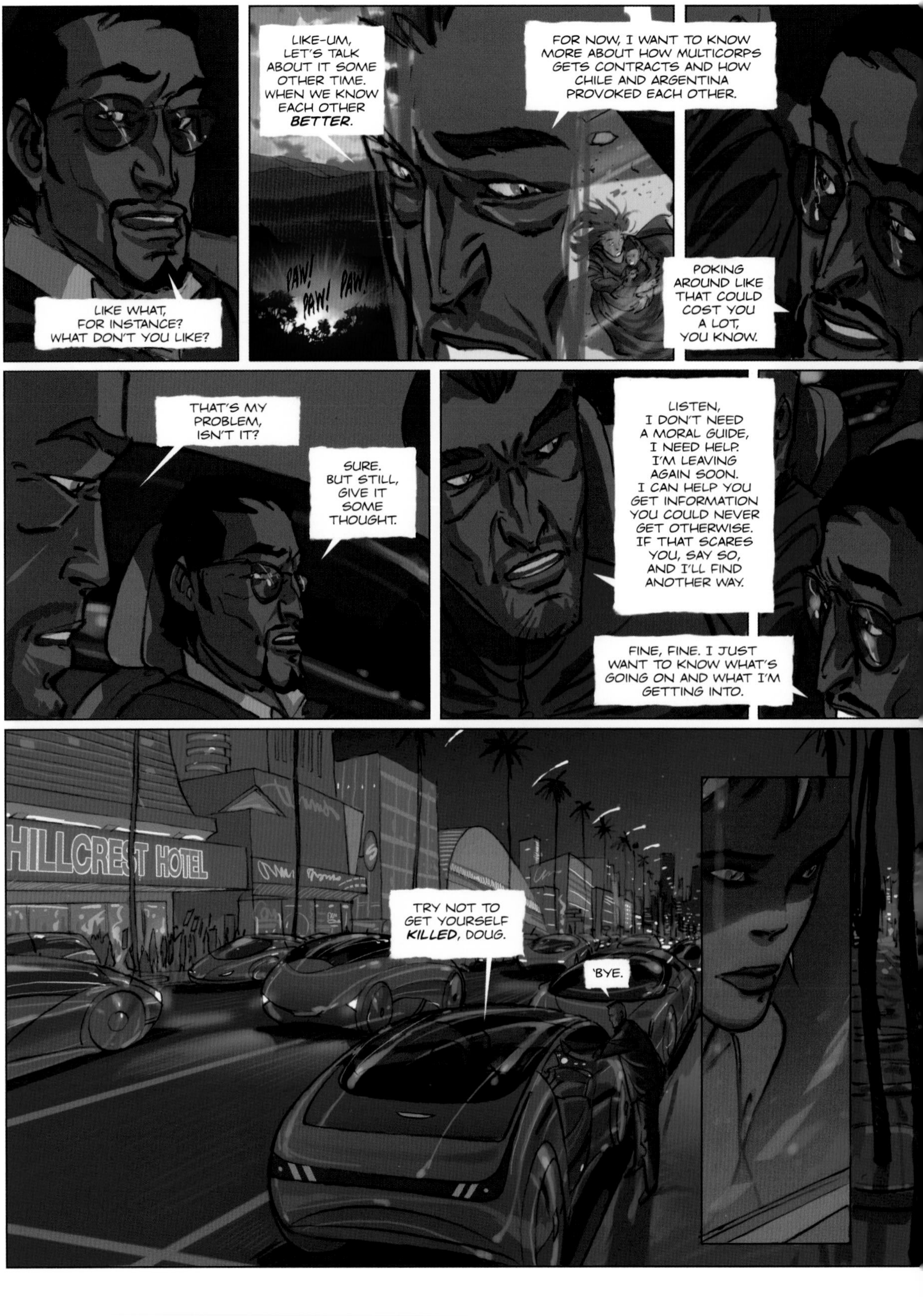
LIKE WHAT, FOR INSTANCE? WHAT DON'T YOU LIKE?
LIKE-UM, LET'S TALK ABOUT IT SOME OTHER TIME. WHEN WE KNOW EACH OTHER **BETTER**.
PAW! PAW! PAW!
FOR NOW, I WANT TO KNOW MORE ABOUT HOW MULTICORPS GETS CONTRACTS AND HOW CHILE AND ARGENTINA PROVOKED EACH OTHER.
POKING AROUND LIKE THAT COULD COST YOU A LOT, YOU KNOW.
THAT'S MY PROBLEM, ISN'T IT?
SURE. BUT STILL, GIVE IT SOME THOUGHT.
LISTEN, I DON'T NEED A MORAL GUIDE, I NEED HELP. I'M LEAVING AGAIN SOON. I CAN HELP YOU GET INFORMATION YOU COULD NEVER GET OTHERWISE. IF THAT SCARES YOU, SAY SO, AND I'LL FIND ANOTHER WAY.
FINE, FINE. I JUST WANT TO KNOW WHAT'S GOING ON AND WHAT I'M GETTING INTO.
HILLCREST HOTEL
TRY NOT TO GET YOURSELF **KILLED**, DOUG.
'BYE.

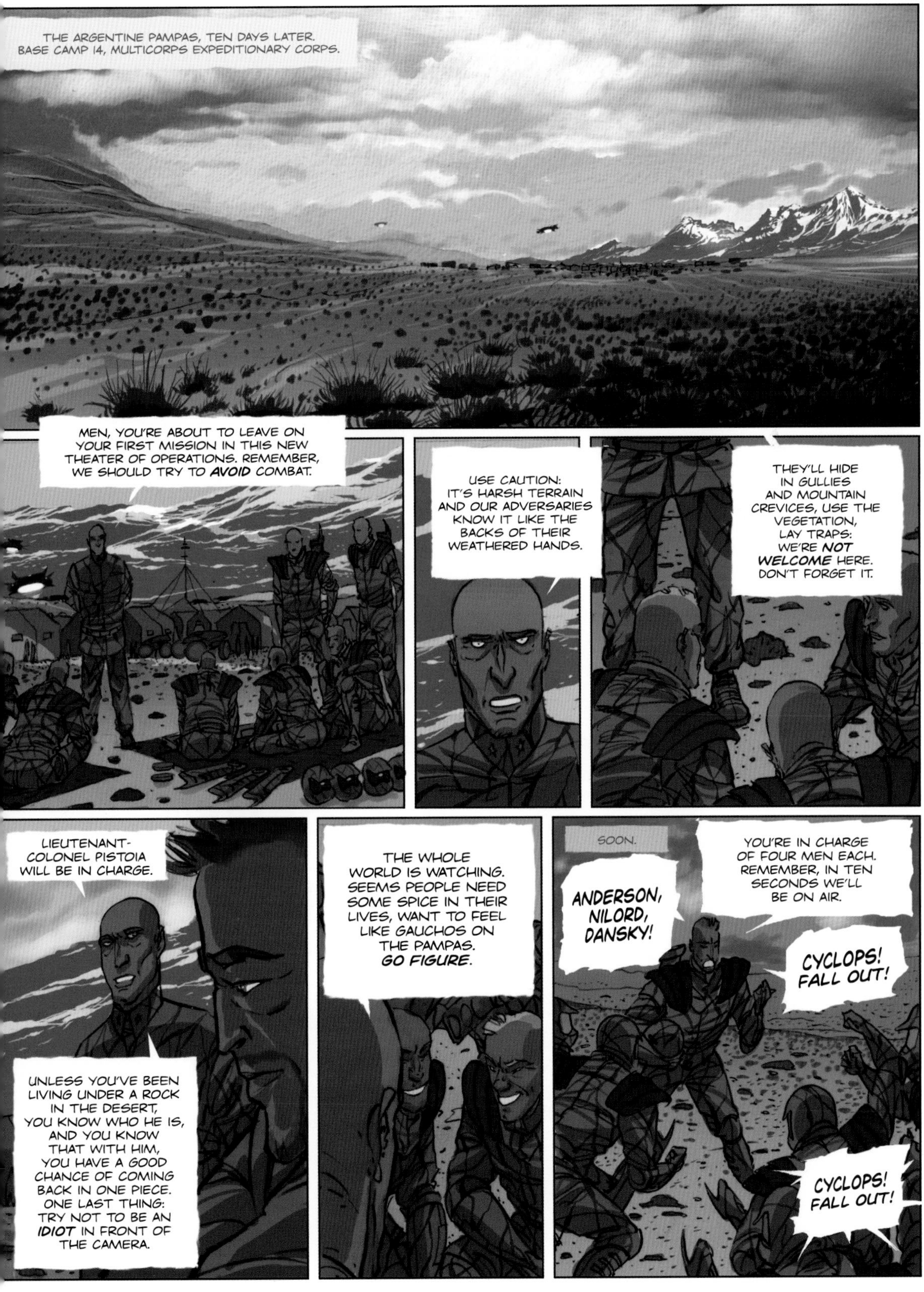
THE ARGENTINE PAMPAS, TEN DAYS LATER.
BASE CAMP 14, MULTICORPS EXPEDITIONARY CORPS.
MEN, YOU'RE ABOUT TO LEAVE ON YOUR FIRST MISSION IN THIS NEW THEATER OF OPERATIONS. REMEMBER, WE SHOULD TRY TO AVOID COMBAT.
USE CAUTION: IT'S HARSH TERRAIN AND OUR ADVERSARIES KNOW IT LIKE THE BACKS OF THEIR WEATHERED HANDS.
THEY'LL HIDE IN GULLIES AND MOUNTAIN CREVICES, USE THE VEGETATION, LAY TRAPS: WE'RE NOT WELCOME HERE. DON'T FORGET IT.
LIEUTENANT-COLONEL PISTOIA WILL BE IN CHARGE.
UNLESS YOU'VE BEEN LIVING UNDER A ROCK IN THE DESERT, YOU KNOW WHO HE IS, AND YOU KNOW THAT WITH HIM, YOU HAVE A GOOD CHANCE OF COMING BACK IN ONE PIECE. ONE LAST THING: TRY NOT TO BE AN IDIOT IN FRONT OF THE CAMERA.
THE WHOLE WORLD IS WATCHING. SEEMS PEOPLE NEED SOME SPICE IN THEIR LIVES, WANT TO FEEL LIKE GAUCHOS ON THE PAMPAS. GO FIGURE.
SOON.
YOU'RE IN CHARGE OF FOUR MEN EACH. REMEMBER, IN TEN SECONDS WE'LL BE ON AIR.
ANDERSON, NILORD, DANSKY!
CYCLOPS! FALL OUT!
CYCLOPS! FALL OUT!

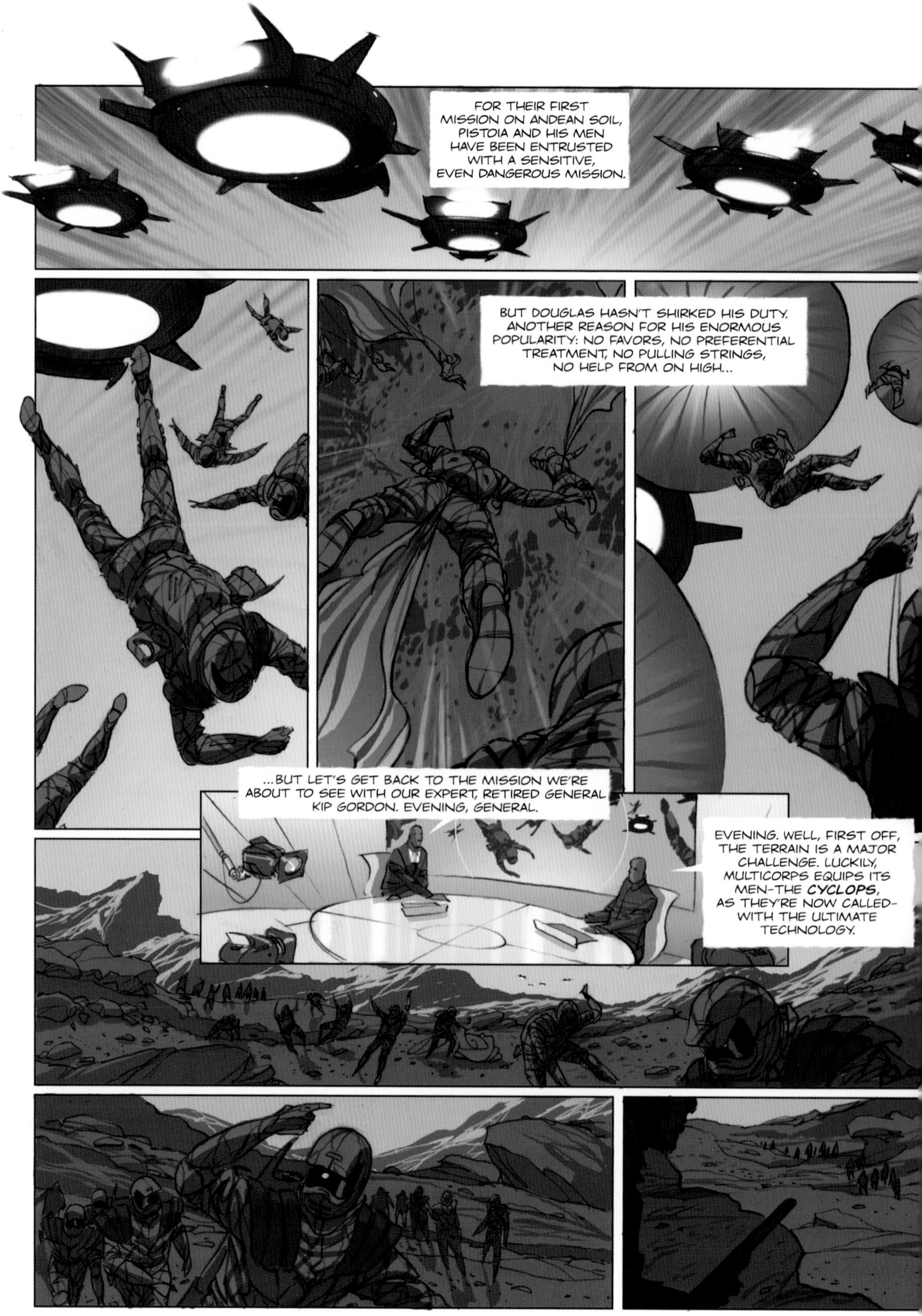
FOR THEIR FIRST MISSION ON ANDEAN SOIL, PISTOIA AND HIS MEN HAVE BEEN ENTRUSTED WITH A SENSITIVE, EVEN DANGEROUS MISSION.
BUT DOUGLAS HASN'T SHIRKED HIS DUTY. ANOTHER REASON FOR HIS ENORMOUS POPULARITY: NO FAVORS, NO PREFERENTIAL TREATMENT, NO PULLING STRINGS, NO HELP FROM ON HIGH...
...BUT LET'S GET BACK TO THE MISSION WE'RE ABOUT TO SEE WITH OUR EXPERT, RETIRED GENERAL KIP GORDON. EVENING, GENERAL.
EVENING. WELL, FIRST OFF, THE TERRAIN IS A MAJOR CHALLENGE. LUCKILY, MULTICORPS EQUIPS ITS MEN–THE ***CYCLOPS***, AS THEY'RE NOW CALLED–WITH THE ULTIMATE TECHNOLOGY.

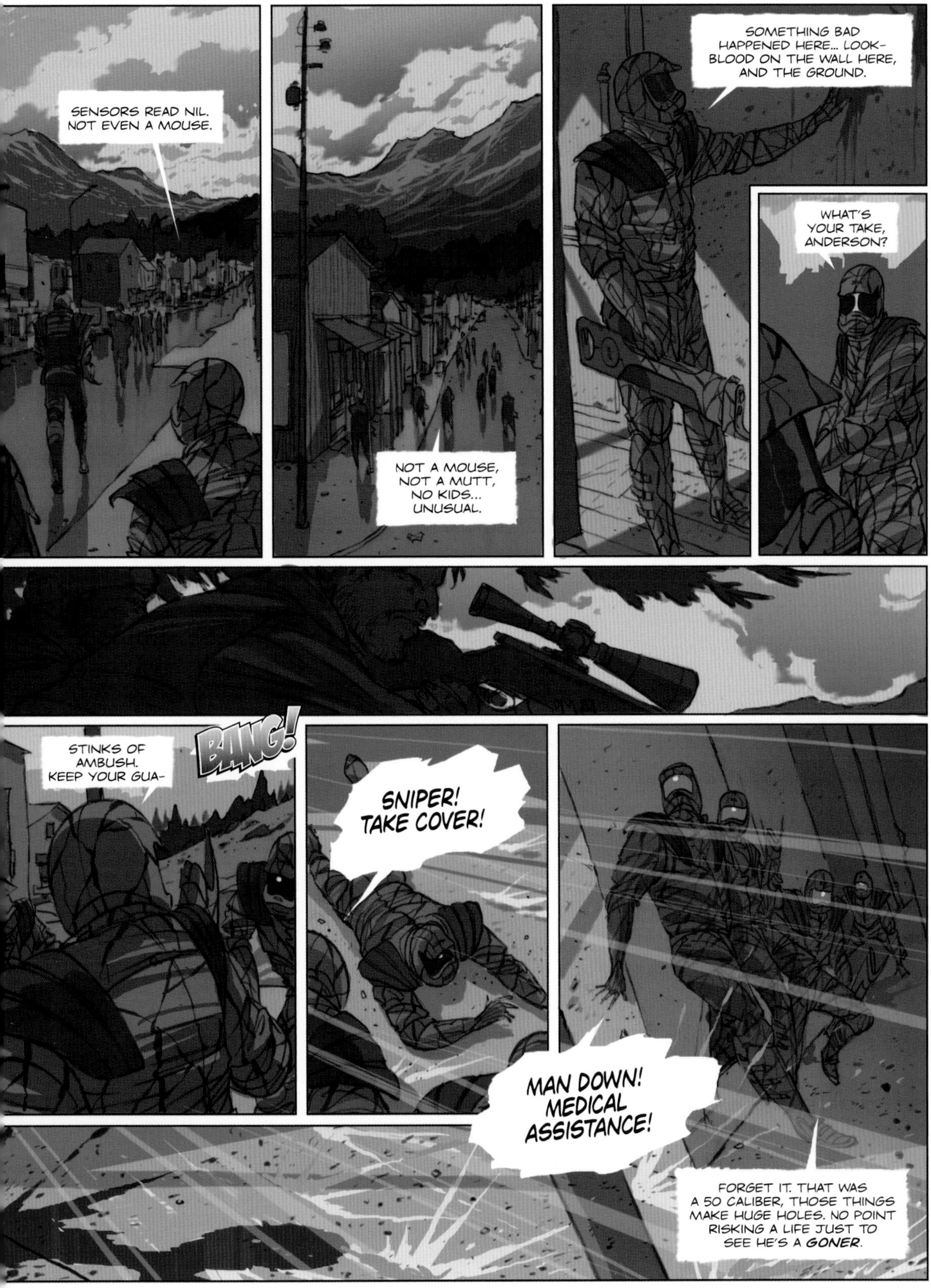
SENSORS READ NIL. NOT EVEN A MOUSE.
NOT A MOUSE, NOT A MUTT, NO KIDS... UNUSUAL.
SOMETHING BAD HAPPENED HERE... LOOK-BLOOD ON THE WALL HERE, AND THE GROUND.
WHAT'S YOUR TAKE, ANDERSON?
STINKS OF AMBUSH. KEEP YOUR GUA-
BANG!
SNIPER! TAKE COVER!
MAN DOWN! MEDICAL ASSISTANCE!
FORGET IT. THAT WAS A 50 CALIBER, THOSE THINGS MAKE HUGE HOLES. NO POINT RISKING A LIFE JUST TO SEE HE'S A ***GONER***.

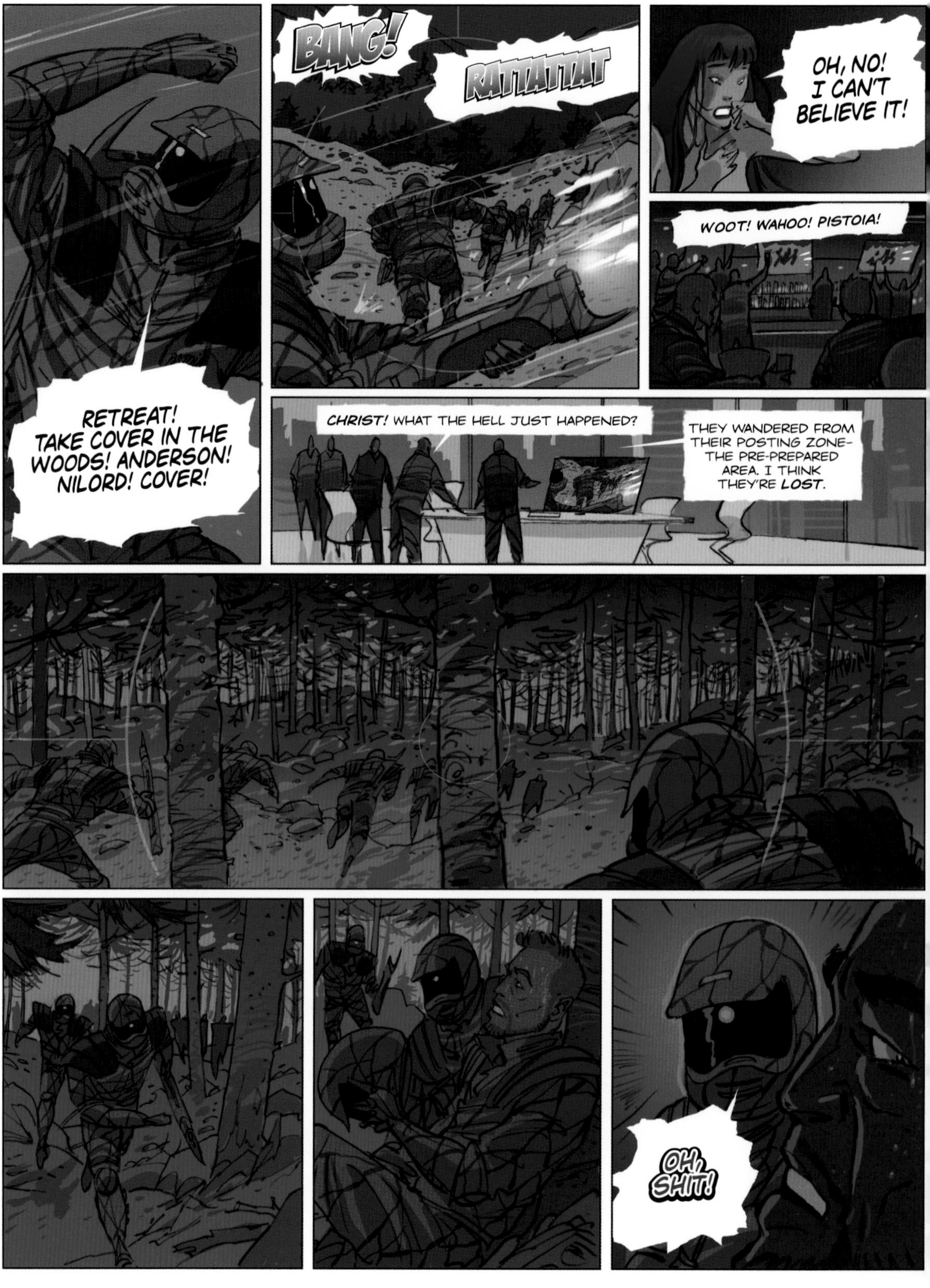
BANG!
RATTATTAT
OH, NO! I CAN'T BELIEVE IT!
WOOT! WAHOO! PISTOIA!
RETREAT! TAKE COVER IN THE WOODS! ANDERSON! NILORD! COVER!
CHRIST! WHAT THE HELL JUST HAPPENED?
THEY WANDERED FROM THEIR POSTING ZONE- THE PRE-PREPARED AREA. I THINK THEY'RE LOST.
OH, SHIT!

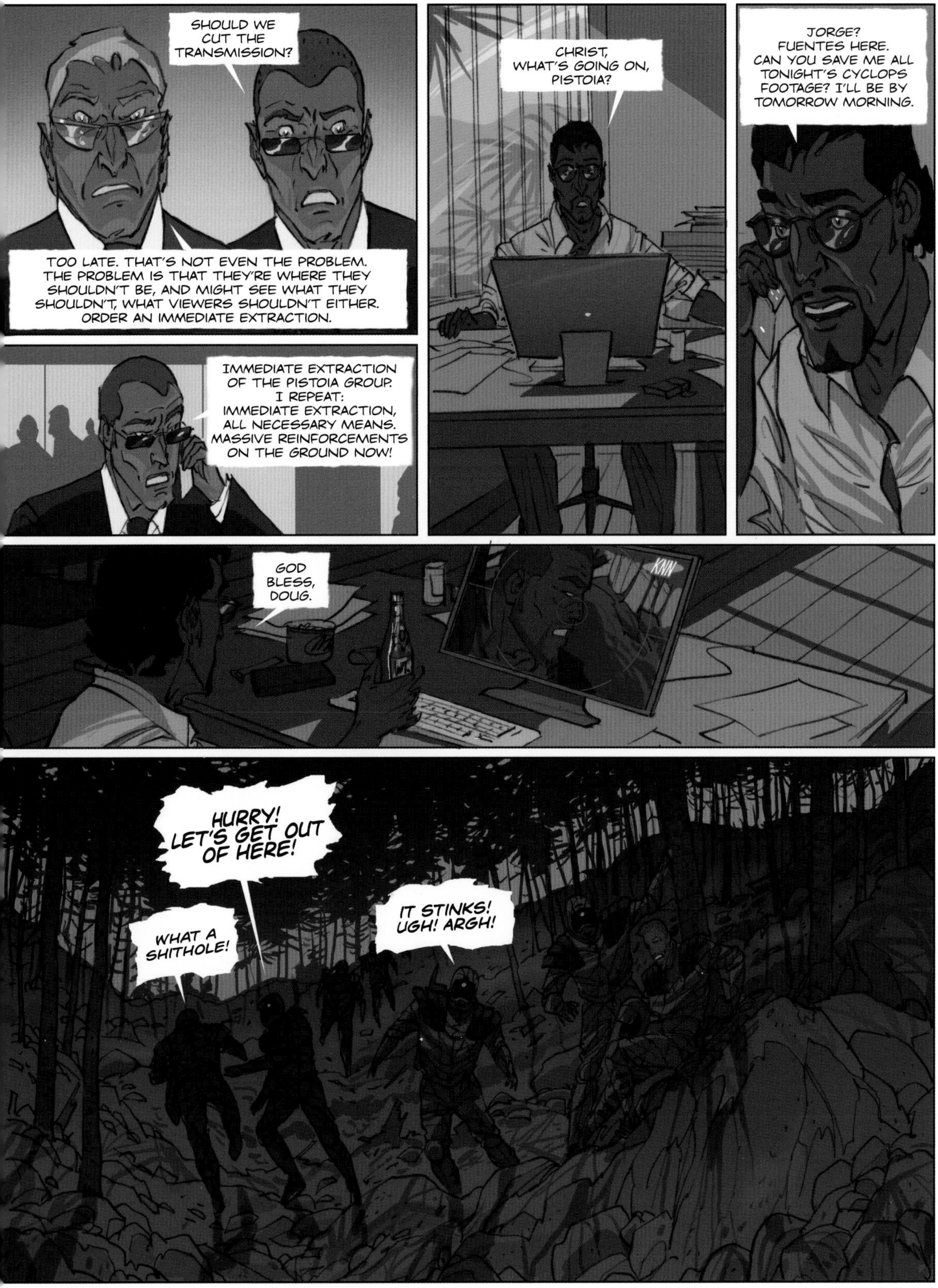
SHOULD WE CUT THE TRANSMISSION?
TOO LATE. THAT'S NOT EVEN THE PROBLEM. THE PROBLEM IS THAT THEY'RE WHERE THEY SHOULDN'T BE, AND MIGHT SEE WHAT THEY SHOULDN'T, WHAT VIEWERS SHOULDN'T EITHER. ORDER AN IMMEDIATE EXTRACTION.
IMMEDIATE EXTRACTION OF THE PISTOIA GROUP. I REPEAT: IMMEDIATE EXTRACTION, ALL NECESSARY MEANS. MASSIVE REINFORCEMENTS ON THE GROUND NOW!
CHRIST, WHAT'S GOING ON, PISTOIA?
JORGE? FUENTES HERE. CAN YOU SAVE ME ALL TONIGHT'S CYCLOPS FOOTAGE? I'LL BE BY TOMORROW MORNING.
GOD BLESS, DOUG.
KNN
HURRY! LET'S GET OUT OF HERE!
WHAT A SHITHOLE!
IT STINKS! UGH! ARGH!

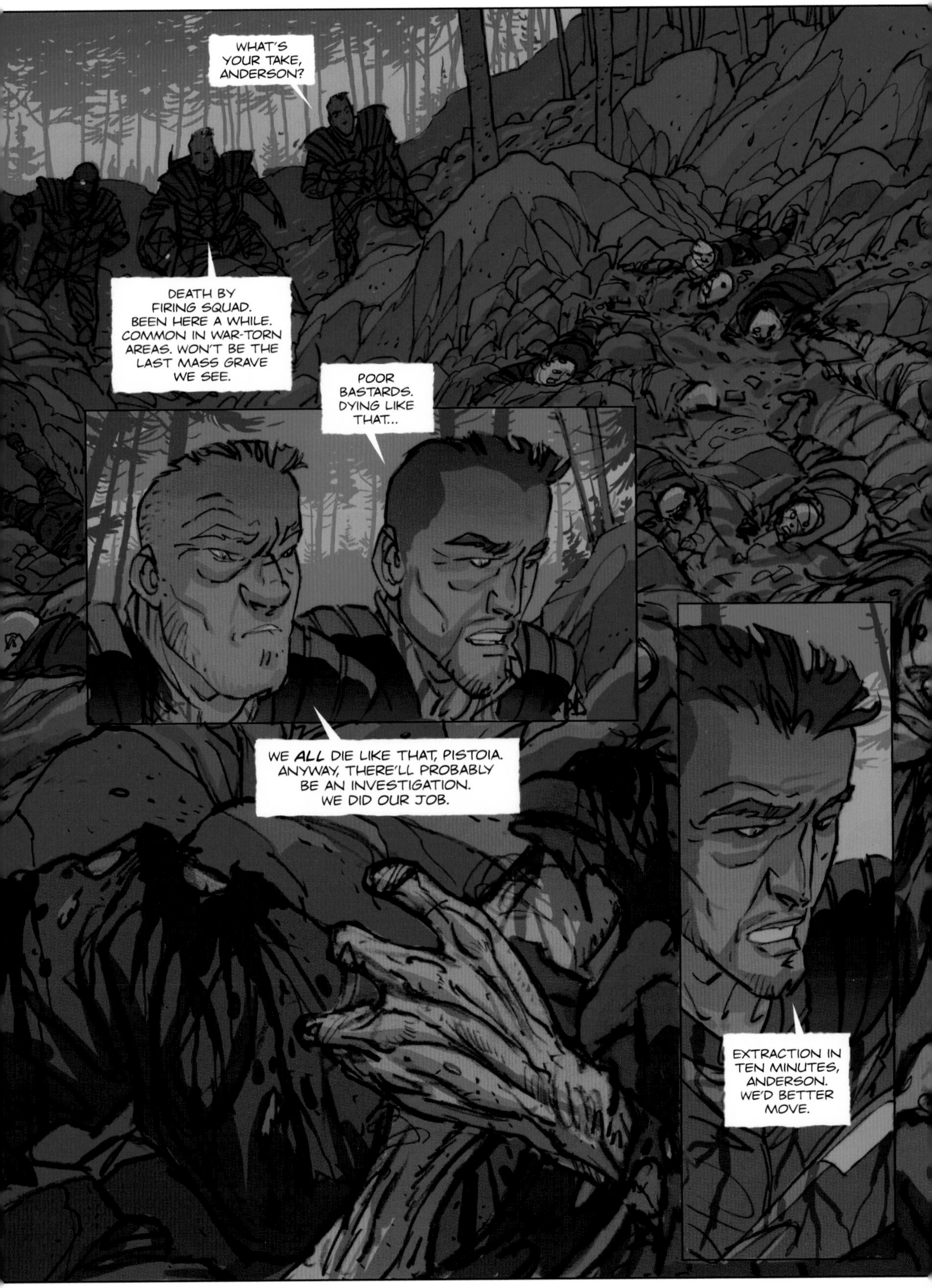
WHAT'S YOUR TAKE, ANDERSON?
DEATH BY FIRING SQUAD. BEEN HERE A WHILE. COMMON IN WAR-TORN AREAS. WON'T BE THE LAST MASS GRAVE WE SEE.
POOR BASTARDS. DYING LIKE THAT...
WE ALL DIE LIKE THAT, PISTOIA. ANYWAY, THERE'LL PROBABLY BE AN INVESTIGATION. WE DID OUR JOB.
EXTRACTION IN TEN MINUTES, ANDERSON. WE'D BETTER MOVE.

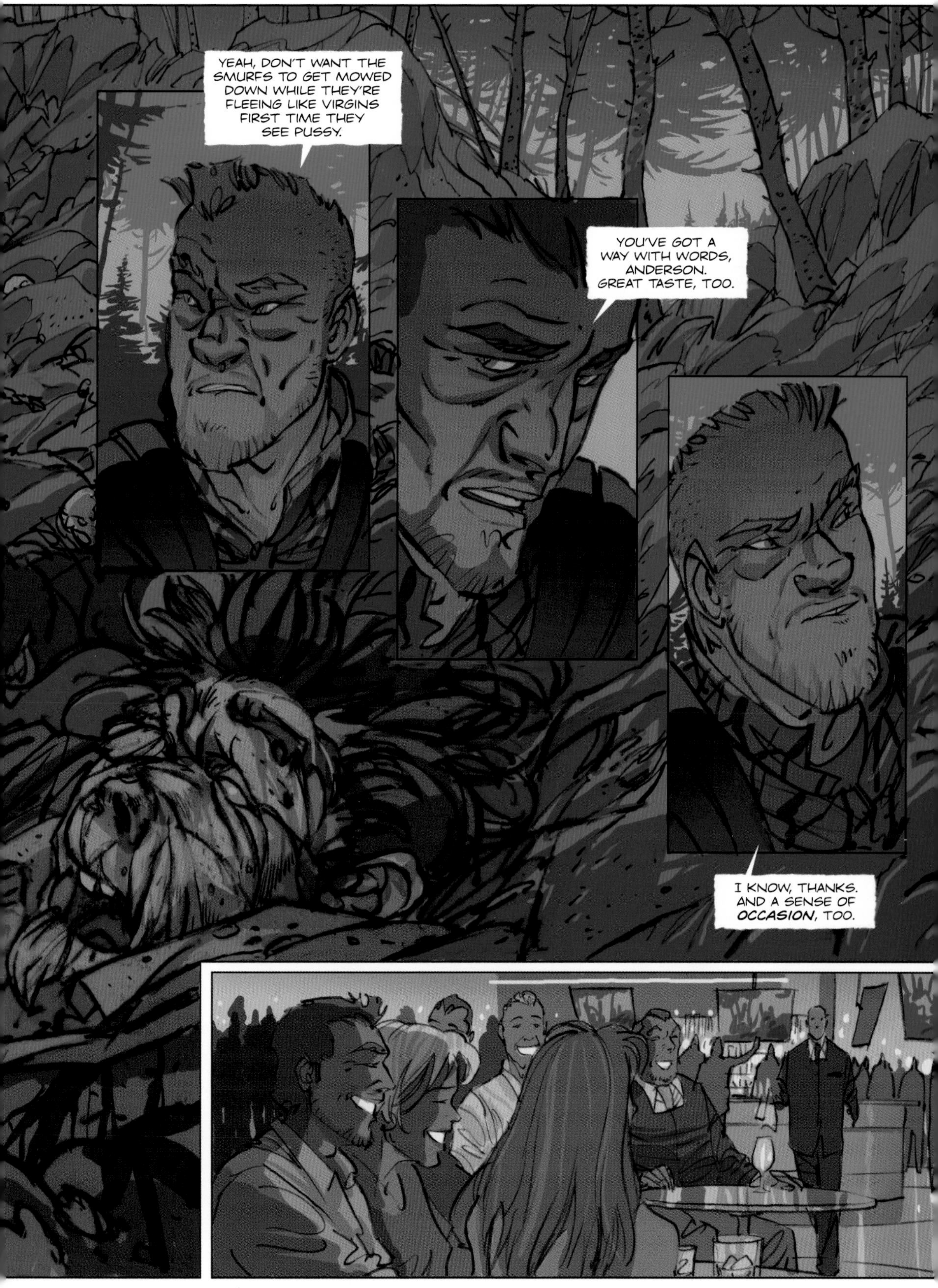
YEAH, DON'T WANT THE SMURFS TO GET MOWED DOWN WHILE THEY'RE FLEEING LIKE VIRGINS FIRST TIME THEY SEE PUSSY.
YOU'VE GOT A WAY WITH WORDS, ANDERSON. GREAT TASTE, TOO.
I KNOW, THANKS. AND A SENSE OF *OCCASION*, TOO.

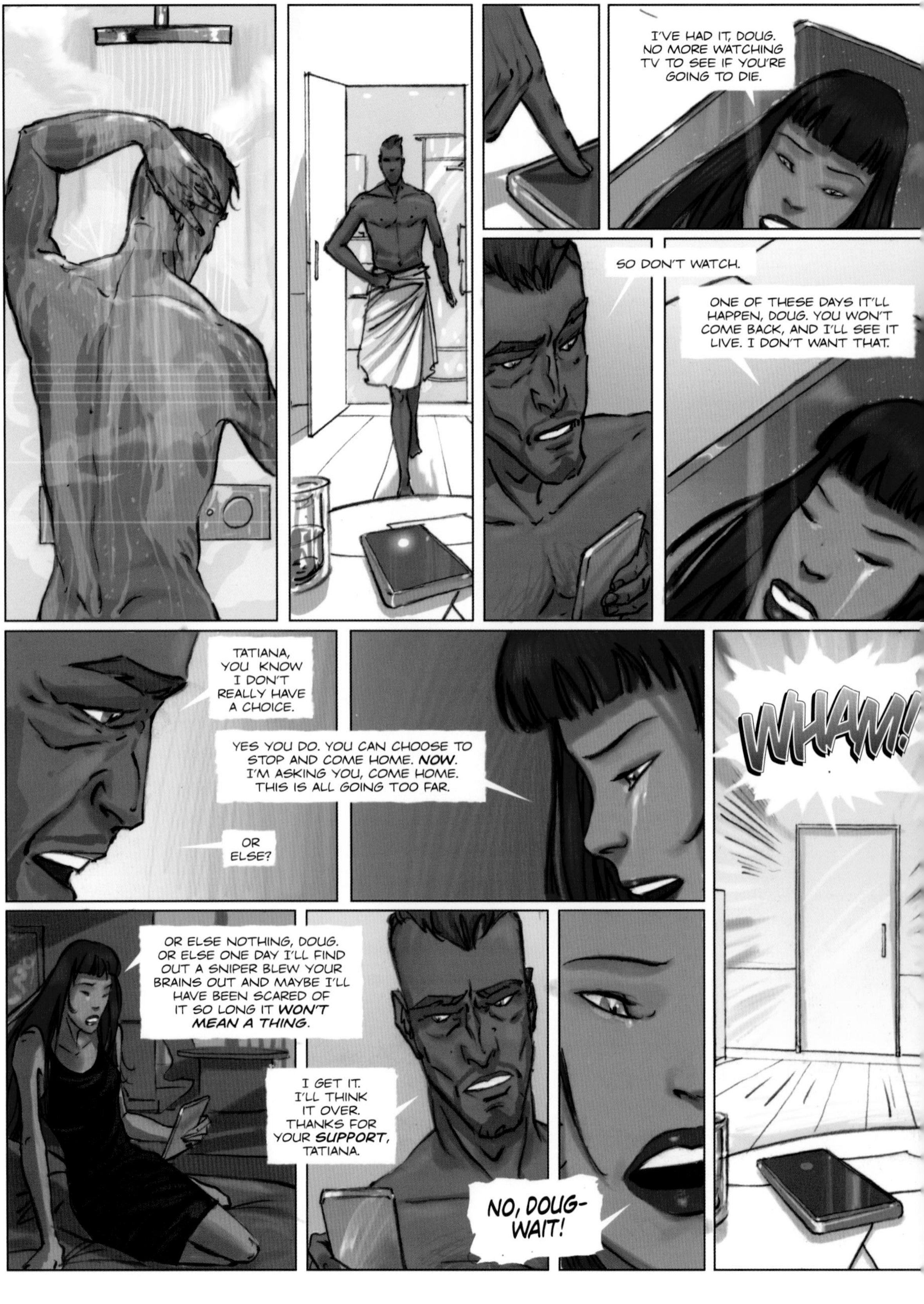
I'VE HAD IT, DOUG. NO MORE WATCHING TV TO SEE IF YOU'RE GOING TO DIE.
SO DON'T WATCH.
ONE OF THESE DAYS IT'LL HAPPEN, DOUG. YOU WON'T COME BACK, AND I'LL SEE IT LIVE. I DON'T WANT THAT.
TATIANA, YOU KNOW I DON'T REALLY HAVE A CHOICE.
YES YOU DO. YOU CAN CHOOSE TO STOP AND COME HOME. **NOW**. I'M ASKING YOU, COME HOME. THIS IS ALL GOING TOO FAR.
OR ELSE?
WHAM!
OR ELSE NOTHING, DOUG. OR ELSE ONE DAY I'LL FIND OUT A SNIPER BLEW YOUR BRAINS OUT AND MAYBE I'LL HAVE BEEN SCARED OF IT SO LONG IT ***WON'T MEAN A THING***.
I GET IT. I'LL THINK IT OVER. THANKS FOR YOUR ***SUPPORT***, TATIANA.
NO, DOUG- WAIT!

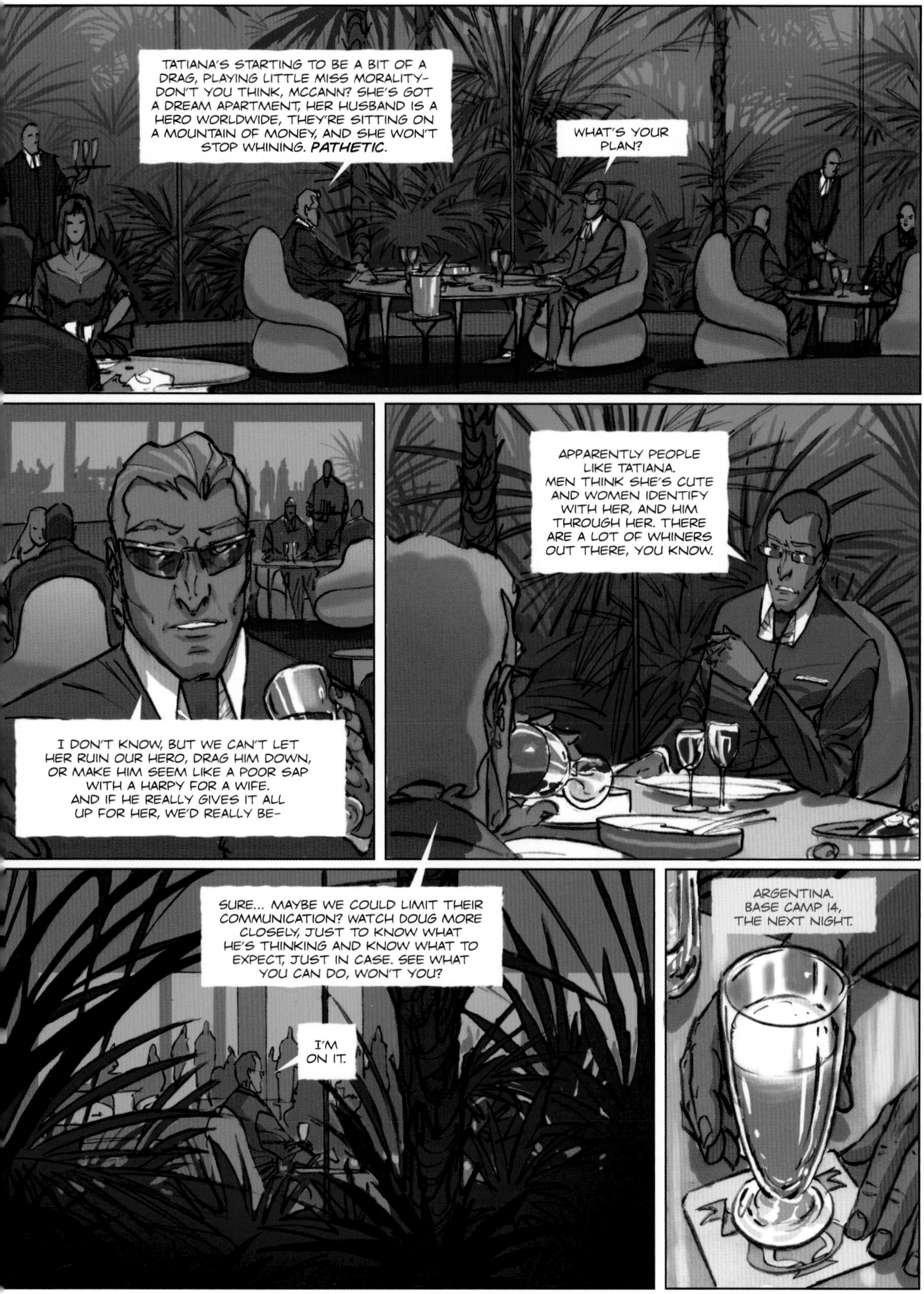
TATIANA'S STARTING TO BE A BIT OF A DRAG, PLAYING LITTLE MISS MORALITY-DON'T YOU THINK, MCCANN? SHE'S GOT A DREAM APARTMENT, HER HUSBAND IS A HERO WORLDWIDE, THEY'RE SITTING ON A MOUNTAIN OF MONEY, AND SHE WON'T STOP WHINING. ***PATHETIC***.
WHAT'S YOUR PLAN?
I DON'T KNOW, BUT WE CAN'T LET HER RUIN OUR HERO, DRAG HIM DOWN, OR MAKE HIM SEEM LIKE A POOR SAP WITH A HARPY FOR A WIFE. AND IF HE REALLY GIVES IT ALL UP FOR HER, WE'D REALLY BE-
APPARENTLY PEOPLE LIKE TATIANA. MEN THINK SHE'S CUTE AND WOMEN IDENTIFY WITH HER, AND HIM THROUGH HER. THERE ARE A LOT OF WHINERS OUT THERE, YOU KNOW.
SURE... MAYBE WE COULD LIMIT THEIR COMMUNICATION? WATCH DOUG MORE CLOSELY, JUST TO KNOW WHAT HE'S THINKING AND KNOW WHAT TO EXPECT, JUST IN CASE. SEE WHAT YOU CAN DO, WON'T YOU?
I'M ON IT.
ARGENTINA. BASE CAMP 14, THE NEXT NIGHT.

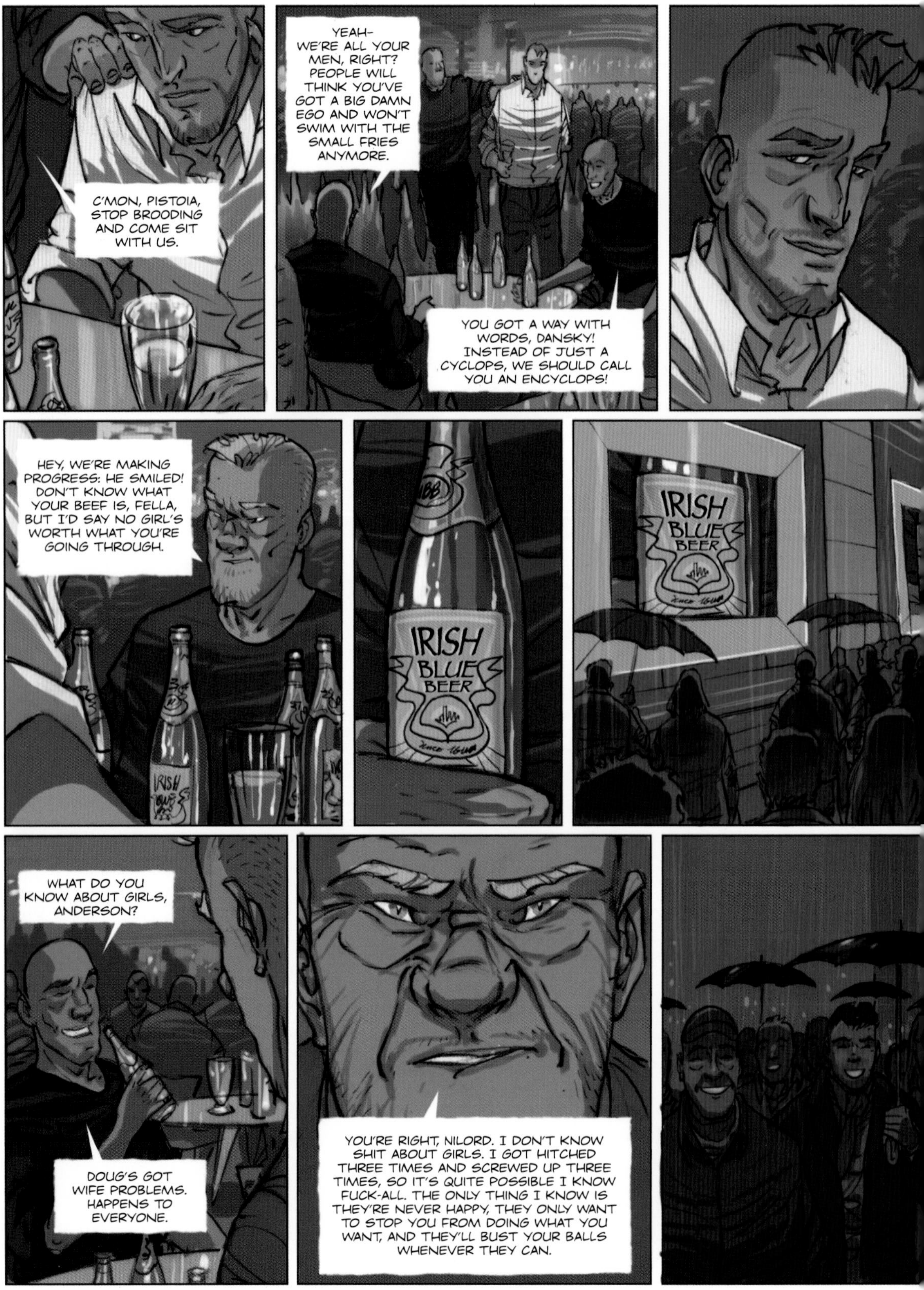
C'MON, PISTOIA, STOP BROODING AND COME SIT WITH US.
YEAH- WE'RE ALL YOUR MEN, RIGHT? PEOPLE WILL THINK YOU'VE GOT A BIG DAMN EGO AND WON'T SWIM WITH THE SMALL FRIES ANYMORE.
YOU GOT A WAY WITH WORDS, DANSKY! INSTEAD OF JUST A CYCLOPS, WE SHOULD CALL YOU AN ENCYCLOPS!
HEY, WE'RE MAKING PROGRESS: HE SMILED! DON'T KNOW WHAT YOUR BEEF IS, FELLA, BUT I'D SAY NO GIRL'S WORTH WHAT YOU'RE GOING THROUGH.
IRISH BLUE BEER
IRISH BLUE BEER
WHAT DO YOU KNOW ABOUT GIRLS, ANDERSON?
DOUG'S GOT WIFE PROBLEMS. HAPPENS TO EVERYONE.
YOU'RE RIGHT, NILORD. I DON'T KNOW SHIT ABOUT GIRLS. I GOT HITCHED THREE TIMES AND SCREWED UP THREE TIMES, SO IT'S QUITE POSSIBLE I KNOW FUCK-ALL. THE ONLY THING I KNOW IS THEY'RE NEVER HAPPY, THEY ONLY WANT TO STOP YOU FROM DOING WHAT YOU WANT, AND THEY'LL BUST YOUR BALLS WHENEVER THEY CAN.

THREE TIMES! SHIT, ANDERSON! YOU NEVER SAID.

BESIDES, HOW DO YOU LET YOURSELF GET MARRIED THREE TIMES? TWO, WHY NOT: ONE MISTAKE, AND THE NEXT TIME YOU THINK IT'LL BE BETTER, BUT THREE? MAKES NO SENSE. YOU GOT KIDS?

FOUR. WASN'T MARRIED THREE TIMES, GOT DIVORCED THREE TIMES. NUANCE.

NOW I KNOW WHY YOU'RE BROKE ALL THE TIME!

WHY DIDN'T YOU EVER TELL US ABOUT IT?

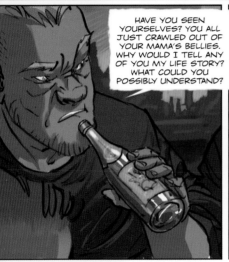

HAVE YOU SEEN YOURSELVES? YOU ALL JUST CRAWLED OUT OF YOUR MAMA'S BELLIES. WHY WOULD I TELL ANY OF YOU MY LIFE STORY? WHAT COULD YOU POSSIBLY UNDERSTAND?

HA HA HA!

GO, ANDERSON!

DON'T STAND FOR IT, DOUG!

YOU'RE RIGHT, ANDERSON. AND SEEING HOW YOUNG I AM, I'D BETTER GO TO BED. YOU COMING, BOYS?

I'M STILL THIRSTY. I GOT A FEW THINGS TO DROWN. SEE YOU TOMORROW, BOYS.

PUB

CYCLOPS! CYCLOPS! FORWARD MARCH! ADVENTURE AWAITS!

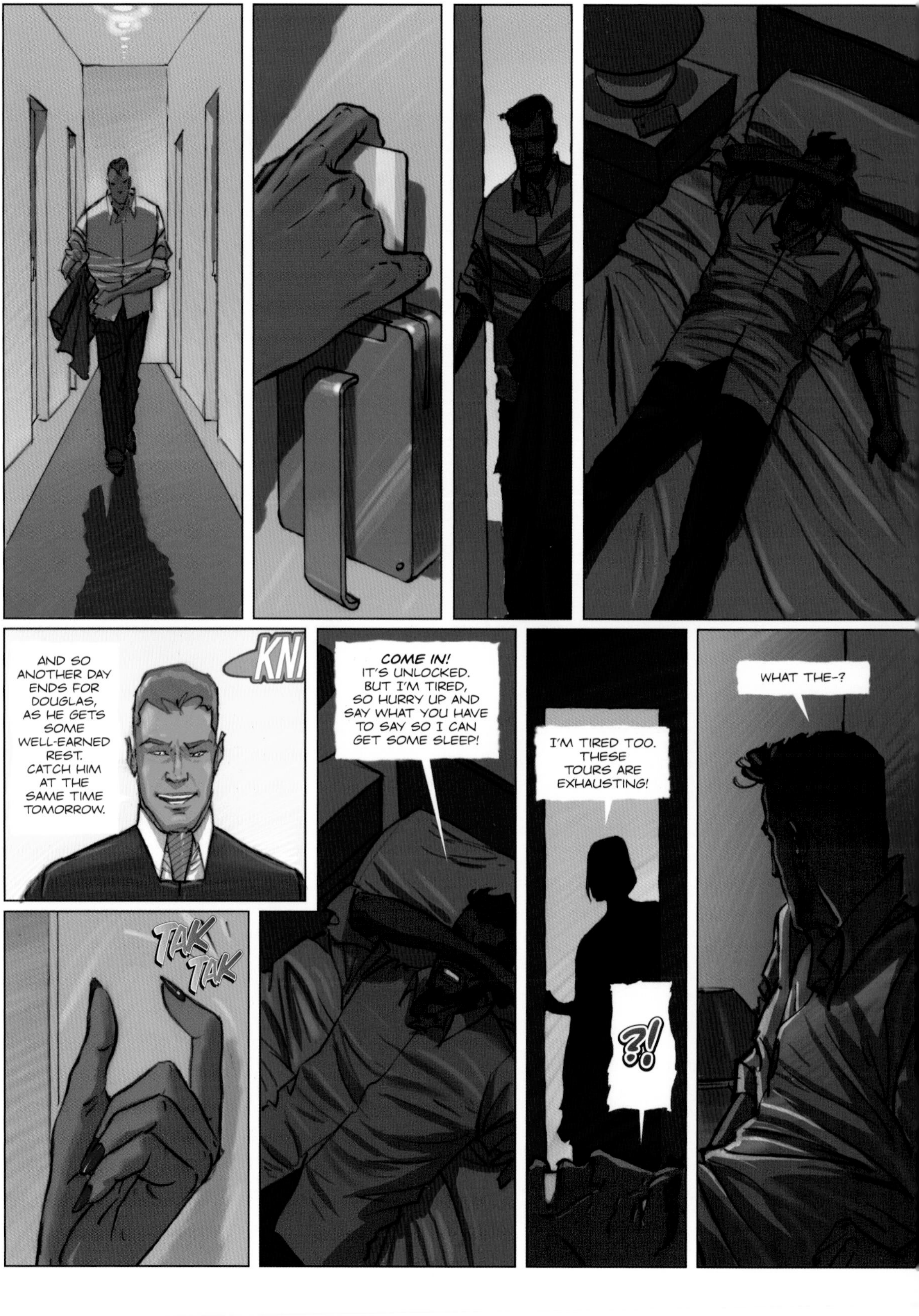
AND SO ANOTHER DAY ENDS FOR DOUGLAS, AS HE GETS SOME WELL-EARNED REST. CATCH HIM AT THE SAME TIME TOMORROW.
KN
TAK TAK
COME IN! IT'S UNLOCKED. BUT I'M TIRED, SO HURRY UP AND SAY WHAT YOU HAVE TO SAY SO I CAN GET SOME SLEEP!
I'M TIRED TOO. THESE TOURS ARE EXHAUSTING!
?!
WHAT THE-?

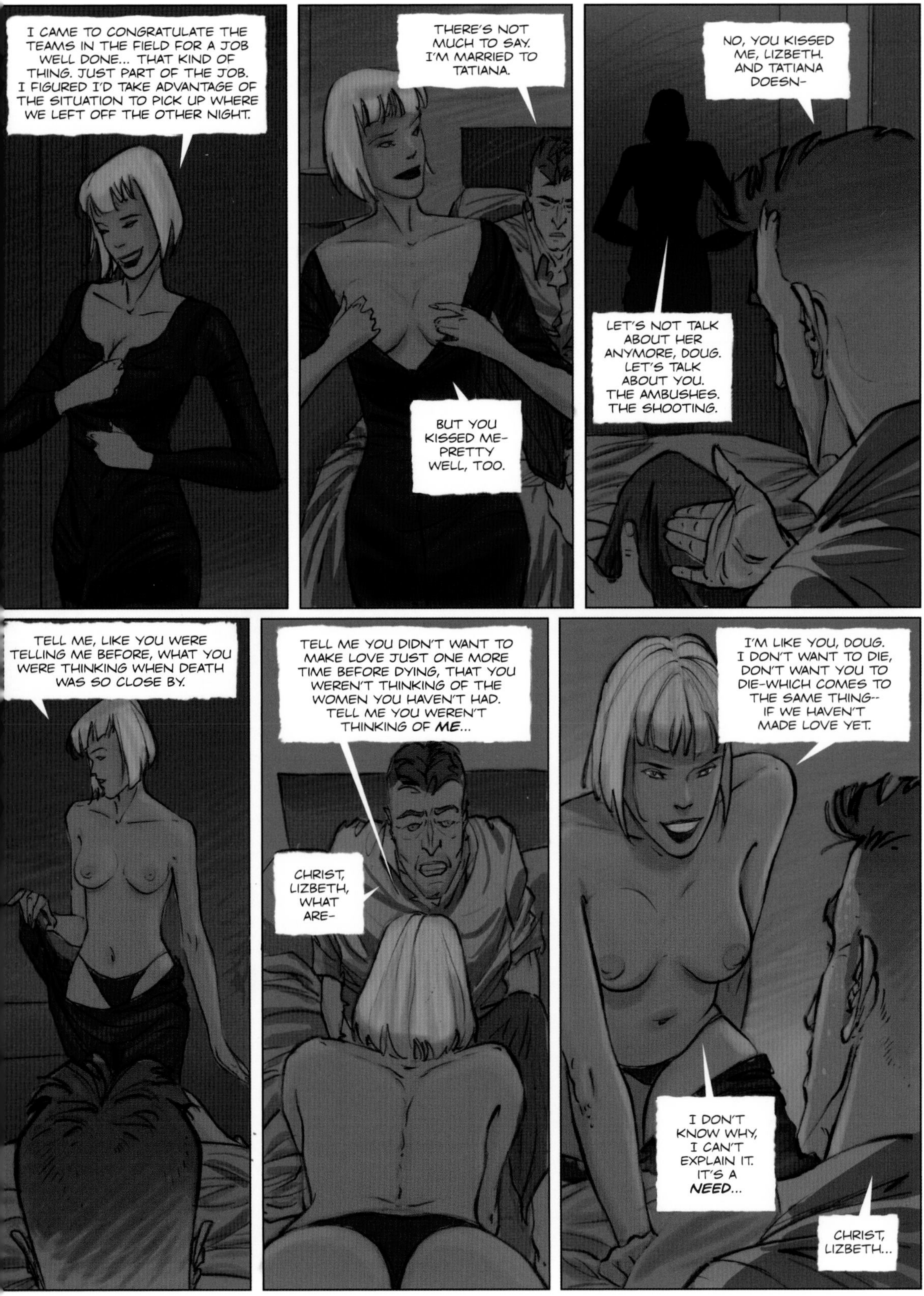
I CAME TO CONGRATULATE THE TEAMS IN THE FIELD FOR A JOB WELL DONE... THAT KIND OF THING. JUST PART OF THE JOB. I FIGURED I'D TAKE ADVANTAGE OF THE SITUATION TO PICK UP WHERE WE LEFT OFF THE OTHER NIGHT.
THERE'S NOT MUCH TO SAY. I'M MARRIED TO TATIANA.
BUT YOU KISSED ME-PRETTY WELL, TOO.
NO, YOU KISSED ME, LIZBETH. AND TATIANA DOESN-
LET'S NOT TALK ABOUT HER ANYMORE, DOUG. LET'S TALK ABOUT YOU. THE AMBUSHES. THE SHOOTING.
TELL ME, LIKE YOU WERE TELLING ME BEFORE, WHAT YOU WERE THINKING WHEN DEATH WAS SO CLOSE BY.
TELL ME YOU DIDN'T WANT TO MAKE LOVE JUST ONE MORE TIME BEFORE DYING, THAT YOU WEREN'T THINKING OF THE WOMEN YOU HAVEN'T HAD. TELL ME YOU WEREN'T THINKING OF ***ME***...
CHRIST, LIZBETH, WHAT ARE-
I'M LIKE YOU, DOUG. I DON'T WANT TO DIE, DON'T WANT YOU TO DIE-WHICH COMES TO THE SAME THING-- IF WE HAVEN'T MADE LOVE YET.
I DON'T KNOW WHY, I CAN'T EXPLAIN IT. IT'S A ***NEED***...
CHRIST, LIZBETH...

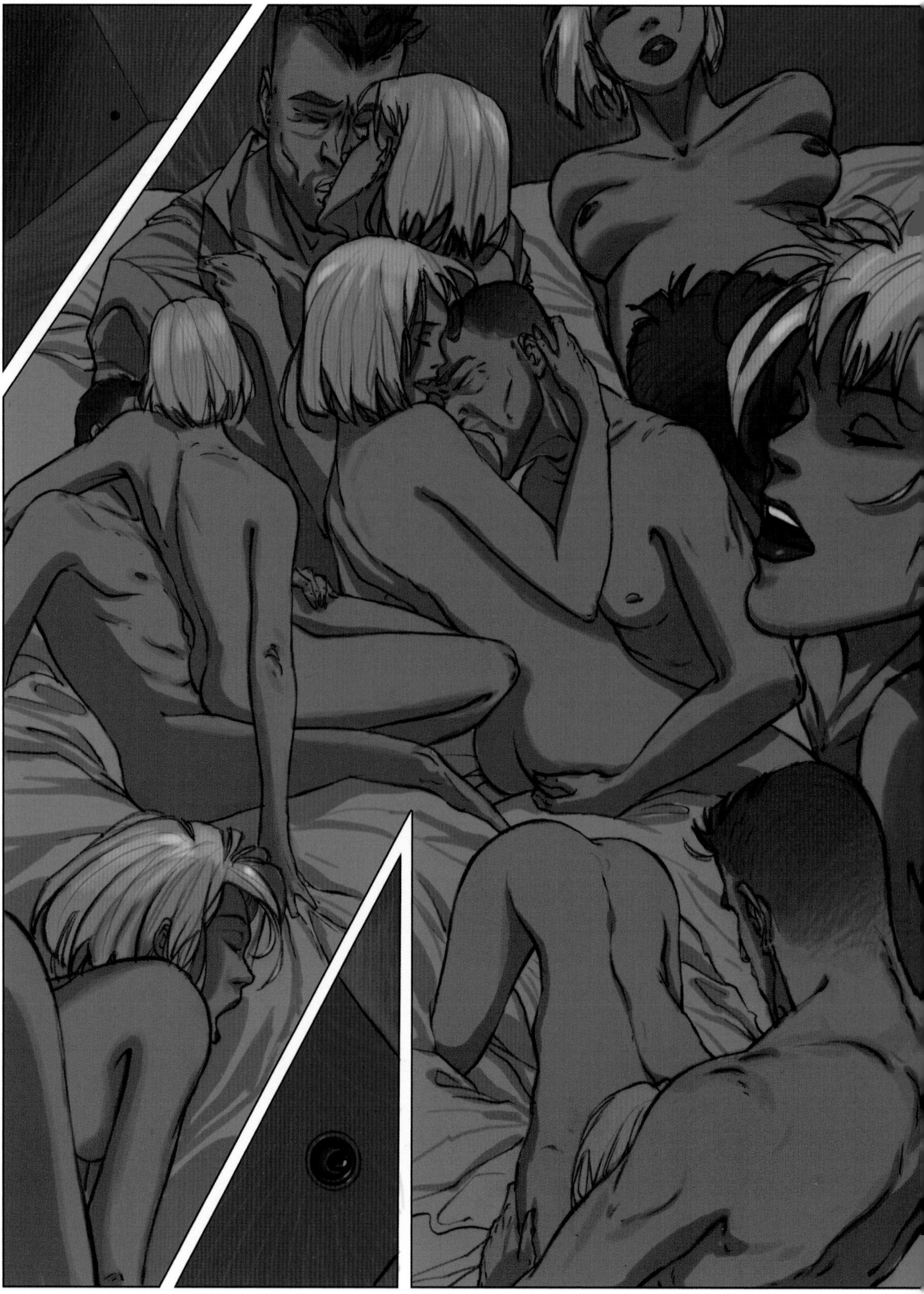

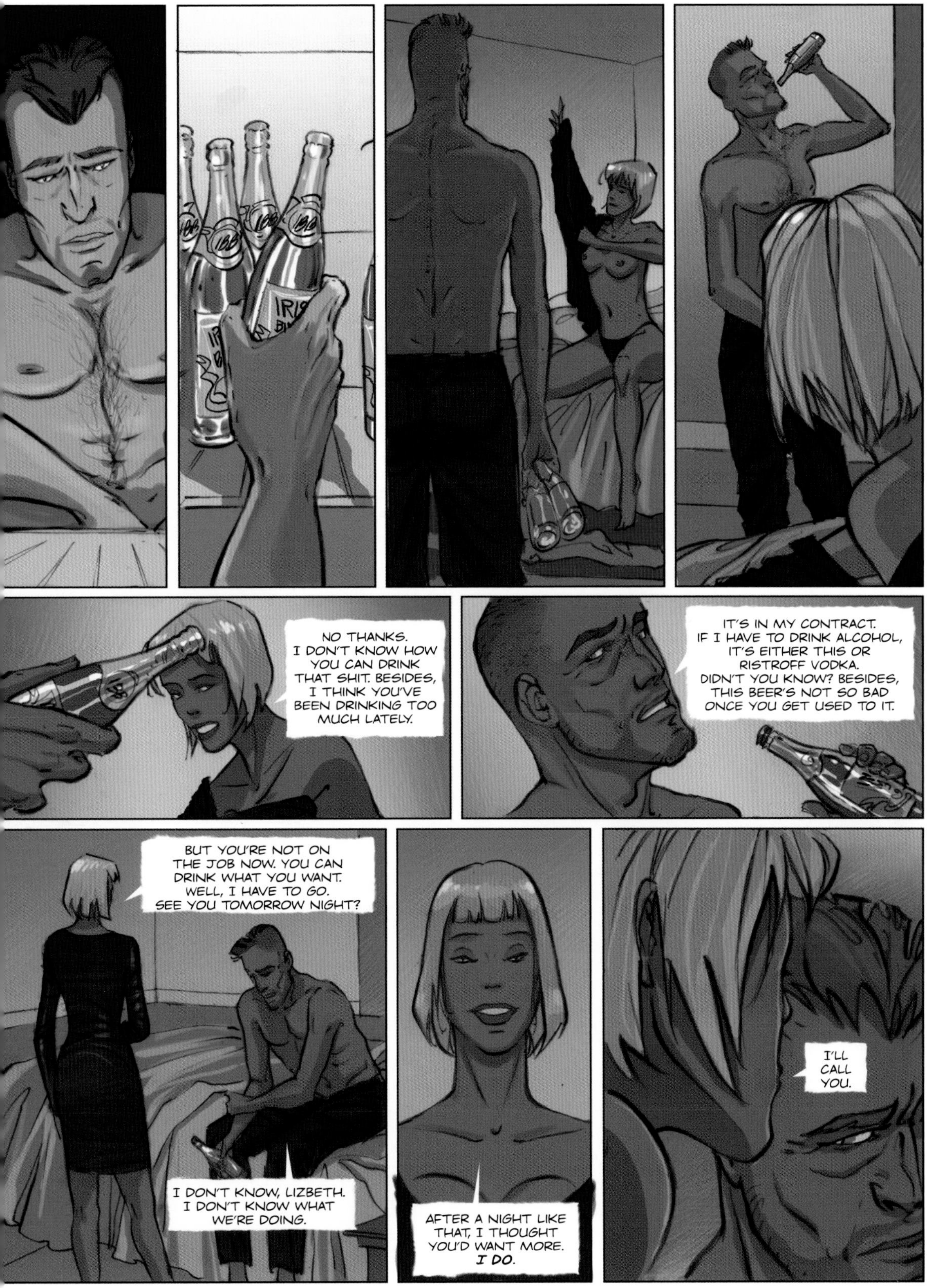
NO THANKS. I DON'T KNOW HOW YOU CAN DRINK THAT SHIT. BESIDES, I THINK YOU'VE BEEN DRINKING TOO MUCH LATELY.
IT'S IN MY CONTRACT. IF I HAVE TO DRINK ALCOHOL, IT'S EITHER THIS OR RISTROFF VODKA. DIDN'T YOU KNOW? BESIDES, THIS BEER'S NOT SO BAD ONCE YOU GET USED TO IT.
BUT YOU'RE NOT ON THE JOB NOW. YOU CAN DRINK WHAT YOU WANT. WELL, I HAVE TO GO. SEE YOU TOMORROW NIGHT?
I DON'T KNOW, LIZBETH. I DON'T KNOW WHAT WE'RE DOING.
AFTER A NIGHT LIKE THAT, I THOUGHT YOU'D WANT MORE. ***I DO***.
I'LL CALL YOU.

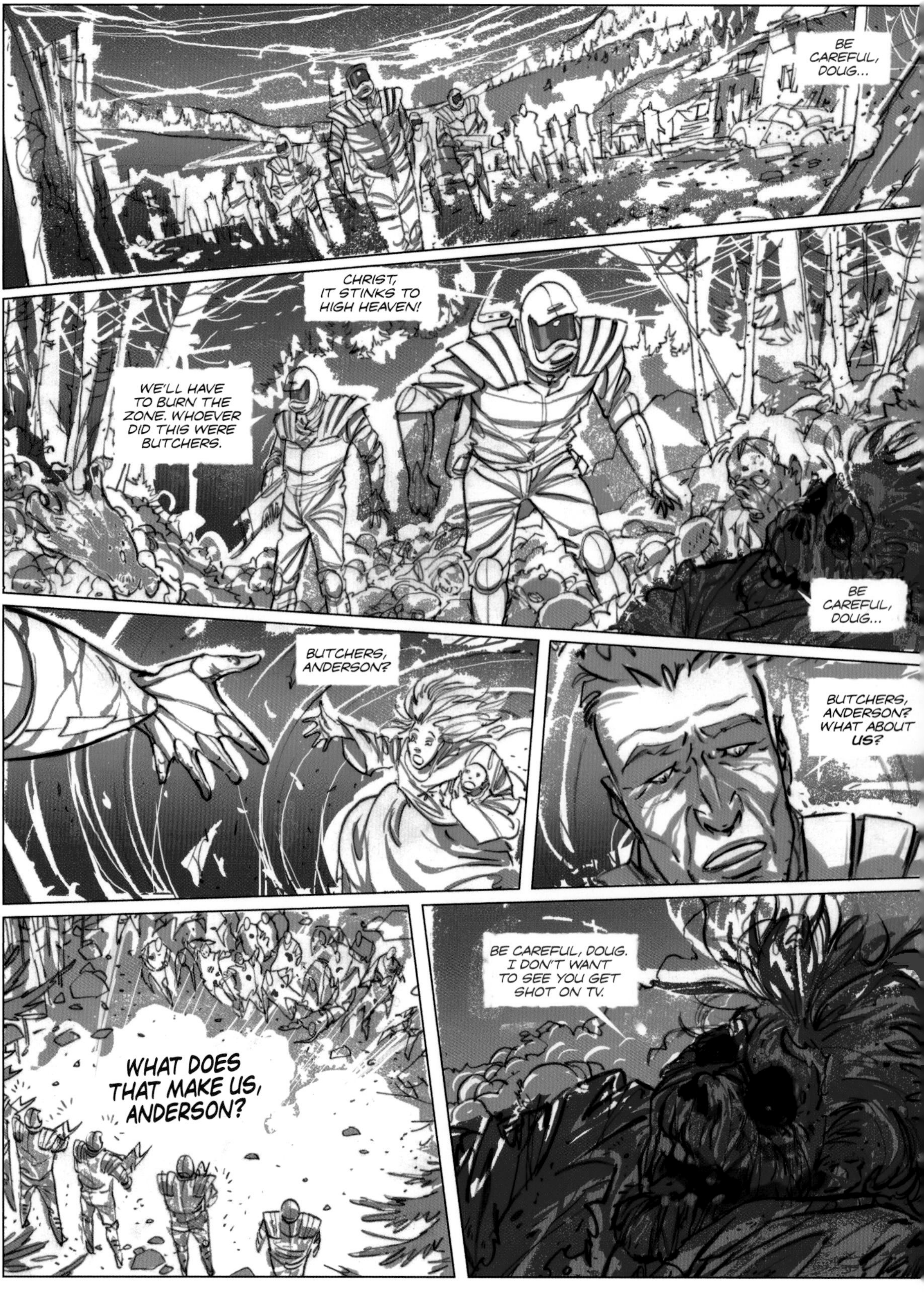
BE CAREFUL, DOUG...
CHRIST, IT STINKS TO HIGH HEAVEN!
WE'LL HAVE TO BURN THE ZONE. WHOEVER DID THIS WERE BUTCHERS.
BE CAREFUL, DOUG...
BUTCHERS, ANDERSON?
BUTCHERS, ANDERSON? WHAT ABOUT US?
WHAT DOES THAT MAKE US, ANDERSON?
BE CAREFUL, DOUG. I DON'T WANT TO SEE YOU GET SHOT ON TV.

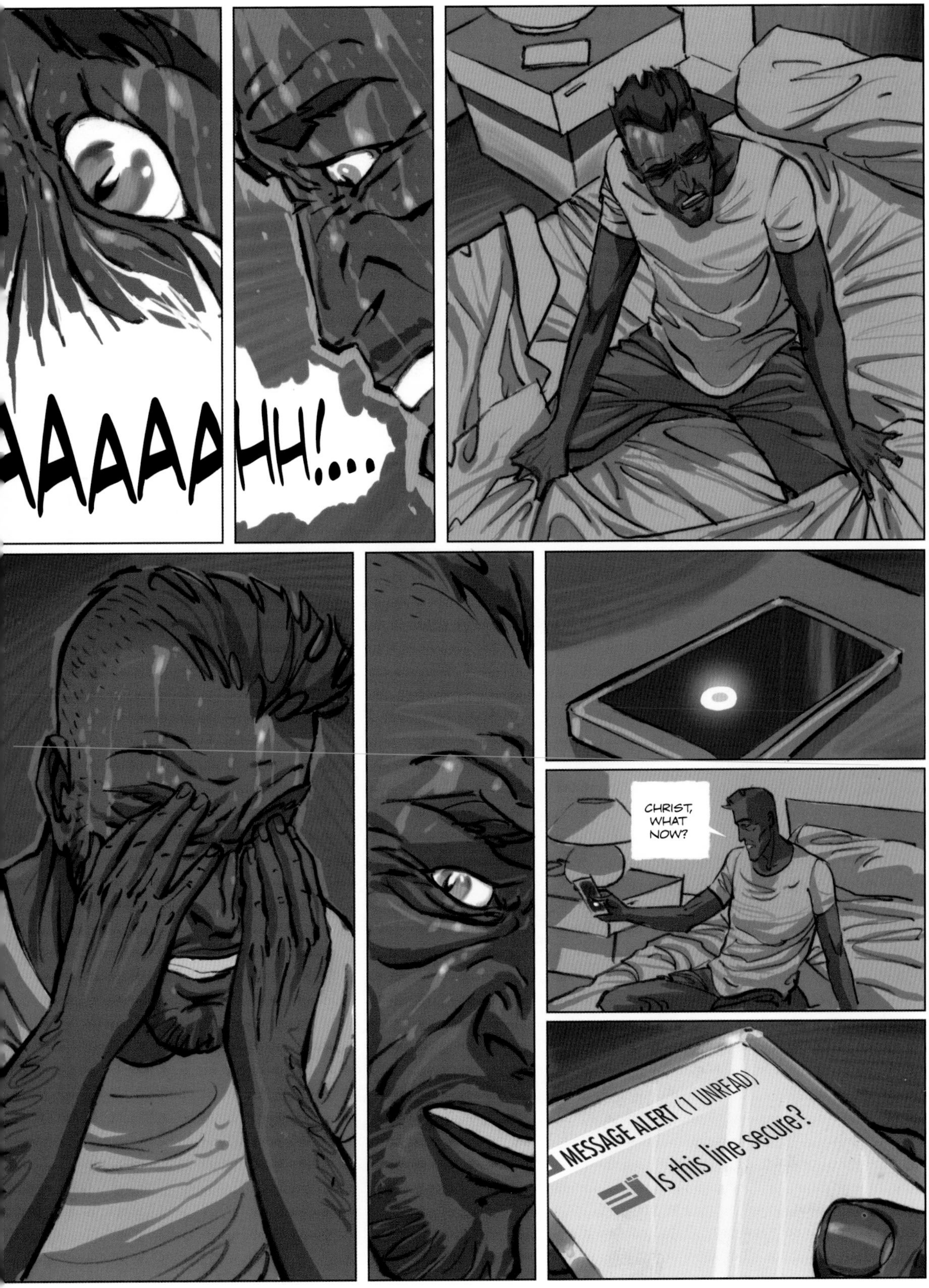
AAAAAAHH!...
CHRIST, WHAT NOW?
MESSAGE ALERT (1 UNREAD)
Is this line secure?

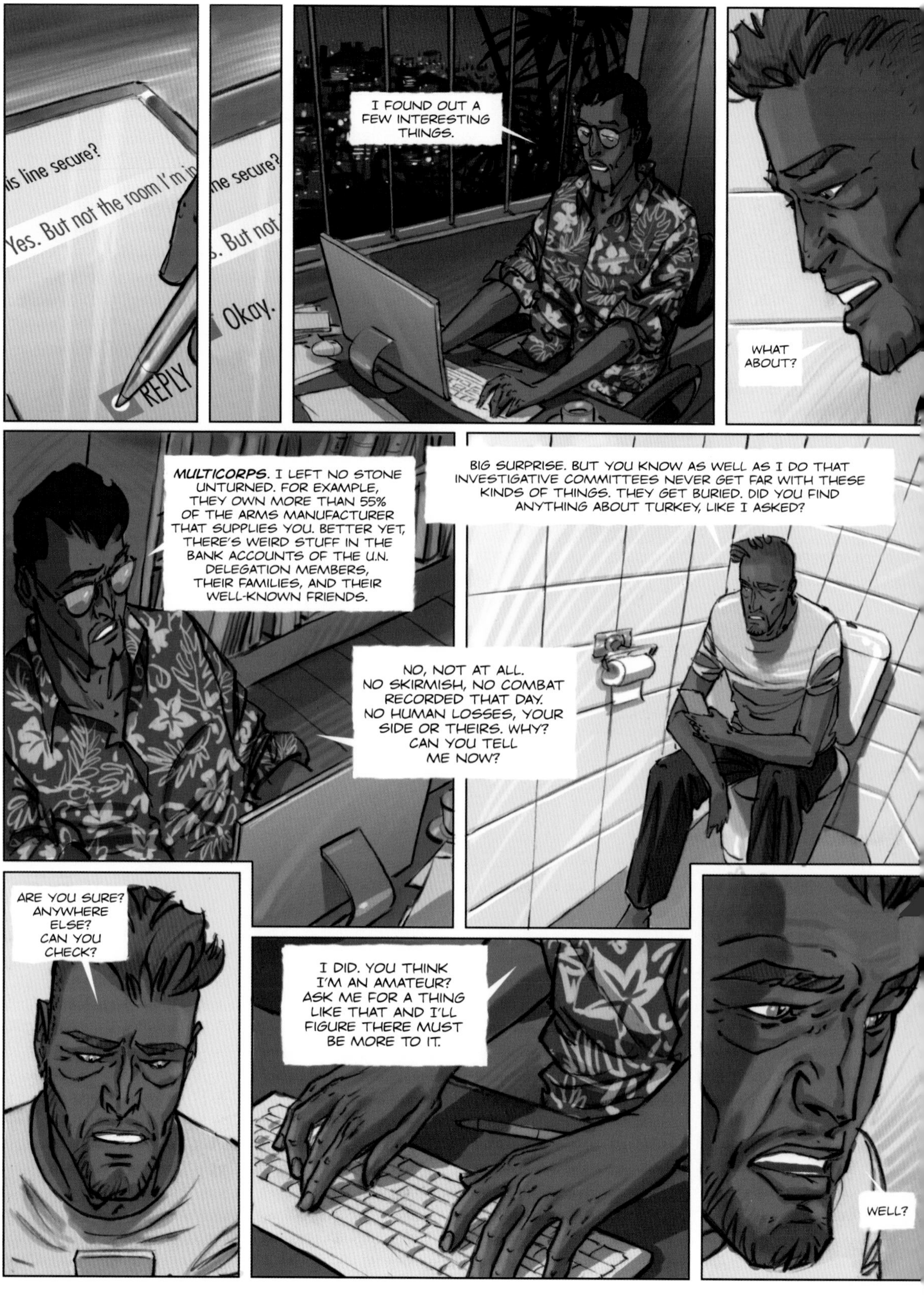
is line secure?
Yes. But not the room I'm in
REPLY
ne secure?
. But not
Okay.
I FOUND OUT A FEW INTERESTING THINGS.
WHAT ABOUT?
MULTICORPS. I LEFT NO STONE UNTURNED. FOR EXAMPLE, THEY OWN MORE THAN 55% OF THE ARMS MANUFACTURER THAT SUPPLIES YOU. BETTER YET, THERE'S WEIRD STUFF IN THE BANK ACCOUNTS OF THE U.N. DELEGATION MEMBERS, THEIR FAMILIES, AND THEIR WELL-KNOWN FRIENDS.
BIG SURPRISE. BUT YOU KNOW AS WELL AS I DO THAT INVESTIGATIVE COMMITTEES NEVER GET FAR WITH THESE KINDS OF THINGS. THEY GET BURIED. DID YOU FIND ANYTHING ABOUT TURKEY, LIKE I ASKED?
NO, NOT AT ALL. NO SKIRMISH, NO COMBAT RECORDED THAT DAY. NO HUMAN LOSSES, YOUR SIDE OR THEIRS. WHY? CAN YOU TELL ME NOW?
ARE YOU SURE? ANYWHERE ELSE? CAN YOU CHECK?
I DID. YOU THINK I'M AN AMATEUR? ASK ME FOR A THING LIKE THAT AND I'LL FIGURE THERE MUST BE MORE TO IT.
WELL?

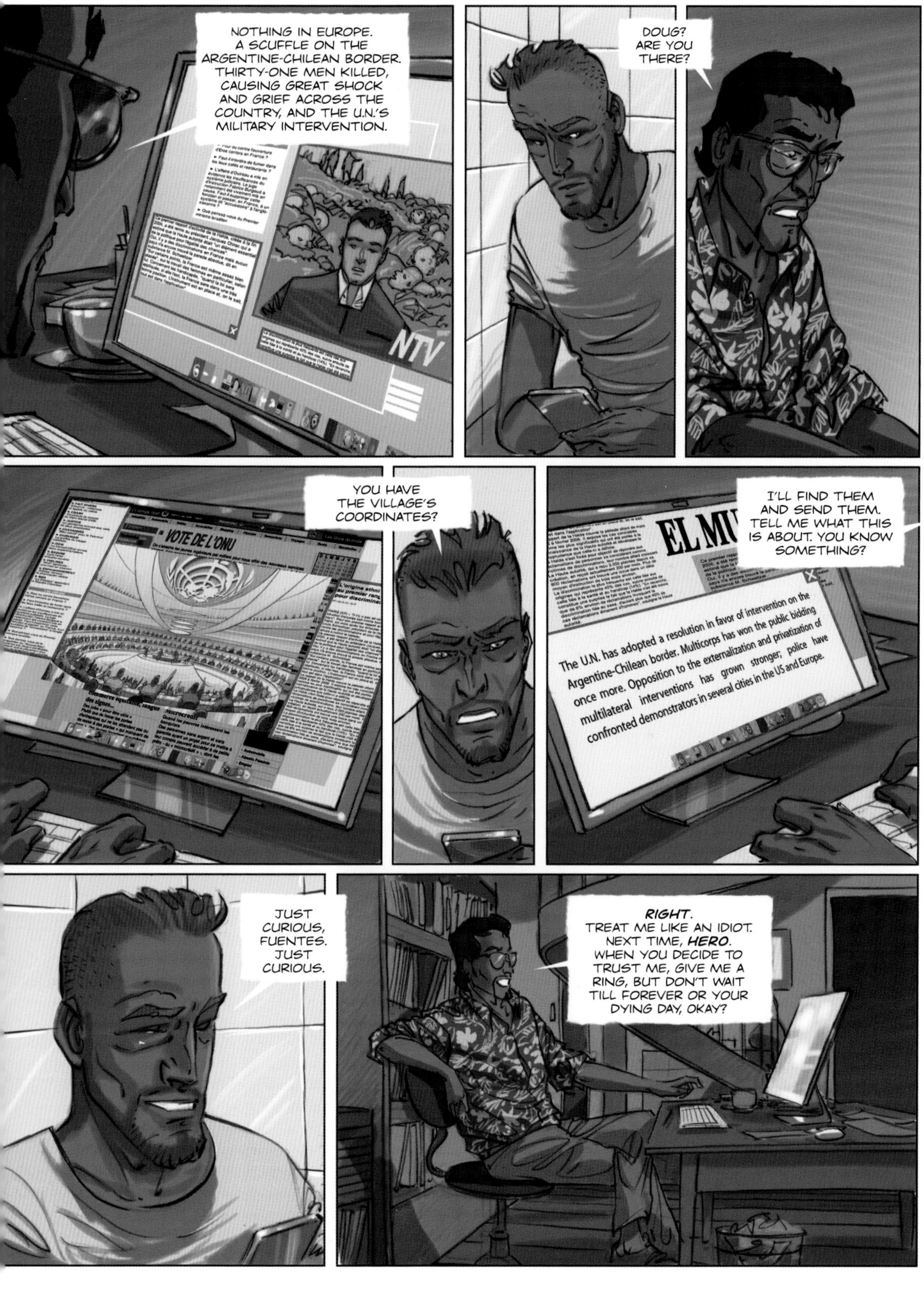
NOTHING IN EUROPE. A SCUFFLE ON THE ARGENTINE-CHILEAN BORDER. THIRTY-ONE MEN KILLED, CAUSING GREAT SHOCK AND GRIEF ACROSS THE COUNTRY, AND THE U.N.'S MILITARY INTERVENTION.
NTV
DOUG? ARE YOU THERE?
VOTE DE L'ONU
YOU HAVE THE VILLAGE'S COORDINATES?
EL MU
I'LL FIND THEM AND SEND THEM. TELL ME WHAT THIS IS ABOUT. YOU KNOW SOMETHING?
The U.N. has adopted a resolution in favor of intervention on the Argentine-Chilean border. Multicorps has won the public bidding once more. Opposition to the externalization and privatization of multilateral interventions has grown stronger; police have confronted demonstrators in several cities in the US and Europe.
JUST CURIOUS, FUENTES. JUST CURIOUS.
RIGHT. TREAT ME LIKE AN IDIOT. NEXT TIME, HERO. WHEN YOU DECIDE TO TRUST ME, GIVE ME A RING, BUT DON'T WAIT TILL FOREVER OR YOUR DYING DAY, OKAY?

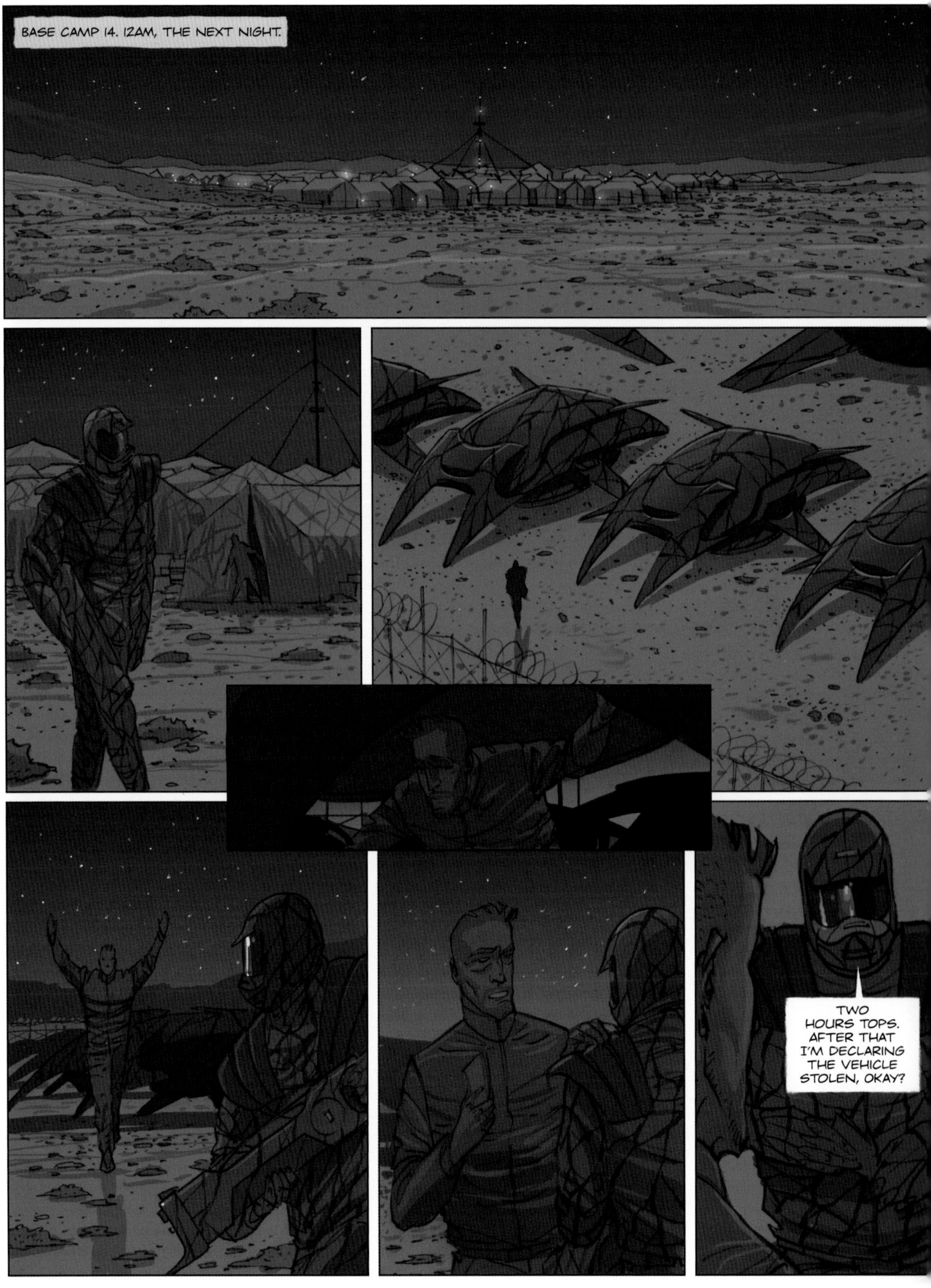
BASE CAMP 14. 12AM, THE NEXT NIGHT.
TWO HOURS TOPS. AFTER THAT I'M DECLARING THE VEHICLE STOLEN, OKAY?

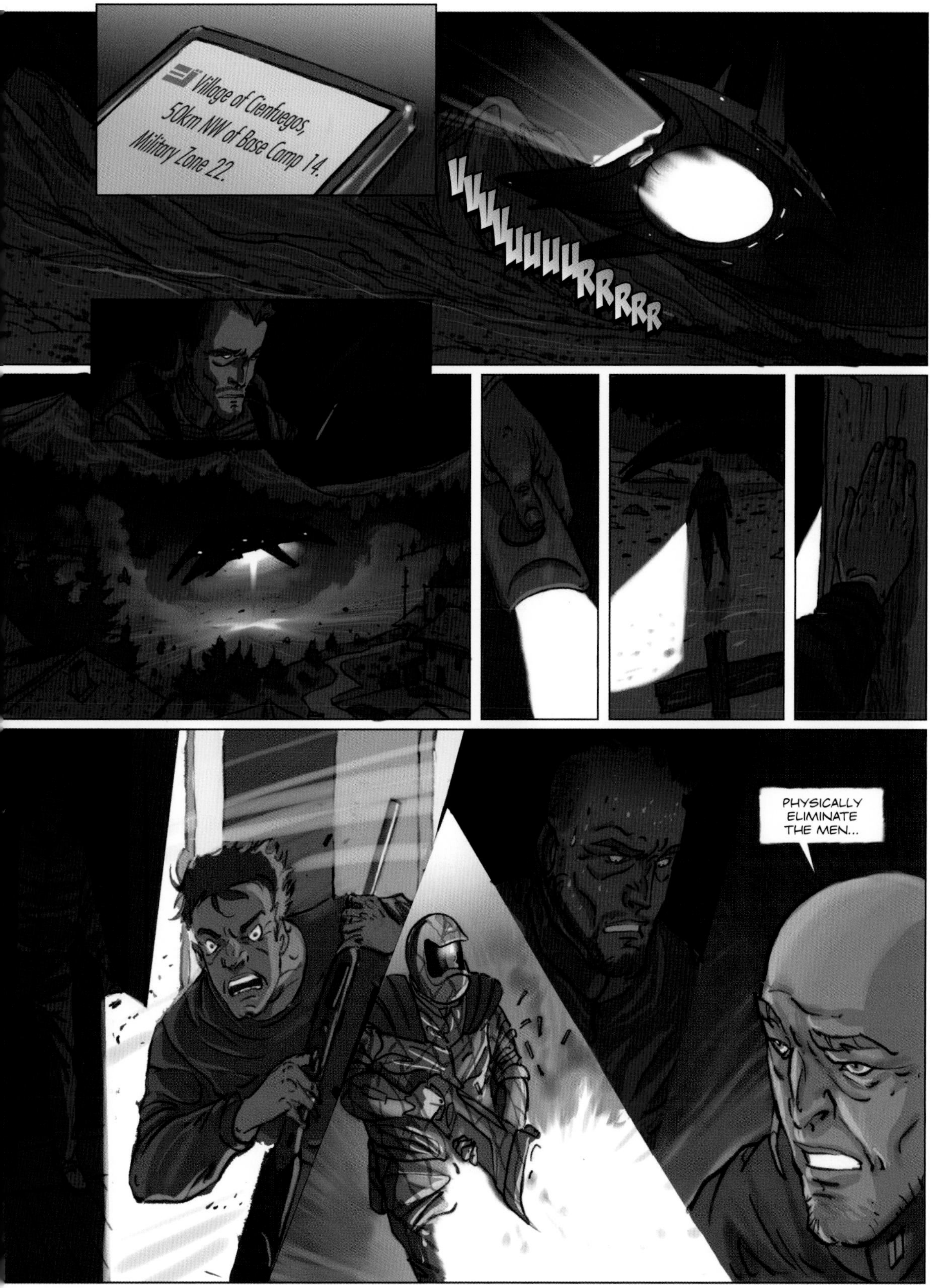
Village of Cienfuegos,
50km NW of Base Camp 14.
Military Zone 22.
VVVVUUUURRRRR
PHYSICALLY ELIMINATE THE MEN...

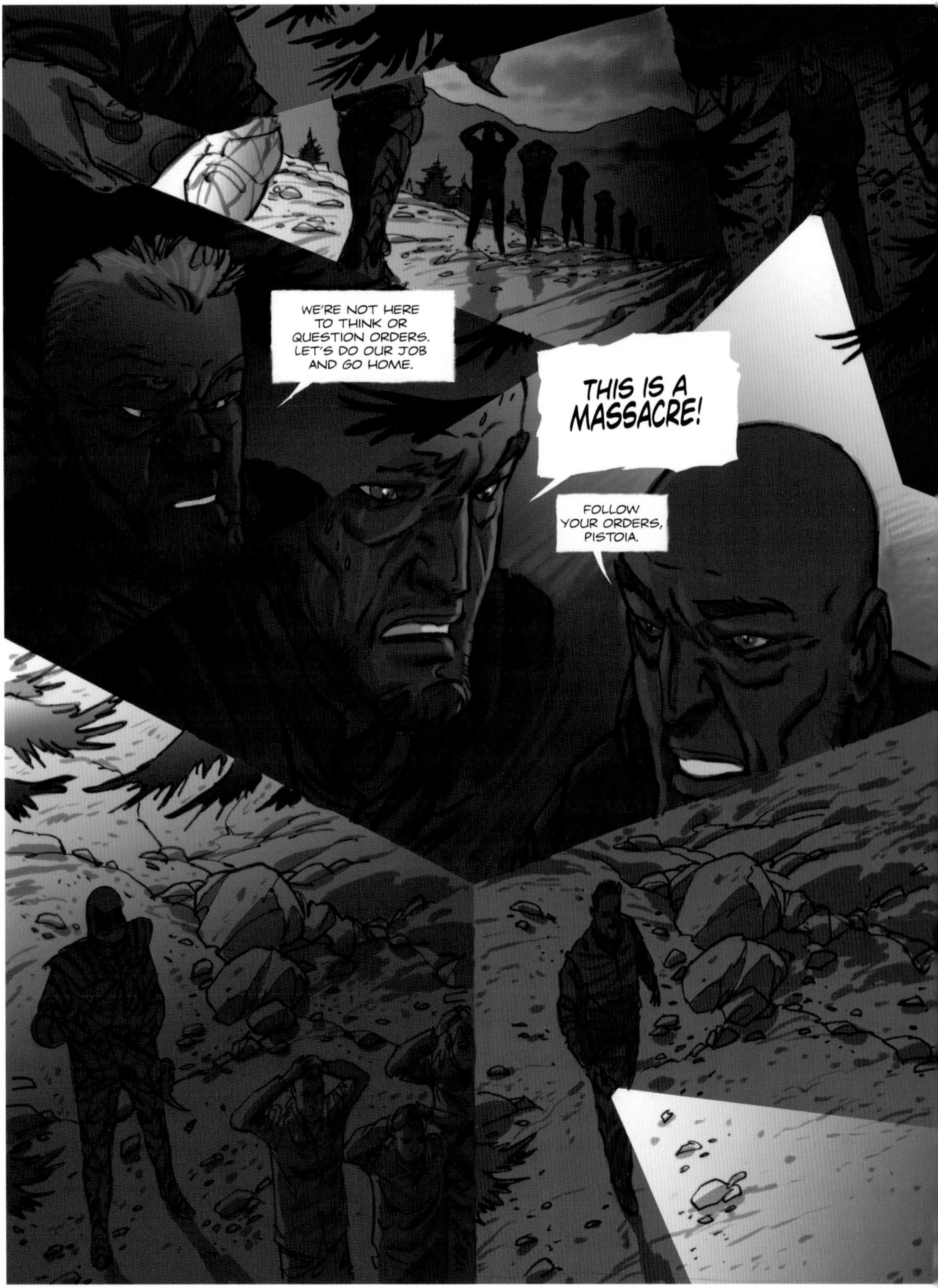
WE'RE NOT HERE TO THINK OR QUESTION ORDERS. LET'S DO OUR JOB AND GO HOME.
THIS IS A MASSACRE!
FOLLOW YOUR ORDERS, PISTOIA.

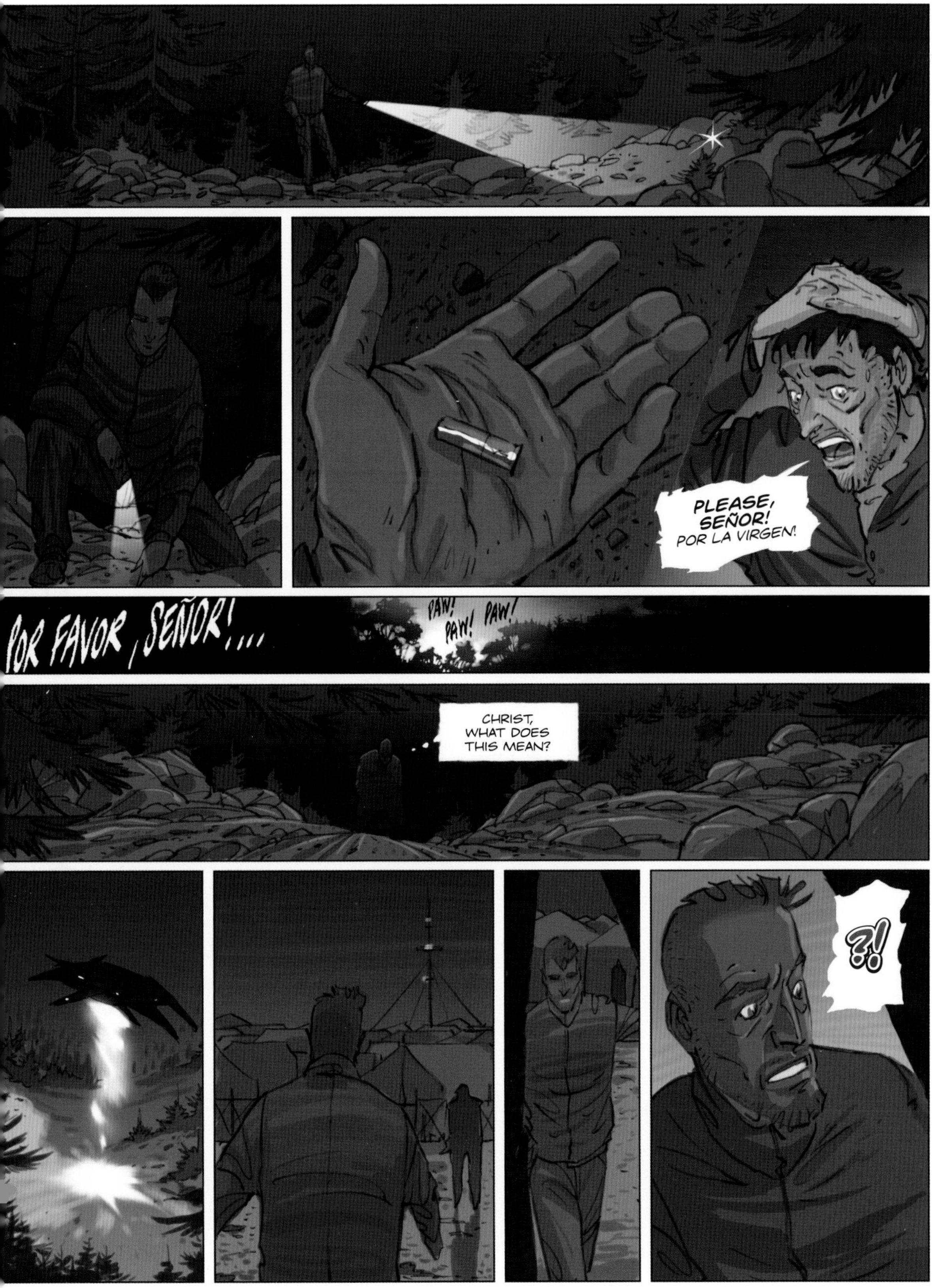
PLEASE, SEÑOR! POR LA VIRGEN!
POR FAVOR, SEÑOR!...
PAW! PAW! PAW!
CHRIST, WHAT DOES THIS MEAN?
?!

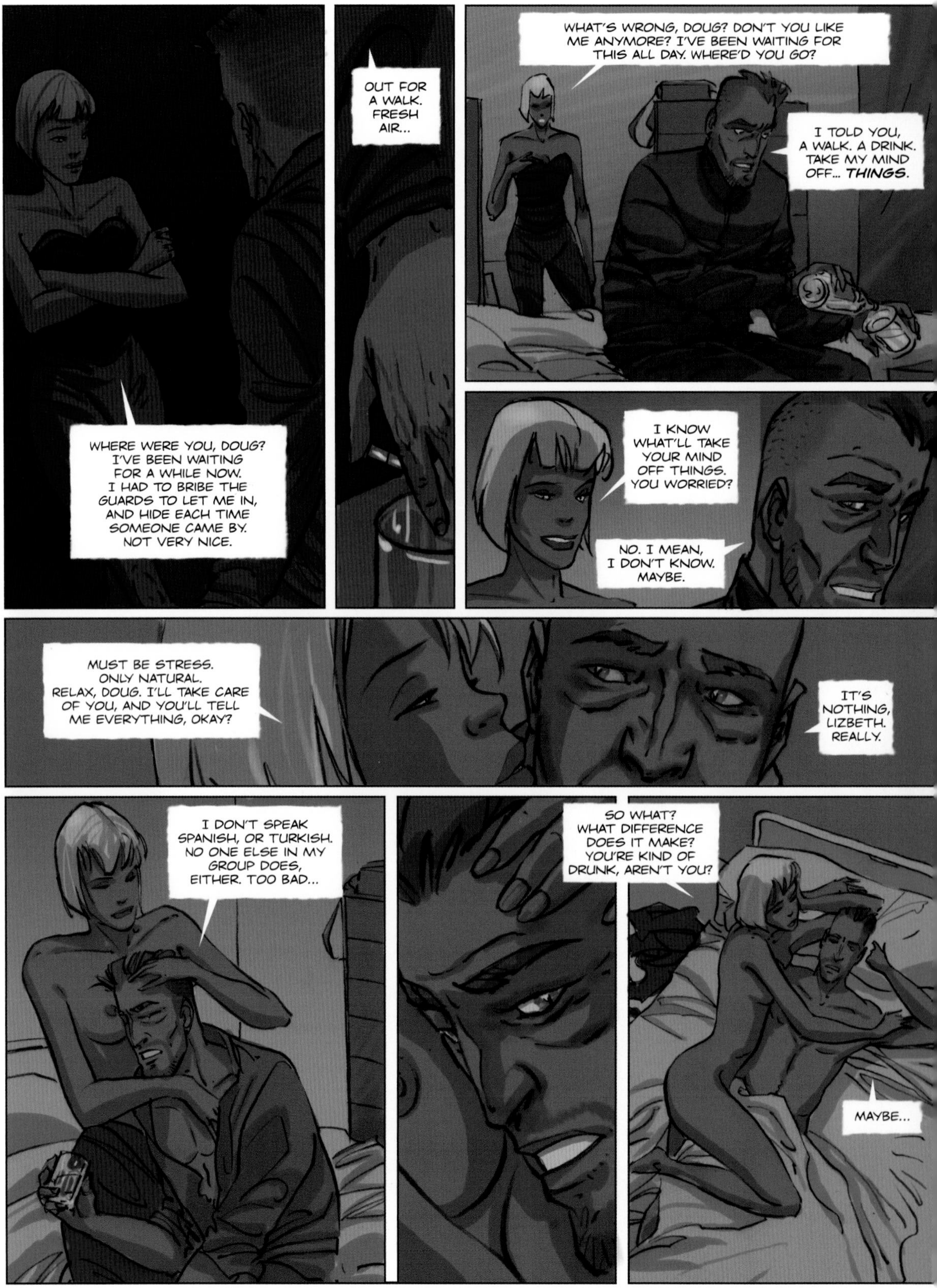
WHERE WERE YOU, DOUG? I'VE BEEN WAITING FOR A WHILE NOW. I HAD TO BRIBE THE GUARDS TO LET ME IN, AND HIDE EACH TIME SOMEONE CAME BY. NOT VERY NICE.
OUT FOR A WALK. FRESH AIR...
WHAT'S WRONG, DOUG? DON'T YOU LIKE ME ANYMORE? I'VE BEEN WAITING FOR THIS ALL DAY. WHERE'D YOU GO?
I TOLD YOU, A WALK. A DRINK. TAKE MY MIND OFF... THINGS.
I KNOW WHAT'LL TAKE YOUR MIND OFF THINGS. YOU WORRIED?
NO. I MEAN, I DON'T KNOW. MAYBE.
MUST BE STRESS. ONLY NATURAL. RELAX, DOUG. I'LL TAKE CARE OF YOU, AND YOU'LL TELL ME EVERYTHING, OKAY?
IT'S NOTHING, LIZBETH. REALLY.
I DON'T SPEAK SPANISH, OR TURKISH. NO ONE ELSE IN MY GROUP DOES, EITHER. TOO BAD...
SO WHAT? WHAT DIFFERENCE DOES IT MAKE? YOU'RE KIND OF DRUNK, AREN'T YOU?
MAYBE...

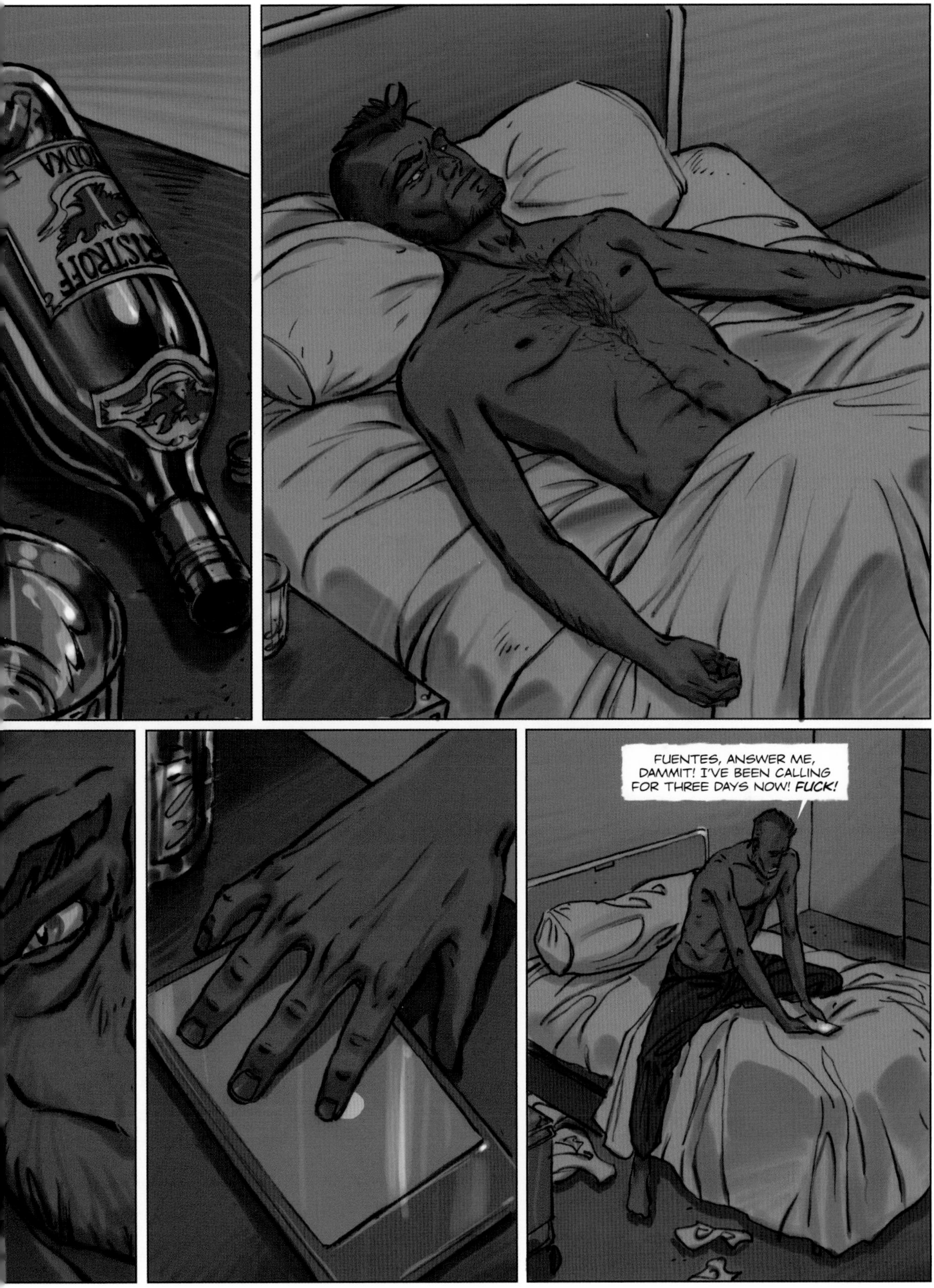
VODKA
KRISTOFF
FUENTES, ANSWER ME, DAMMIT! I'VE BEEN CALLING FOR THREE DAYS NOW! ***FUCK!***

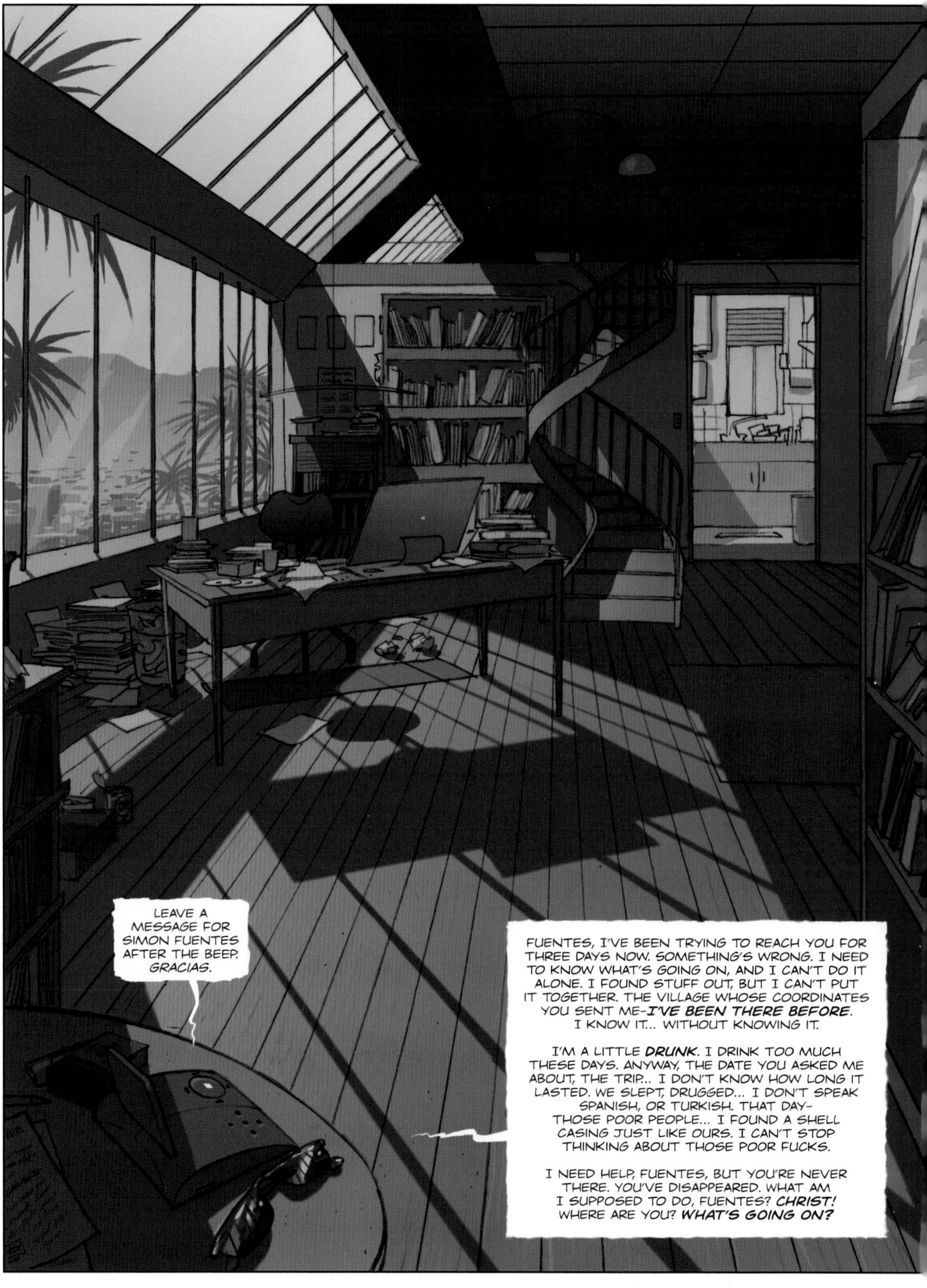
LEAVE A MESSAGE FOR SIMON FUENTES AFTER THE BEEP. GRACIAS.
FUENTES, I'VE BEEN TRYING TO REACH YOU FOR THREE DAYS NOW. SOMETHING'S WRONG. I NEED TO KNOW WHAT'S GOING ON, AND I CAN'T DO IT ALONE. I FOUND STUFF OUT, BUT I CAN'T PUT IT TOGETHER. THE VILLAGE WHOSE COORDINATES YOU SENT ME–I'VE BEEN THERE BEFORE. I KNOW IT... WITHOUT KNOWING IT.
I'M A LITTLE DRUNK. I DRINK TOO MUCH THESE DAYS. ANYWAY, THE DATE YOU ASKED ME ABOUT, THE TRIP... I DON'T KNOW HOW LONG IT LASTED. WE SLEPT, DRUGGED... I DON'T SPEAK SPANISH, OR TURKISH. THAT DAY– THOSE POOR PEOPLE... I FOUND A SHELL CASING JUST LIKE OURS. I CAN'T STOP THINKING ABOUT THOSE POOR FUCKS.
I NEED HELP, FUENTES, BUT YOU'RE NEVER THERE. YOU'VE DISAPPEARED. WHAT AM I SUPPOSED TO DO, FUENTES? CHRIST! WHERE ARE YOU? WHAT'S GOING ON?

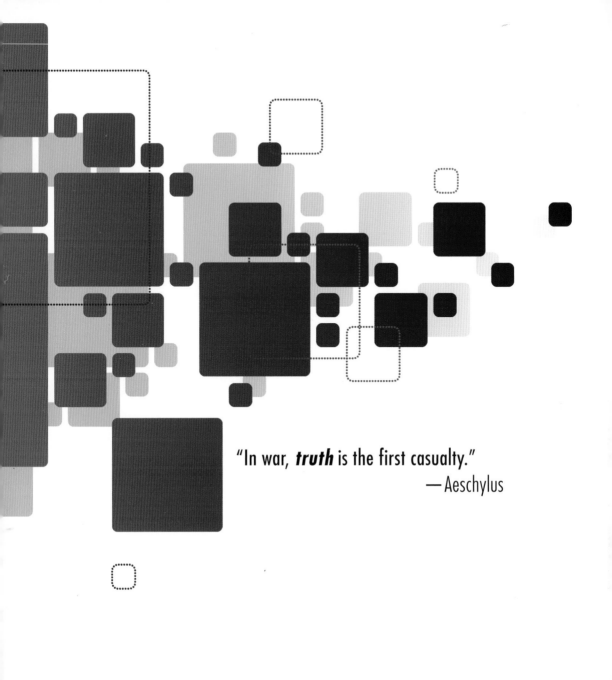

"In war, **truth** is the first casualty."

— Aeschylus

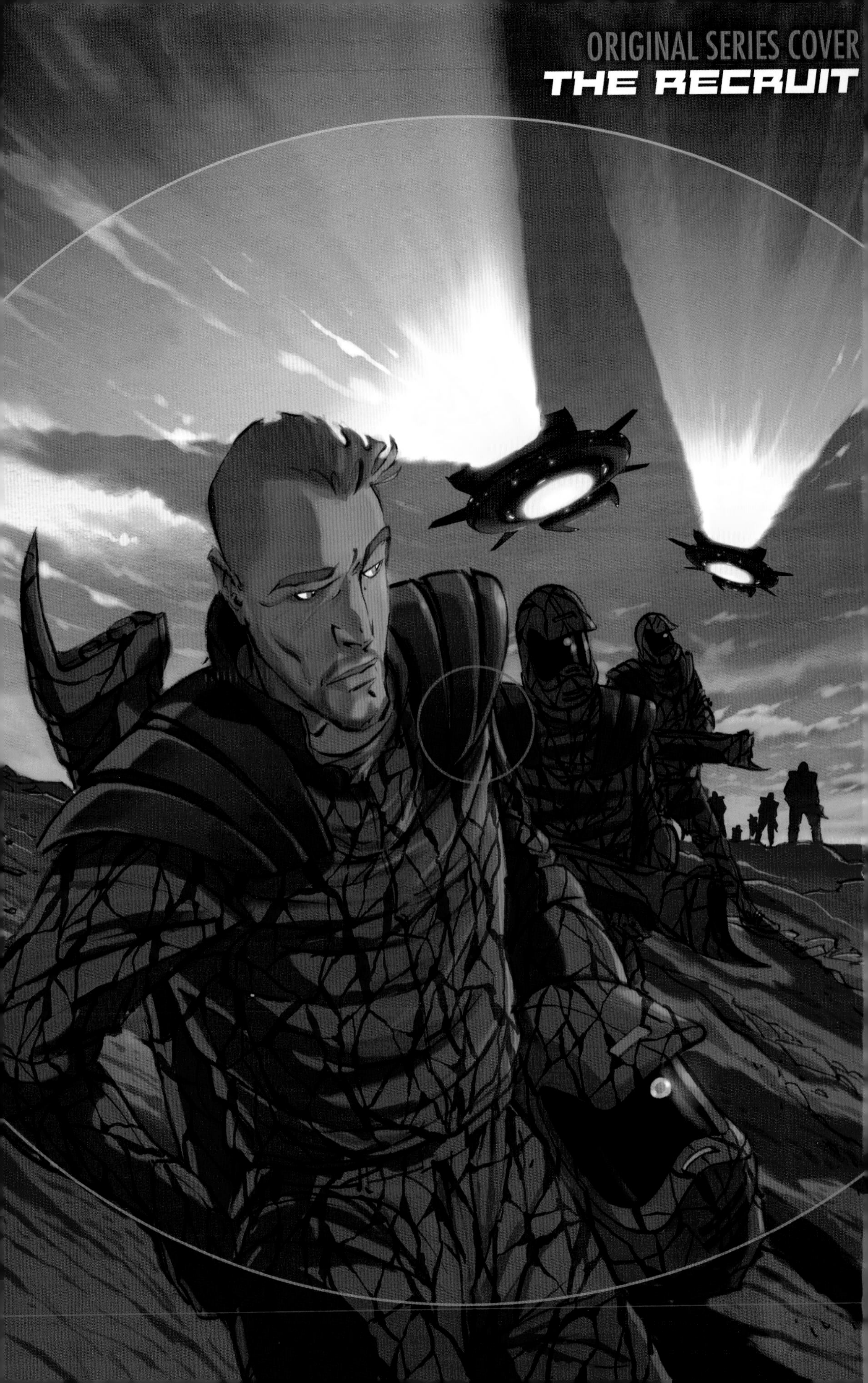
ORIGINAL SERIES COVER
THE RECRUIT

ORIGINAL SERIES COVER
THE HERO

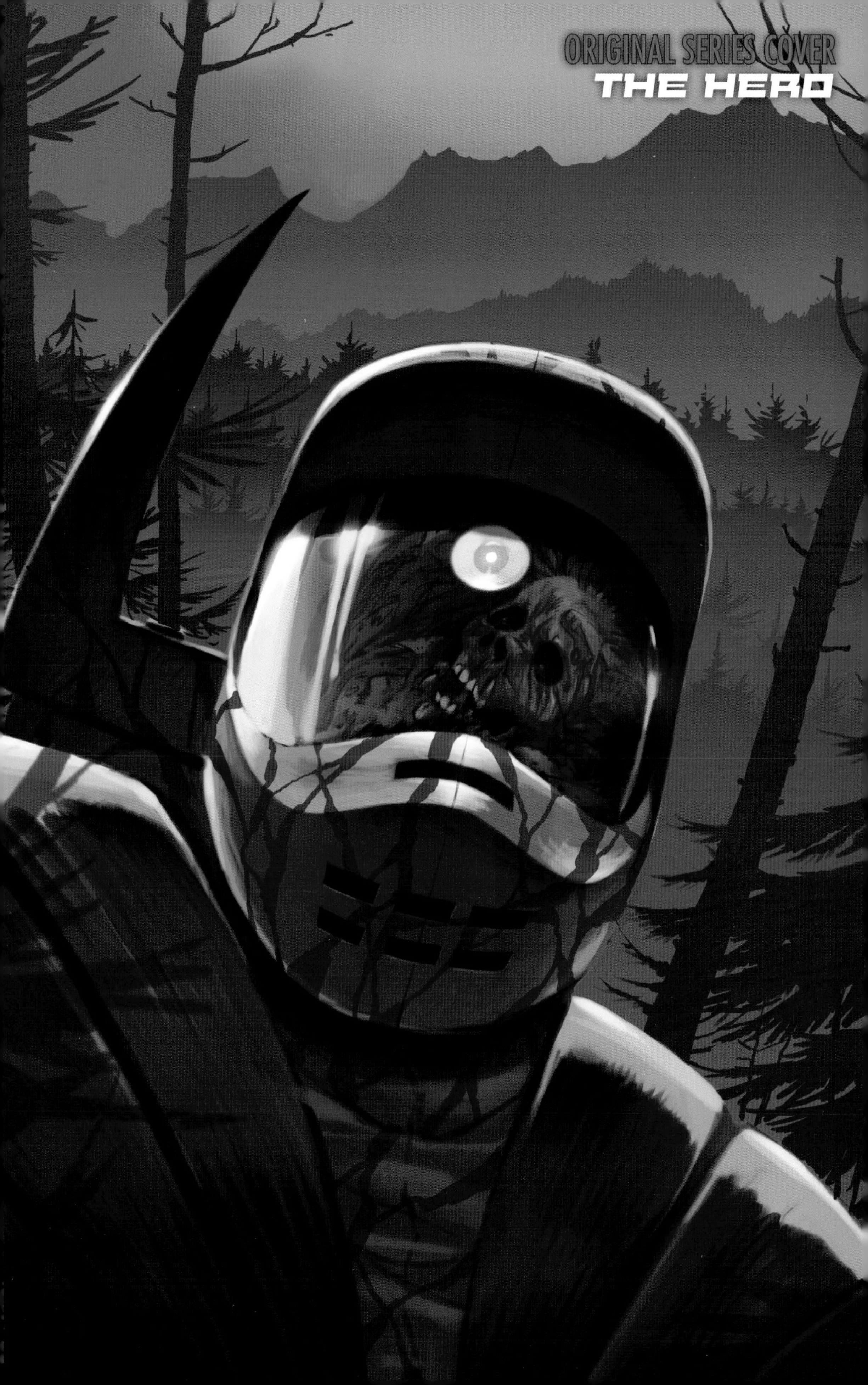

ABOUT THE AUTHORS

Luc Jacamon honed his drawing skills with an Alfred scholarship in 1986. His first published work was the crime thriller *Le Tueur: Long Feu*, also with Matz (published in the US as *The Killer*, where it was nominated for an Eisner Award).

Matz has published various graphic novels including the crime thriller *Le Tueur*; a thriller, *Du Plomb Dans La Tête* (*Headshot*) with renowned New Zealand artist Colin Wilson; *Shandy*, with artist Bertail; and *Peines Perdues* with artist Chauzy, which was nominated for Best Comic and Audience's Choice at Angoulême in 1993. Matz is also, under his real name, an active writer for video games, as well as a published novelist.

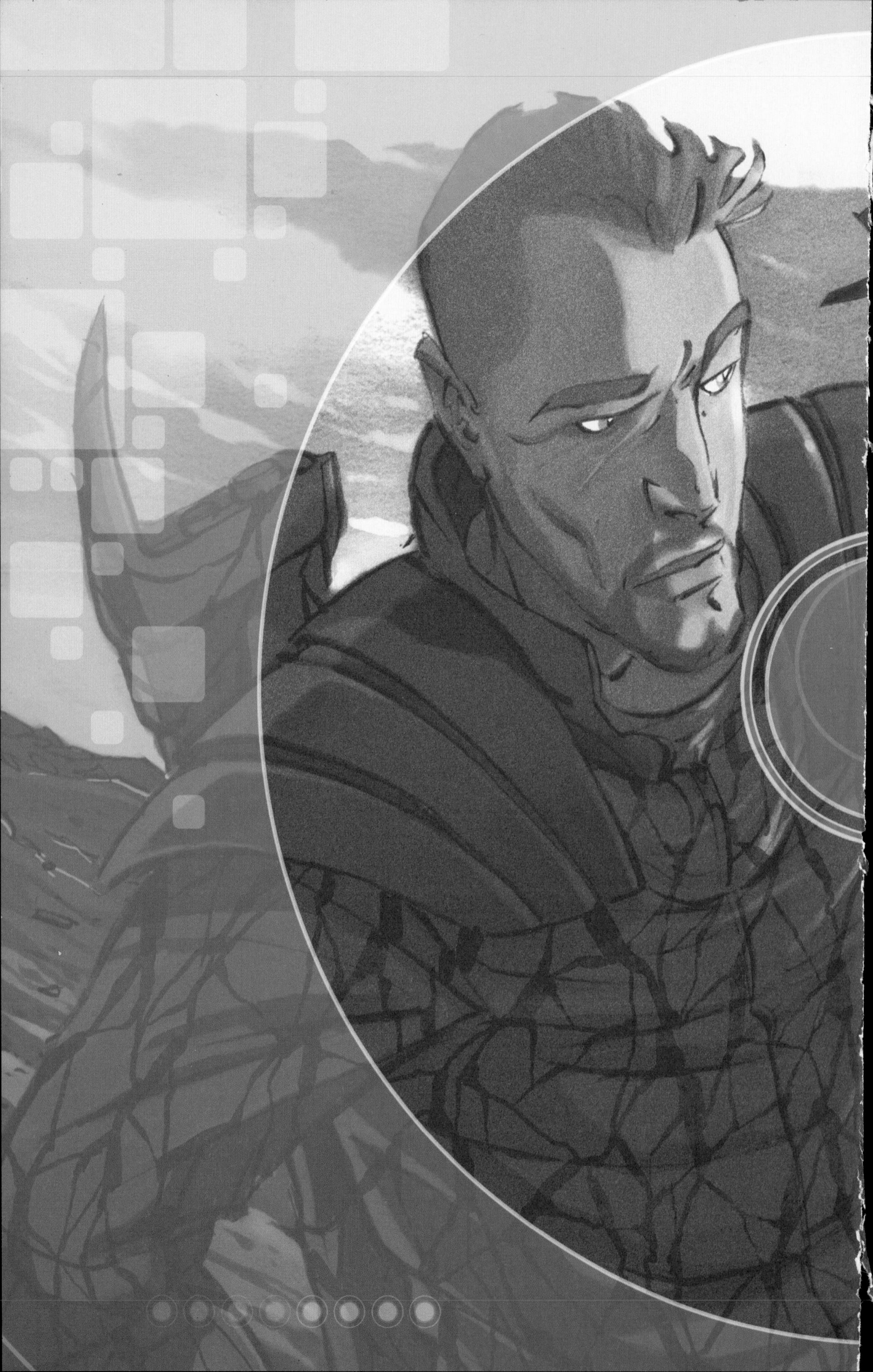